# MULTIPLE REI PSYCHOTHERAPY

MW00800420

This first-of-a-kind analysis will focus exclusively on unavoidable common, and mandated multiple relationships between clients and psychotherapists. The book will cover the ethics of a range of venues and situations where dual relationships are mandated, such as in the military, prisons/jails, and police departments, and settings where multiple relationships are unavoidable or common, such as rural communities; graduate schools and training institutions; faith, spiritual, recovery or 12-step, minority and disabled communities, total institutions, and sport psychology. The complexities of social network ethics and digital dual relationships, such as clients becoming "friends" or "fans" on their therapists' social media pages are discussed. Finally, the book will discuss the complexities of multiple roles that inevitably emerge in supervisory relationships.

**Ofer Zur, PhD**, is a licensed psychologist, fellow of the American Psychological Association, lecturer, ethics consultant, and forensic expert. He is the director of the Zur Institute Inc., which offers over 180 online continuing education courses for mental health practitioners. He also has been practicing psychotherapy in California for over 25 years. Dr. Zur is one of the top experts in the field of psychological ethics, applying a non-dogmatic approach to multiple relationships and therapeutic boundaries. He is the author of numerous articles and four books.

# MULTIPLE RELATIONSHIPS IN PSYCHOTHERAPY AND COUNSELING

Unavoidable, Common, and
Mandatory Dual Relations
in Therapy

### Edited by Ofer Zur

Routledge
Taylor & Francis Group
NEW YORK AND LONDON

First published 2017
by Routledge
711 Third Avenue, New York, NY 10017

and by Routledge
2 Park Square, Milton Park, Abingdon, Oxon OX14 4RN

*Routledge is an imprint of the Taylor & Francis Group, an informa business*

© 2017 Taylor & Francis

The right of Ofer Zur to be identified as the author of the editorial material, and of the authors for their individual chapters has been asserted in accordance with sections 77 and 78 of the Copyright, Designs and Patents Act 1988.

All rights reserved. No part of this book may be reprinted or reproduced or utilized in any form or by any electronic, mechanical, or other means, now known or hereafter invented, including photocopying and recording, or in any information storage or retrieval system, without permission in writing from the publishers.

*Trademark notice*: Product or corporate names may be trademarks or registered trademarks, and are used only for identification and explanation without intent to infringe.

*Library of Congress Cataloging in Publication Data*
A catalog record for this book has been requested

ISBN: 978-1-138-93778-9 (hbk)
ISBN: 978-1-138-93777-2 (pbk)
ISBN: 978-1-315-67613-5 (ebk)

Typeset in ITC Legacy Serif
by Swales & Willis Ltd, Exeter, Devon, UK

# CONTENTS

# CONTRIBUTORS

Jude Austin, Ph.D., Old Dominion University, Norfolk, VA, USA

Julius Austin, Ph.D., Nicolls State University, Thibodaux, LA, USA

Jeffrey E. Barnett, Psy.D., ABPP, Affiliation Associate Dean, Loyola College of Arts and Sciences; Professor, Department of Psychology, Loyola University Maryland, Baltimore, MD, USA

Lindsey Boone, M.A., LMFT, Los Angeles, CA, USA

Steven F. Bucky, Ph.D., ABPP, Distinguished Professor, Director, Professional Training, CSPP at Alliant/San Diego, CA, USA

Gerald Corey, Ed.D., Professor Emeritus, Human Services and Counseling, California State University at Fullerton, USA

Carol A. Falender, Ph.D., Clinical Professor, UCLA Department of Psychology, USA

Michael Gottlieb, Ph.D., ABPP, Clinical Professor, University of Texas Health Science Center, San Antonio, TX, USA

Shannon J. Johnson, Ph.D., CDR USN MSC, Clinical Psychologist, Director Mental Health, Naval Medical Center Portsmouth, Assistant Specialty Leader, Navy Psychology, Portsmouth, VA, USA

W. Brad Johnson, Ph.D., Professor of Psychology, Department of Leadership, Ethics and Law, United States Naval Academy, Annapolis, MD, USA

Keely Kolmes, Ph.D., Licensed Psychologist, San Francisco, CA, USA

**Gerald P. Koocher**, Ph.D., Dean and Professor, College of Science and Health, DePaul University, Chicago, IL, USA

**Jeni L. McCutchen**, Psy.D. M.S.C.P., ABPP, Board Certified in Police and Public Safety Psychology National Chair of Examinations (NCE), Phoenix, AZ, USA

**Michelle Muratori**, Ph.D., Johns Hopkins University, Baltimore, MD, USA

**Frederic G. Reamer**, Ph.D., Professor, School of Social Work, Rhode Island College, Providence, RI, USA

**Randolph K. Sanders**, Ph.D., Clinical Psychologist, New Braunfels, TX, USA

**Marianne Schneider Corey**, M.A., Consultant, Idyllwild, CA, USA

**David L. Shapiro**, Ph.D., J.D., Professor, Nova Southeastern University. Fort Lauderdale, FL, USA

**Adam Silberstein**, Ph.D., Psychologist, Tarzana, CA, USA

**Patricia Keith Spiegel**, Ph.D., Professor Emerita, Ball State University, Muncie, IN, USA

**Ronald A. Stolberg**, Ph.D., Assistant Professor, Alliant International University, San Diego, San Diego, CA, USA

**Lenore E.A. Walker**, Ed.D., Professor, Nova Southeastern University, Fort Lauderdale, FL, USA

**Alex S. Ward**, Postgraduate, Victoria University of Wellington, Wellington, New Zealand

**Tony Ward**, Ph.D, Professor and Clinical Director, School of Psychology, Victoria University of Wellington, Wellington, New Zealand

**Jeffrey Younggren**, Ph.D., ABPP Clinical Professor, University of Missouri, Columbia, MO, USA

**Ofer Zur**, Ph.D., Director, Zur Institute, Inc., Sebastopol, CA, USA

# ACKNOWLEDGMENTS

I would like to thank my patients of the last quarter-century who taught me so much that graduate school, ethics seminars, and risk management workshops did not. They modeled to me how to be flexible and human in my interactions with them in the small town where we lived. They did not hesitate to join a basketball league that I played in; or to sign up, with me and other parents, to chaperone our young children on a field trip. One client even loudly told the cashier in the supermarket, pointing at me standing at the end of the line, "That psychologist saved our marriage." Many of them told me that they chose me as their therapist "because" they knew me within the community.

I would also like to thank my colleague and co-author, the late Dr. Arnold Lazarus, and my colleagues, Dr. Jeffrey Barnett and Dr. Jeffrey Younggren, who encouraged, supported, as well as challenged my work, and helped me sharpen my views and find platforms where I could share my ideas about the importance of flexibility and clinical integrity rather than fear, when it comes to boundaries and multiple relationships.

I want to express particular thanks and appreciation to my dear friend and colleague, Sam Keen, who initiated me in regard to unexpected and unavoidable multiple relationships in a small town. He consistently reminded me that healing takes place in one's community and people had chosen to consult with me, the way they had chosen to consult with him, because they know us, have been familiar with our work, and respect us.

Special thanks to my colleague, Bruce Ecker, the founder of Coherence Therapy, for his support—and also for creatively suggesting to name this book, *Polishing the Monument*. I would also like to acknowledge Mimi Capes, my editor for the last 30 years, for her consistent support, editorial skills, and unfailing enthusiasm. I would also like to thank Ilan Zur for his help in the final editing.

Finally, thanks to my publisher, George Zimmer, who encouraged and urged me to publish this book. In his long and valiant career as a publisher, he has not shied away from controversies and inspired me and his many other authors to employ critical thinking and personal integrity and conviction to bravely challenge false, but commonly held, professional beliefs wherever they are encountered in our profession.

# INTRODUCTION

## The Multiple Relationships Spectrum: Mandated-Unavoidable-Common-Ethical-Unethical ... and Beyond

*Ofer Zur*

Back in the 1980s, on a hot summer's day, my friend and colleague, best-selling author Sam Keen, and I were working, shirtless, repairing a bridge over a creek on his property. To his surprise, I suddenly took off, up into the hills when I spotted one of my patients driving down the hill towards the bridge we were working on. After my client drove over the bridge and was out of sight, I reappeared and joined Sam, who, by that time had figured out the cause of my disappearance. It was in these unlikely circumstances that I was initiated into the idea that some multiple relationships are unexpected and unavoidable and can be not only ethical, but also helpful. Seriously annoyed with me, he said something like, "You describe yourself as a 'secular priest' and you lived in Israel where the rabbis not only lead the congregations and conduct sermons and weddings, but also conduct pastoral counseling, marital therapy, and help individuals and couples in their congregations to work out their spiritual, mental health, and other problems." He then added something to the time of, "You also lived with the Maasai in Africa where you would never see a Maasai, in need of medical, mental or spiritual help, take a raft and float three villages down the river to find a medicine man who doesn't know him or his tribe. The suffering man would turn to the medicine man or the wise woman of his very own village for help, because they know him, they know his family, his ancestors, and the spirits of the tribe. Healing takes place in one's own community, by a familiar healer." His exasperation was a turning point for me and irreversibly shaped my attitudes towards healing in general and multiple relationships in particular.

Not too long thereafter, I moved to a small town and soon found out the truth of Sam's words. I discovered that people chose me as their psychotherapist because they knew me and were familiar with me from our children's school, the local synagogue, basketball court, gym, or local rotary club. It was not unusual, after a day of chaperoning our young children on a field trip, that a parent would seek me out for personal or marital counseling. A couple of clients sought my services after playing with me or against me on the basketball court; others attended lectures I offered in our community.

When I turned to experts to inquire how to handle these kinds of situations, I received a uniformly negative response and a clear warning that multiple relationships are unethical. Period. Some experts added that dual relationships are not only below the standard of care but are harmful and may even lead to . . . sex. I was not sure if they were referring to sex with the men, the women, or both. These reactions were a true reflection of the attitudes to multiple relationships prevalent at that time.

The concept of multiple relationships, or what is often also called "dual relationships," refers to the fact that psychotherapists or counselors, besides their clinical-therapeutic roles, may also have additional non-therapeutic relationships with their clients. As I subsequently learned, this subject has been a source of' disagreements and misunderstandings for a long time and generally part of the broader discussion and debate concerning crossing therapeutic boundaries in psychotherapy, such as gift giving, physical touch, home visits, self-disclosure, use of language, therapy outside the office, and a variety of others.

In this book you will find a wide range of the venues and situations where multiple relationships are either mandated, such as in the military and prisons/jails, and, at times, police departments; and settings where multiple relationships are generally unavoidable, such as rural and small communities, faith, spiritual, recovery or 12-step communities, wilderness therapy, residential treatment programs, and behavioral health programs in boarding schools; or where dual relationships are common, such as graduate schools and postgraduate professional training institutions.

Additionally, there are unique, cutting-edge chapters, which also discuss the complexities of modern-day digital ethics and the increasingly common digital multiple relationships in online social networking, such as Facebook. Furthermore, the book examines the complexities that often emerge in the multiple roles and duties of supervisory relationships. Most chapters also offer an ethical decision-making process to effectively and ethically handle multiple relationships in a variety of settings and situations.

My colleague, Bruce Ecker, the founder of Coherence Therapy, has suggested naming this book *Polishing the Monument*, by which he meant that this book puts a cap on the now finally established idea that not all dual relationships are unethical, some multiple relationships are mandated, unavoidable, and common, and some can be healthy and beneficial. Indeed, with the persistence and, at times, forceful presentations, by myself and a few colleagues, the mental health field's understanding and attitudes towards multiple relationships have significantly changed. In recent times, the field has gradually moved in the direction where there is less fear and more critical thinking and context-based analysis when it comes to multiple relationships. This book indeed refutes the misguided assertions by ethicists and so-called experts and risk management instructors that multiple relationships not only are forbidden, but are likely to lead to sexual relationships between therapists and clients. But it likewise goes well beyond the more recent popular cliché, "not all dual relationships are unethical." The book clearly transcends both these opposing stances and hopefully will finally and firmly move our field towards a flexible and informed attitude and the employment of critical thinking towards multiple relationships. This is especially important when such relationships take place in the settings and within the practices that are the focus of this book, i.e., where psychotherapists are mandated or have no choice but to engage in multiple relationships.

## Codes of Ethics

This gradual shift in the direction of flexibility is reflected in the present codes of ethics. The American Psychological Association (APA) *Code of Ethics* (2010), in section 3.05, defines multiple relationships as:

(a) A multiple relationship occurs when a psychologist is in a professional role with a person and (1) at the same time is in another role with the same person, (2) at the same time is in a relationship with a person closely associated with or related to the person with whom the psychologist has the professional relationship, or (3) promises to enter into another relationship in the future with the person or a person closely associated with or related to the person.

Most other professional organizations' codes of ethics define multiple relationships in a similar way, with the exception of APA's code that includes in its definition of multiple relationships situations where the psychotherapist or the counselor promises the client that they will establish or enter into multiple relationships after therapy has ended.

The *Ethical Principles of Psychologists and Code of Conduct* (APA Ethics Code; APA, 2010) addresses the nature and extent of multiple relationships in Standard 3.05, Multiple Relationships, stating:

A psychologist refrains from entering into a multiple relationship if the multiple relationship could reasonably be expected to impair the psychologist's objectivity, competence or effectiveness in performing his or her functions as a psychologist, or otherwise risks exploitation or harm to the person with whom the professional relationship exists.

As noted above, the APA code (2010), like most other codes, also adds: "Multiple relationships that would not reasonably be expected to cause impairment or risk exploitation or harm are not unethical" (p. 6).

Clearly, the codes of ethics are very straightforward and explicit in stating that not all multiple relationships are unethical and must be avoided. What is obvious, as this book illustrates, is that there are situations and venues in which multiple relationships are actually mandated or unavoidable. Even though the codes state that multiple relationships which place the client at significant risk of harm should be avoided, this book discusses the fact that avoiding harm to clients due to multiple relationships is not always possible, especially in environments such as the military and prisons.

## TYPES OF MULTIPLE RELATIONSHIPS

Multiple relationships come in many colors and shapes and there are several ways to categorize the various forms. They can be ethical or unethical, legal or illegal, concurrent or sequential, avoidable or unavoidable, voluntary or mandatory, uncommon or common, expected or unexpected, and low-intensity or high-intensity.

Another way to categorize multiple relationships is by their types, such as:

- social/communal multiple relationships, which involve a therapist and client engaging socially in the community;
- professional multiple relationships, where, for example, the therapist is also a co-author of a book or is also co-presenter or co-attendee in a conference;
- business multiple relationships, such as where the client is also a business partner, the therapist's plumber, or the fellow who sold a car to the therapist;

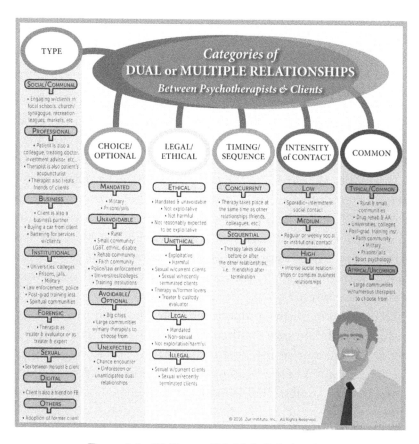

Figure 0.1: 26 Types of Multiple Relationships

- institutional multiple relationships take place when therapist and client are also colleagues in the same university or working in the same prison facility or military base;
- forensic dual relationships take place where the therapist acts as a treater, as well as custody evaluator, or an evaluator of the client's sanity or capacity to stand trial;
- sexual multiple relationships take place when therapist and client are also involved sexually (obviously, sexual relationships with current clients are always unethical);
- a digital multiple relationship is when client and therapist are, for instance, also friends on Facebook, interact on Second Life, or are on the same online dating website;
- additional unique types of multiple relationships, such as when a therapist adopts a former client or acts as a matchmaker between two current or former clients.

## The Evolution of Attitudes and Ethical Guidelines Regarding Multiple Relationships

As alluded to above, the fields of psychotherapy and counseling have seen numerous shifts in attitudes towards boundaries, in general, and multiple relationships in psychotherapy, in particular. Conflicts, debates, and disagreements have abounded since the inception of the discipline. Paradoxically, Freud, who laid the foundations for strict, analytically based, therapeutic boundaries, crossed many of them himself earlier in his career. Besides giving his patients gifts and offering a meal to the patient known as the "Rat Man," he was involved in multiple relationships with his clients when he arranged a match with two of his clients, and provided financial support to others. Most interesting and egregious in today's, or any day's norms, he was involved in the most unique multiple relationships when they psychoanalyzed their own children. However, in the early 1930s, this attitude shifted among psychoanalysts as Freud became concerned with the reputation of the budding new discipline of psychoanalysis. To preserve the professional standing of psychoanalysis, as well as for theoretical-clinical reasons, he instituted a clear ban on almost all boundary crossing, including multiple relationships (Lazarus & Zur, 2002; Zur, 2008).

The concerns with therapeutic boundaries in general, and more specifically, sexual multiple relationships, came to the forefront of the field during the sexual revolution period of the 1960s. Sexual multiple relationships and other boundary violations were openly conducted in California and other states, where therapists and clients often became playmates and lovers. In response to the sexually and culturally permissive attitudes of the 1960s and 1970s, there was pressure within the culture at large, including the mental health world, to provide more specific guidelines regarding therapists' conduct *vis-à-vis* their clients. As a result, consumer protection agencies, licensing boards, and legislators joined ethicists in establishing clear restrictions with regard to therapist-client sexual dual relationships and other boundaries issues (Gutheil & Gabbard, 1993).

Not only did sexual multiple relationships become illegal, but therapists were also urged, or even instructed, to make every effort to avoid any kind of boundary crossing, because, as the myth or flawed belief went, such boundary crossings could place them on the slippery slope towards harm and sexual dual relationships (Lazarus & Zur, 2002; Zur, 2007, 2008).

The increasingly litigious culture of the 1980s and 1990s and thereafter, as well as the increased focus on risk management in general medicine, led to more spoken and unspoken injunctions against any deviation from hands-off, only-in-the-office, "no self-disclosure" therapy. Most boundary crossings, including dual relationships, were generally viewed as hazards from a risk management standpoint and that first step towards supposedly inevitable sexual relationships, also known as the "slippery slope." Enforcing this view was the pervasive influence of psychoanalytic practice, which held that multiple relationships in all their forms contaminated the psychoanalytic concept of transference. In parallel to all this, there was a wider cultural counter-reaction to the feminist, free-speech movement, civil rights movement, and the sexual revolution of the 1970s. As a result, licensing boards, ethicists, and consumer affairs agencies frowned upon multiple relationships and other boundary crossings—especially touch (Zur, 2008).

In the mid-1990s, we saw an intensification and polarization of the debate around multiple relationships and other boundary issues. On one side of the debate, consumer protection agencies, licensing boards, so-called risk management experts, many ethicists, and psychoanalytically oriented therapists continued to advocate clearly defined, distinct, and rigid boundaries around the therapeutic relationship and between therapists and clients. This approach clearly advocated the avoidance of all forms of boundary crossing—in short and obviously, the avoidance of all multiple relationships. On the other side of the debate, there were a few publications at this time that discussed the fact that non-sexual dual relationships are neither always avoidable, such as those in small rural communities, nor always unethical or harmful (Barnett & Yutrenzka, 1994; Williams, 1997).

The practice of so-called risk management is one of the reasons why so many experts advocate avoidance of all forms of multiple relationships. "Risk management" may sound like a sensible and reasonable practice, which it can be; however, in fact, it is often a label for a practice in which fear of attorneys and licensing boards, rather than clinical considerations, dictates the course of therapy (Lazarus & Zur, 2002). As this book clearly illuminates, in many situations therapists have no choice but to engage in multiple relationships, like it or not. The book discusses these situations and proposes ways for therapists to navigate the often convoluted terrain of mandated, unavoidable, and common multiple relationships. Furthermore, the book illustrates that there are ethical ways to practice risk management, which are not based on fear of attorneys and boards, but are based on sound clinical judgment, ethical conduct, and the importance of the use of informed consent.

By the turn of the 21st century, we saw—at least in the literature and in the major professional organizations' codes of ethics—more contemplative attitudes towards multiple relationships and the beginning of the acknowledgment that they are sometimes mandated and/or unavoidable, and not all of them are harmful (Gottlieb & Younggren, 2009; Lazarus & Zur, 2002; Pope & Wedding, 2007; Schank & Skovholt, 2006; Sonne, 2006; Younggren & Gottlieb, 2004; Zur, 2007). It is significant that, also at that time, some of the most prominent promoters of the rigid application of therapeutic boundaries, and those who had promulgated the myth of the slippery slope, seemed to change their positions and present more balanced and flexible views of therapeutic boundaries.

Some literature, during this same period, had gone further than merely tolerating unavoidable multiple relationships by mapping their potential benefits under a variety of circumstances (Lazarus & Zur, 2002; Zur, 2007). At the same time, the mental health professional organizations' codes of ethics were also gradually becoming more sensible and realistic regarding multiple relationships. For example, as noted above, the 2002 APA *Code of Conduct* states that, "Multiple relationships that would not reasonably be expected to cause impairment or risk exploitation or harm are not unethical." Similarly, the American Counseling Association (ACA) *Code of Ethics* of 2005 discussed in section A.5.d the "Potentially Beneficial Interactions" of multiple relationships. Similar language appears in the revised APA *Code of Conduct* of 2010 and the revised ACA *Code of Ethics* of 2014. The ethics codes of the American National Association of Social Workers, California Association of Marriage and Family Therapists, and other codes also followed suit.

While still unacknowledged by many risk-management experts and some ethicists and licensing boards, the second decade of the 21st century has presented more textbooks and articles that have taken less rigid and more open, reasonable, just realistic, and context-based views of multiple relationships with less focus on fear and risk management (Herlihy & Corey, 2015; Koocher & Keith-Spiegel, 2016; Reamer, 2012). This book is testimony to that trend and brings us to where we are today, i.e., that, with the exception of unethical and sexual relationships, ethical multiple relationships are almost universally accepted. And finally, the 21st century has also introduced us to the new, but increasingly common and ever-evolving, form of digital multiple relationships.

## MULTIPLE RELATIONSHIPS IN DIFFERENT SETTINGS

Earlier in this chapter, we looked at all the types of multiple relationships; however, the main goal of this book is to focus on the mandated, unavoidable, and common multiple relationships in their different configurations and this is accomplished by some of the most renowned experts in the field, in great detail and specificity. The contributors discuss the nature of such multiple relationships, with the complexities, benefits, and risks involved. Included in their guidance is the importance of informed consent and ethical decision making for these numerous types of multiple relationships.

Following are brief descriptions of circumstances where multiple relationships are mandated, unavoidable, and common, as well as descriptions of some of the basic complexities of multiple relationships in these different settings.

9

Prisons and jails are clear examples of venues where there will be mandated multiple relationships; where the clinicians' first loyalty, duty and legal responsibility are to the institutions, primarily regarding concerns with security and safety, and a secondary responsibility is to their incarcerated clients. For example, a clinician, in these settings, who hears about an escape plan or potential violence within the prison must report it to the correctional staff. Such reporting may result in punishment and/or isolation of the client. Obviously, the concern with prison security and safety supersedes the clinician's loyalty or responsibility to the welfare of the prisoner patients.

Mandated multiple relationships also take place in the military, where psychologists experience mixed agency because their loyalties are first to the Department of Defense, then to the local commanding officer, and lastly to the individual service members to whom they provide therapy. These mandated multiple relationships can be extremely complex and prone to conflicts because helping clients overcome psychiatric impairment, including symptoms of trauma and posttraumatic stress disorder, may result in their being declared fit to rejoin their combat unit, which may mean that they could engage in combat, where they may be wounded or even killed. Additionally, as will be detailed in this book, at times embedded military psychologists share sleeping quarters with their clients, and some are required to evaluate fellow officers, or even their own commanders, for fitness for duty/combat. Obviously, such evaluations are likely to constitute complex multiple relationships and conflicting roles.

Police psychology frequently presents complex, mandated, and unavoidable multiple roles, multiple loyalties, and multiple relationship situations in which the psychologists may be concurrently involved in providing clinical services, as well as training, fitness-for-duty evaluations, pre-employment screenings, consultations with SWAT units, hostage negotiations, debriefings, consultations on suicide prevention, and other roles. Needless to say, these diverse responsibilities and multiple loyalties (i.e., to their own clients, the department, officers, public, courts, own safety) can easily present conflicts of interests, conflicts of loyalties, and complex ethical, clinical, and legal dilemmas.

Like psychologists in the military, police, and prison environments, school psychologists must also cope with mandated multiple relationships wherein they have concurrent obligations to students, their families, and their employer, i.e., the school district. Reporting laws that are applied to minors add complexity as they present multiple duties, responsibilities, and loyalties, which can translate into unavoidable and conflicting multiple relationships.

While multiple relationships are mandated in prison, military settings, and often in the police department and school settings, they are unavoidable in a variety of other settings, such as rural, small, ethnic, faith, and drug rehabilitation communities, as well as in higher educational institutions and sport psychology.

It has been long recognized that multiple relationships are unavoidable in small rural communities where there is limited number of clinicians. In this setting, a clinician's involvement in the community also frequently involves engagement with clients in the community, which may include co-participating in school or sports activities, attending religious ceremonies, or attending local events or celebrations where clients are also present. Multiple relationships are also established when the therapist buys products, such as groceries or cars, in local stores and businesses which are owned or operated by clients. Familiarity with the clinician in the community is often a factor in clients choosing a certain clinician as their therapist.

In drug rehabilitation programs, most psychotherapists and counselors are active in their own recovery; therefore, it is not uncommon for them to encounter current, former, or future clients at 12-step meetings or other recovery programs. This inevitably creates concurrent or sequential dual relationships between clients and therapists. These multiple relationships are often reported to have positive effects on clients, as the therapists model, encourage, and support their clients' sobriety via 12-step or similar rehab programs.

Educational institutions are another context in which multiple relationships abound. Some professors or teaching assistants are also on the staff of the college mental health clinics, increasing the possibility of multiple relationships with clients who attend, or attended, their classes, or may attend in future. Some group process classes involve leaders in a dual role of leading a group dynamics class, as well as handling students' therapeutic disclosures and working through students' clinical issues. Therapists and clients may encounter each other at social, sport, and other school events or, as in a small town, find themselves next to each other in the pool or the gym, or even the gym shower.

Sport psychologists who often travel with the team find themselves, in addition to formal therapy in a consulting room, conducting informal therapy on the plane, on the bus, or even on the field. In order to create trust, they often hang out with the players, whom they counsel, in hotel lobbies or bars in far-away cities where the games take place.

Faith and spiritual communities are other milieus where multiple relationships are common. Therapists and clients may attend services in the same church, synagogue, ashram, or other places of worship. Their children may go to the same Sunday school and therapists may, knowingly or unknowingly, end up volunteering to serve on the same committees as their clients. In fact, congregation members often choose a psychotherapist who they know shares their spiritual orientation. Similarly, priests, rabbis, swamis, and other heads of faith communities often refer people in their congregations to therapists from the congregation whom they know, trust, and respect. Priests and other leaders often conduct not only spiritual or pastoral counseling, but also traditional counseling with members of their congregations, which clearly creates multiple relationships.

Cyberspace provides rich and fertile ground for all sorts of multiple relationships. Most common are the social-digital multiple relationships on social networks that are created, for example, when therapists accept their clients as friends on Facebook or co-participate in Second Life. Similarly, LinkedIn or any social networking programs create social multiple relationships when therapists and clients knowingly or unknowingly interact. Sometimes clients may join a social network where the therapist is involved under a pseudonym, which also creates multiple relationships that the therapists may not even know exist.

Supervision inherently involves supervisors in multiple roles, duties, and responsibilities, or what may constitute multiple relationships. Supervisors have duties and responsibilities for the supervisees' clients, and for the supervisees themselves; additionally, as gatekeepers, they have a duty to the mental health profession, future clients, and to the public at large. Reporting laws may add another layer of multiple duties to the supervisor's roster of duties and can create additional and complex, and potentially enhancing and/or conflicting, multiple relationships

## THE BOOK

The book is composed of 17 chapters by some of the most renowned ethicists of our time, who have written extensively, have helped shape the field of psychotherapy ethics, and were part of developing the codes of ethics for different professional organizations, such as the American Psychological Association, National Association of Social Workers, and American Counseling Association. These include Dr. Gerald Koocher, Dr. Jeffrey Younggren, Dr. Frederic Reamer, Dr. Jeffrey Barnett, Dr. Michael Gottlieb, Dr. David Shapiro, Dr. Lenore Walker, Dr. Gerald Corey, Dr. Marianne Schneider Corey, and Dr. Patricia Keith Spiegel. Together with these distinguished ethicists-scholars, the book includes the work of top experts on the ethical complexities and multiple relationships in their specific fields: Dr. Carol Falender on supervision, Dr. Steven Bucky on sport psychology, Dr. Brad Johnson and Dr. Shannon Johnson on military psychology, Dr. Keely Kolmes on digital ethics, Dr. Jeni McCutchen on police psychology, Dr. Alex Ward and Dr. Tony Ward on forensic psychology, and Dr. Randolph Sanders on faith communities. Additional chapters were co-authored by Dr. Adam Silberstein and Ms. Lindsey Boone on rehabilitation communities and Mr. Jude Austin and colleagues on multiple roles and relationships in counseling education.

This is not a book that needs to be read from cover to cover. After this introduction and the first two general chapters—which define multiple relationships, refer to different codes of ethics on multiple relationships, and discuss the process of ethical decision making—the rest of the chapters, with the exception of Chapter 11 on total institutions, examine those specific settings where multiple relationships are mandated, unavoidable, or common. Readers are invited to find the situations, circumstances, and settings that are most relevant to their work and focus on those chapters.

## REFERENCES

American Counseling Association. (2005). *Code of Ethics*. Alexandria, VA: Author.
American Counseling Association. (2014). *Code of Ethics*. Alexandria, VA: Author.
American Psychological Association (2002). *Ethical Principles of Psychologists and Code of Conduct*. Washington, D.C: Author
American Psychological Association. (2010). *Ethical Principles of Psychologists and Code of Conduct*. Retrieved from http://www.apa.org/ethics (accessed July 27, 2016).
Barnett, J. E., & Yutrenzka, B. (1994) Nonsexual dual relationships in professional practice with special applications to rural and military communities. *The Independent Practitioner*, 14(5), 243-248.

Gottlieb, M. C., & Younggren, J. N. (2009). Is there is a slippery slope? Considerations regarding multiple relationships and risk management. *Professional Psychology: Research and Practice*, 40, 564–571.

Gutheil, T. G., & Gabbard, G. O. (1993). The concept of boundaries in clinical practice: theoretical and risk-management dimensions. *American Journal of Psychiatry*, 150, 188–196.

Herlihy, B., & Corey, G. (2015). *Boundary Issues in Counseling: Multiple Roles and Responsibilities* (3rd ed.). Alexandria, VA: American Counseling Association.

Koocher, G. P., & Keith-Spiegel, P. C. (2016). *Ethics in Psychology and the Mental Health Professions: Professional Standards and Cases* (4th ed.). New York: Oxford University Press.

Lazarus, A. A., & Zur, O. (Eds.). (2002). *Dual Relationships and Psychotherapy*. New York: Springer.

Pope, K. S., & Wedding, D. (2007). Nonsexual multiple relationships and boundaries in psychotherapy. In R. Corsini and D. Wedding (Eds) *Current Psychotherapies* (8th ed.). New York: Brooks/Cole.

Reamer, F. G. (2012). *Boundary Issues and Dual Relationships in the Human Services*. New York: Columbia University Press.

Schank, A. J., & Skovholt, T. M. (2006). *Ethical Practice in Small Communities: Challenges and Rewards for Psychologists*. Washington, DC: APA Books.

Sonne, J. L. (2006) Nonsexual multiple relationships: a practical decision-making model for clinicians. *The Independent Practitioner*, Fall, 187–192.

Williams, M. H. (1997). Boundary violations: do some contended standards of care fail to encompass commonplace procedures of humanistic, behavioral, and eclectic psychotherapies? *Psychotherapy*, 34, 238–249.

Younggren, J. N., & Gottlieb, M. C. (2004). Managing risk when contemplating multiple relationships. *Professional Psychology: Research and Practice*, 35, 255–260.

Zur, O. (2007). *Boundaries in Psychotherapy: Ethical and Clinical Explorations*. Washington, DC: APA Books.

Zur, O. (2008). Historical shifts in the debate on therapeutic boundaries. *California Psychologist*, 41 (1), 6–9.

# Part I

## Introduction and Ethical Decision Making for Boundaries and Multiple Relationships in Psychotherapy and Counseling

# INTRODUCTION

*Ofer Zur*

Part I (Chapters 1 and 2) provides a general introduction to the ethics of multiple relationships and puts them into the context of other therapeutic boundaries, such as gift giving and receiving, bartering, touch, self-disclosure, and language.

In Chapter 1, Dr. Barnett introduces the constructs of boundaries and contrasts boundary crossing with boundary violations. He defines the term multiple relationships and discusses how the codes of ethics delineate ethical multiple relationships. The chapter discusses ethical decision making and the importance of informed consent, especially in settings where multiple relationships are unavoidable. It concludes with a list of recommendations that can serve therapists as guidelines for handling multiple relationships.

In Chapter 2, Dr. Younggren and Dr. Gottlieb provide one of the most inclusive lists available of settings and situations where therapists face multiple relationships, multiple duties, or multiple loyalties. The chapter differentiates between mandated dual relationships, administrative duality, and civil duties, including reporting laws, criminal duality, and other types of mandated multiple relationships, and unavoidable multiple duties. It ends with a discussion about risk management and informed consent regarding mandatory multiple relationships and multiple duties.

# Chapter 1

# AN INTRODUCTION TO BOUNDARIES AND MULTIPLE RELATIONSHIPS FOR PSYCHOTHERAPISTS

## Issues, Challenges, and Recommendations

*Jeffrey E. Barnett*

Boundaries are defined as the ground rules of the professional relationship that help establish, and provide guidance on, acceptable and unacceptable behaviors by psychotherapists (Knapp & VandeCreek, 2012). Boundaries provide "a therapeutic frame which defines a set of roles for the participants in the therapeutic process" (Smith & Fitzpatrick, 1995, p. 499) and, when effectively and appropriately applied, they "provide a foundation for this relationship by fostering a sense of safety and the belief that the clinician will always act in the client's best interest" (p. 500). In essence, the thoughtful and appropriate application of boundaries helps psychotherapists to most appropriately and effectively assist their clients in an ethical and clinically effective manner (Moleski & Kilesica, 2005; Zur, 2007).

Psychotherapists have a significant responsibility to do their best to ensure that their actions serve their clients' best interests and that clients are not exploited or harmed. This responsibility has been described by Jorgenson, Hirsch, and Wahl (1997) as a fiduciary responsibility to one's clients. This means that the psychotherapist agrees to act in the client's best interests. Yet, as this book will clearly illustrate, doing so is

17

not always easy and straightforward. Depending on the setting and context, mental health practitioners may have multiple obligations, roles, and allegiances that make applying our responsibilities to clients and others quite complex and challenging.

BOUNDARIES IN PSYCHOTHERAPY: AVOIDING, CROSSING, AND VIOLATING BOUNDARIES

There exists a wide range of boundaries that are relevant to the psychotherapy relationship. Examples include touch, self-disclosure, time and place of treatment, interpersonal space, gifts, clothing, language, finances, and multiple relationships.

Each of these boundaries falls on a continuum that ranges from avoiding it completely to participating in it actively in a variety of ways. Depending on the specific situation, a particular action or behavior by the psychotherapist may be found to be helpful, harmful, or benign, appropriate or inappropriate, and ethical or unethical.

A widely used way of conceptualizing the boundaries continuum is to view them as being avoided, crossed, or violated (Smith & Fitzpatrick, 1995). For the boundary of touch, an example of avoiding this boundary would be having a policy that forbids engaging in any physical contact with clients. While such an approach would be counterproductive and inappropriate for many clients, in some settings and situations this may be necessary. For example, such a prohibition against physical touch might be seen on inpatient units or in prison settings.

To violate a boundary means that the boundary is traversed but that it is done in a way that holds a significant potential for exploitation of, or harm to, the client; that is clinically contraindicated, that is not consistent with the client's treatment plan or history, that violates legal and/or ethics standards, that violates social or cultural norms or mores for the client, and that takes advantage of the client's dependence and trust. With the boundary of touch, an example of a boundary violation is engaging in sexual or intimate touch with a client.

To cross a boundary means that the boundary has been traversed (e.g., engaging in touch with a client), but that it is done in a way that is not clinically contraindicated, that is consistent with the client's treatment needs and history, that is culturally appropriate and responsive to the client's background and preferences, that does not exploit or harm the client, and that does not violate the client's dependence and trust. Additional considerations include the psychotherapist's intent and motivations for engaging in the behavior in question, how this action or behavior is perceived by the client (Barnett, Lazarus, Vasquez, Moorehead-Slaughter, & Johnson, 2007a; Zur, 2007), the psychotherapist's theoretical orientation, and the nature of the treatment being provided (Williams, 1997). An example of boundary crossing with touch is to shake a client's extended hand.

## Boundary Challenges

As is hopefully evident from the above discussion, an absolute avoidance of all boundaries is neither desired nor possible. In fact, boundary crossing can be seen as essential to developing and maintaining an effective psychotherapy relationship (Zur, 2007; Zur & Lazarus, 2002). In an effort to avoid unethical and harmful behaviors, some psychotherapists may take an overly conservative approach to boundaries in the psychotherapy relationship. But, a rigid risk-avoidance application of boundaries (i.e., rejecting a client's small symbolic gift or a handshake) can actually result in harm to the client by creating a sterile or even shaming relationship that does not promote a positive therapeutic alliance (Barnett et al., 2007a, Gottlieb & Younggren, 2009).

To determine if certain actions are boundary crossings or boundary violations one must consider the client's age, gender, culture, history, and diagnosis, as well as the therapeutic approach employed, the psychotherapist's age, gender, culture, training, and, as was noted above, the setting in which treatment takes place.

## Multiple Relationships

An important boundary issue of relevance for many psychotherapists is that of multiple relationships, the focus of this book. Multiple relationships involve participating in one or more additional relationships or roles with clients, former clients, or significant others in their lives in addition to the psychotherapy relationship or beginning psychotherapy with an individual with whom a psychotherapist has previously maintained an additional relationship. A range of multiple relationships is possible. Examples include business relationships, personal or social relationships, and romantic or sexually intimate relationships, among others.

The *Ethical Principles of Psychologists and Code of Conduct* (American Psychological Association (APA) Ethics Code; APA, 2010) addresses the nature and extent of multiple relationships in Standard 3.05, Multiple Relationships, stating:

> A psychologist refrains from entering into a multiple relationship if the multiple relationship could reasonably be expected to impair the psychologist's objectivity, competence or effectiveness in performing his or her functions as a psychologist, or otherwise risks exploitation or harm to the person with whom the professional relationship exists.
>
> Multiple relationships that would not reasonably be expected to cause impairment or risk exploitation or harm are not unethical.
>
> (p. 6)

Thus, the APA Ethics Code, like most other codes of ethics, is very clear in stating that not all multiple relationships are unethical and must be avoided. It is only those that hold a significant potential to adversely impact the psychotherapist's objectivity and judgment and/or to place the client at significant risk of harm that should be avoided. These admonitions are consistent with the guidance provided above on how to successfully navigate boundaries, yet, at times may prove challenging for psychotherapists.

Other standards in the APA Ethics Code (APA, 2010) that provide additional guidance relevant to multiple relationships include Standard 3.04, Avoiding Harm, and Standard 3.06, Conflicts of Interest. Standard 3.04 states "Psychologists take reasonable steps to avoid harming their clients/patients ... and others with whom they work, and to minimize harm where it is foreseeable and unavoidable" (p. 6). Standard 3.06 adds:

> Psychologists refrain from taking on a professional role when personal, scientific, professional, legal, financial, or other interests or relationships could reasonably be expected to (1) impair their objectivity, competence, or effectiveness in performing their functions as psychologists or (2) expose the person or organization with whom the professional relationship exists to harm or exploitation.
>
> (p. 6)

As will be seen, each of these standards plays a significant role in each psychotherapist's decision-making process when considering if a planned multiple relationship is acceptable and appropriate. To complicate the matter, as this book illustrates, avoiding multiple relationships, even those that may hold the potential to be harmful to clients, is not always possible in settings where multiple relationships at times are mandatory, such as in the military and correctional facilities.

Mental health professionals should be aware that some multiple relationships are avoidable, some are unavoidable, and some are mandated. Those multiple relationships that hold great potential to exploit or harm clients and that are easily avoidable should definitely be avoided (e.g., becoming partners in a real-estate business with a client, engaging in a sexual relationship with a client). In settings where multiple relationships are mandated or unavoidable, mental health professionals must carefully consider their divided allegiance and how to best meet potentially conflicting agendas and obligations.

Military psychologists, for example, must provide clinical services in a system where their "client" is not the person sitting across from them seeking mental health treatment. In fact, their client is actually the Department of Defense and their ultimate obligation is the combat-readiness of the service members to whom they provide clinical services. Furthermore, at times, commanders will refer service members for treatment with the clear goal being to get the service member combat-ready (regardless of what the service member's goals are). Many military psychologists will experience the tension of divided loyalties or what Kennedy and Johnson (2009) call "mixed agency," due to the owing of obligations to both the individual service member and the military service overall. This can create frequent dilemmas regarding treatment planning and goal setting, treatment decisions, and confidentiality. Many of these issues may be addressed in the informed-consent process.

Additional multiple relationship challenges in insular or isolated communities, such as rural communities, isolated military bases, and certain ethnic or racial and LGBT communities, include being in multiple relationships and not having other options. A military psychologist on an aircraft carrier or a remote base may be required to provide treatment to her or his commander, the individual who is her or his boss, or even his or her bunk mate. Similarly, a child psychologist may be the only one with such specialty in a remote rural community and may need to evaluate or provide treatment to his or her child's classmates or friends. While making a referral might be desirable, at times there are no referral options and the decision to be made is how to best manage the multiple relationship, not if this situation is optimal.

As with boundaries in general, there will be those multiple relationship situations that will be clearly appropriate and those that will be clearly inappropriate. For example, a psychotherapist in a rural setting where there are few other professionals to whom one may refer a client may agree to treat a member of his or her religious congregation. This may be seen as quite different from entering into an intimate romantic relationship with a current client or providing marital therapy to one's parents in law. But, not all multiple relationship decisions are so clear and straightforward. Most frequently, they are more ambiguous and the decision-making process is more complex and challenging.

## ETHICAL DECISION MAKING

Important guidance to consider when deciding if a planned multiple relationship is acceptable is found in the aspirational ethical ideals of the profession, as articulated in the General Principles of the APA Ethics Code (APA, 2010).

### Beneficence and Non-maleficence

This involves providing help and assistance to clients while avoiding harm to them. Further, psychologists "are alert to and guard against personal, financial, social, organizational, or political factors that might lead to misuse of their influence" (p. 3).

### Fidelity and Responsibility

Under these principles, psychologists fulfill expected obligations to clients and only act in ways that serve their clients' best interests. This includes that psychologists "seek to manage conflicts of interest that could lead to exploitation or harm" (p. 3).

## Integrity

Psychologists should act ethically and honestly; not mislead, manipulate, or take advantage of others; and endeavor to "avoid unwise or unclear commitments" (p. 3).

## Justice

These guidelines cover treating each individual fairly and ensuring that each individual has "access to and benefit from the contributions of psychology and to equal quality in the processes, procedures, and services being conducted by psychologists" (p. 3).

## Respect for People's Rights and Dignity

Psychologists should respect and value all individuals regardless of individual differences and minimize the effects of biases one may have. Additionally, "Psychologists are aware that special safeguards may be necessary to protect the rights and welfare of persons or communities whose vulnerabilities impair autonomous decision making" (p. 4).

Additional considerations in determining if a multiple relationship is acceptable or should be avoided include:

- availability of options and alternatives;
- the potential for exploitation of, or harm to, the client(s);
- the relevance of the secondary relationship to the goals of treatment and the potential benefit to the client (Younggren & Gottlieb, 2004);
- the ability to keep separate, or compartmentalize, the multiple roles and relationships so that the secondary relationship does not adversely impact the psychotherapy relationship (Barnett & Yutrenzka, 1994);
- obligations to various individuals and organizations and any conflicts between their requirements and expectations;
- the potential for impaired judgment or objectivity on one's part in this decision-making process.

## THE ROLE OF INFORMED CONSENT

Informed consent is a shared decision-making process in which the psychotherapist provides the client with sufficient information so the client may make an informed decision about participating in the proposed course of treatment. The informed-consent process, when implemented effectively, has several benefits of particular relevance to this discussion of multiple relationships. Snyder and Barnett (2006) report the benefits of a timely and thorough informed consent process as follows:

- It reduces the risk of exploitation of, and harm to, clients by providing them with sufficient information so they will have realistic expectations for the relationship and treatment to come.
- It reduces the power differential in the relationship by providing clients with needed information for making their own decisions, thus reducing their dependence on the psychotherapist for decision making and promoting clients' autonomous functioning (Beahrs & Gutheil, 2001).
- It promotes a more effective therapeutic relationship by increasing clients' understanding of the treatment and relationship being proposed, helping to establish realistic expectations in roles, responsibilities, and behaviors (Beahrs & Gutheil, 2001).
- It establishes the foundation for a collaborative decision-making process and working relationship throughout the course of psychotherapy (Barnett, Wise, Johnson-Greene, & Bucky, 2007b).
- It promotes ethical practices.

Thus, open and ongoing discussions with clients is an expected part of the informed consent process. Out of respect for clients and consistent with the goals of informed consent articulated above, multiple relationships should only be entered into after an open discussion as part of the ongoing informed-consent process. This process includes discussion of the proposed course of treatment, confidentiality and its exceptions, responsibilities the psychotherapist has to others, techniques to be used, options and alternatives reasonably available, the relative risks and benefits of each option, the client's right to decline participation in any part of the treatment, and, depending on the setting, the fact that consent must be given voluntarily and not in any way be coerced. Additionally, informed-consent discussions should be documented as part of the client's treatment record and updated as changes in these agreements are made over the course of treatment.

## Risks for Psychotherapists

It is highly unlikely that psychotherapists enter the profession with the intention of violating boundaries or harming clients. Yet, at times, these do occur. In fact, even thoughtful, caring, and well-intentioned psychotherapists may violate boundaries and engage in inappropriate and harmful multiple relationships. It is widely accepted that psychotherapists, like all individuals, have personal vulnerabilities and blind spots. Individual vulnerabilities may lead to professional blind spots, areas where the psychotherapist is acting on these unresolved issues or perpetuating these longstanding patterns, inadvertently transgressing boundaries without conscious forethought or awareness. Additionally, the practice of psychotherapy can be demanding and isolating for the psychotherapist. Clinicians may spend many hours each day and week focusing on, and being the receptacle for, their clients' emotions, difficulties, traumas, and crises. While assisting and supporting clients may be very rewarding, it may also be quite stressful and emotionally demanding for psychotherapists and result in the psychotherapist suffering vicarious traumatization (Figley, 1995; Pearlman & Saakvitne, 1995).

Failure to adequately manage the ongoing stresses in one's personal and professional lives may result in decreased quality of judgment and reduced decision-making ability, with these possibly occurring outside the psychotherapist's awareness. Furthermore, one risk for psychotherapists who have not adequately attended to these issues is to seek emotional support and comfort from clients, engaging in a role reversal that is a clear boundary violation.

These concerns highlight the need for participation and ongoing consultation with colleagues or clinical supervision. It is also of vital importance that each psychotherapist practice ongoing self-care to help ensure emotional, physical, relationship, and, if relevant, spiritual wellness in her or his life (Coster & Schwebel, 1997). Taking care of one's self helps each of us to take better care of our clients, helping to minimize the risk of impaired objectivity and judgment developing, and enabling us to ensure that treatment decisions are motivated not by our own needs but rather, by our clients' best interests.

## RECOMMENDATIONS

Readers are encouraged to give thoughtful consideration to how they manage and address boundaries and multiple relationships with psychotherapy clients. While many boundary crossings are commonplace and do not raise any concerns, and at times multiple relationships may be appropriate, often, the certain behaviors that will be helpful or potentially harmful or exploitative are not always clear. As was noted above, in some settings and contexts multiple relationships cannot be avoided; the challenge is then how to best manage these multiple relationships keeping in mind the best interests of those involved. Differing or competing needs and expectations among the various parties involved can create challenging ethical dilemmas for mental health practitioners. Simply seeking to do no harm or to "follow the ethics code" will prove quite lacking when faced with such difficult situations. As with all ethical dilemmas, it is recommended that an ethical decision-making process (e.g., Younggren & Gottlieb, 2004) be used to assist in determining the appropriateness of intended actions.

Additional steps that may prove helpful when the appropriateness of a boundary incursion is not immediately clear include the following:

- Openly discuss anticipated boundary incursions with clients.
- Honestly consider one's own issues, needs, and motivations that may be influencing the decision to engage in a particular behavior.
- Practice ongoing self-care to promote ongoing wellness and to reduce the risk of impaired functioning as a result of burnout and vicarious traumatization.
- Consider each client's mental health and treatment histories, the nature of the current treatment, one's theoretical orientation, cultural factors, and the likely impact of anticipated actions on the client.
- Consider the context of psychotherapy and how it may impact therapeutic boundaries and multiple loyalties and multiple relationships.
- Discuss concerns with multiple relationships openly with clients as part of the informed-consent process.
- Review relevant ethics and legal standards and remain focused on aspirational ethical ideals.

- Seek out clinical supervision or consult with a knowledgeable colleague.
- Participate in personal psychotherapy to attend to blind spots and vicarious traumatization.
- Document all boundary and multiple relationship decisions or mandates to include options and alternatives considered, your assessment of the likely potential risks and benefits for the client, discussions with the client about these issues, consultations sought, and actual outcomes achieved after engaging in the contemplated actions or behaviors.

Psychotherapists should not be motivated by a risk management or risk avoidance approach to clinical practice (i.e., Knapp, Younggren, Vandecreek, Harris, & Matrin, 2013; Zur, 2002; Zur & Lazarus, 2002) that is likely to stifle creativity and limit treatment options for clients. Thus, the focus should be on each client's best interests. While treatment decisions should be made with relevant ethical, legal, and clinical standards in mind, psychotherapists should always take into consideration client preferences and needs, personal histories, cultural differences, expectations and requirements of each setting, and community standards. One client's boundary crossing may be another client's boundary violation.

Similarly, multiple relationships cannot be viewed simply as being either good or bad. A wide range of possible multiple relationships exist. While, of course, those that hold a clear potential for harm to or exploitation of clients should be avoided, whenever possible (e.g., sexually intimate relationships with clients), there are numerous settings and circumstances where multiple relationships are a way of life and are unavoidable. In settings such as rural and isolated communities, in the military, and in religious, ethnic, rehabilitation, or LGBT communities where the psychotherapist is a member of the community and both lives and works in it, multiple relationships are not just unavoidable, but as will be discussed in several chapters to follow, are often helpful to clients in their treatment. Additionally, in these settings referral options may be quite limited so that meeting the client's treatment needs may necessitate participation in a multiple relationship. Thus, learning how to compartmentalize roles and responsibilities in multiple relationships is

27

essential (Barnett & Yutrenzka, 1994) so that the multiple relationship is managed successfully and does not interfere with the client's treatment goals being met. Boundary crossings and appropriately managed multiple relationships should most definitely be seen as consistent with these ideals and objectives.

## REFERENCES

American Psychological Association (2010). *Ethical Principles of Psychologists and Code of Conduct*. Retrieved from http://www.apa.org/ethics (accessed July 27, 2016).

Barnett, J. E. & Yutrenzka, B. (1994). Nonsexual dual relationships in professional practice with special applications to rural and military communities. *The Independent Practitioner, 14*(5), 243-248.

Barnett, J. E., Lazarus, A. A., Vasquez, M. J. T., Moorehead-Slaughter, O., & Johnson, W. B. (2007a). Boundary issues and multiple relationships: fantasy and reality. *Professional Psychology: Research and Practice, 38*(4), 401-405. doi: 10.1037/073-7028.38.4.401.

Barnett, J. E., Wise, E. H., Johnson-Greene, D., & Bucky, S. F. (2007b). Informed consent: too much of a good thing or not enough? *Professional Psychology: Research and Practice, 38*, 179-186. doi: 10.1037/0735-7028.38.2.179.

Beahrs, J. O., & Gutheil, T. G. (2001). Informed consent in psychotherapy. *American Journal of Psychiatry, 158*, 4-10.

Coster, J. S., & Schwebel, M. (1997). Well-functioning in professional psychologists. *Professional Psychology: Research and Practice, 28*, 5-13.

Figley, C. R. (1995). *Compassion Fatigue: Secondary Traumatic Stress from Treating the Traumatized*. New York, NY: Bruner/Mazel.

Gottlieb, M. C., & Younggren, J. N. (2009). Is there a slippery slope? Considerations regarding multiple relationships and risk management. *Professional Psychology: Research and Practice, 40*(6), 564-571. doi: 10.1037/a0017231.

Jorgenson, L. M., Hirsch, A. B., & Wahl, K. M. (1997). Fiduciary duty and boundaries: acting in the client's best interest. *Behavioral Sciences and the Law, 15*, 49-62.

Kennedy, C. H., & Johnson, W. B. (2006). Mixed agency in military psychology: applying the American Psychological Association Ethics Code. *Psychological Services, 6*, 22-31.

Knapp, S. J., & VandeCreek, L. D. (2012). *Practical Ethics for Psychologists: A Positive Approach* (2nd ed.). Washington, DC: APA Books.

Knapp, S., Younggren, J. N., Vandecreek, L., Harris, E., & Matrin, J. N. (2013). *Assessing and Managing Risk in Psychological Practice: An Individualized Approach* (2nd ed.). Washington, DC: American Psychological Association Insurance Trust.

Moleski, S. M., & Kiselica, M. S. (2005). Dual relationships: a continuum ranging from the destructive to the therapeutic. *Journal of Counseling and Development, 83*(1), 3-11. doi: 10.1002/j.1556-6678.2005.tb00574.x.

Pearlman, L. A., & Saakvitne, K. W. (1995). *Trauma and the Therapist—Counter-transference and Vicarious Traumatization in Psychotherapy with Incest Survivors.* New York, NY: Norton.

Smith, D., & Fitzpatrick, M. (1995). Patient-therapist boundary issues: an integrative review of theory and research. *Professional Psychology: Research and Practice, 26*(5), 499–506. doi: 10.1037/0735-7028.26.5.499.

Snyder, T. A., & Barnett, J. E. (2006). Informed consent and the psychotherapy process. *Psychotherapy Bulletin, 41,* 37–42.

Williams, M. H. (1997). Boundary violations: do some contended standards of care fail to encompass commonplace procedures of humanistic, behavioral, and eclectic psychotherapies? *Psychotherapy, 34,* 238–249.

Younggren, J. N., & Gottlieb, M. C. (2004). Managing risk when contemplating multiple relationships. *Professional Psychology: Research and Practice, 35,* 255–260. doi: 10.1037/0735-7028.35.3.25.

Zur, O. (2002). In celebration of dual relationships. In A. Lazarus & O. Zur (Eds.), *Dual Relationships and Psychotherapy* (pp. 44–51). New York, NY: Springer.

Zur, O. (2007). *Boundaries in Psychotherapy: Ethical and Clinical Explorations.* Washington, DC: American Psychological Association.

Zur, O. & Lazarus, A. A. (2002). Six arguments against dual relationships and their rebuttals. In A. Lazarus & O. Zur (Eds.), *Dual Relationships and Psychotherapy* (pp. 3–24). New York, NY: Springer.

CHAPTER 2

# MANDATED MULTIPLE RELATIONSHIPS AND ETHICAL DECISION MAKING

*Jeff Younggren and Michael Gottlieb*

We would like to thank Dr. Ofer Zur for asking us to contribute to this very valuable book. We were surprised that he asked us to write this chapter since we have often disagreed with him regarding how psychologists should manage duality in professional practice. That is not to say he is wrong and we are right; rather, the discussion about multiple relationships in professional practice has many gray areas that create forums for productive, though differing, debates regarding what is acceptable practice and what is not. Choosing us to assist in the writing of this book reflects his commitment to insuring that this volume is balanced and provides the reader with a fair and thorough discussion of this very important topic.

Multiple or dual relationships can be a type of conflict of interest (American Psychological Association (APA), 2010). In professional practice they are a common occurrence, and are not unethical *per se* or a violation of the standards of professional practice (APA, 2010; Gottlieb, 1993; Gottlieb & Younggren, 2009; Lazarus & Zur, 2002; Younggren & Gottlieb, 2004; Zur, 2007). However, the guidelines for their management are not always clearcut but contextually and conceptually driven (e.g., Knapp et al., 2007). Consequently, solutions for managing specific dual relationships can be quite different, depending upon the circumstance. Among these situations are those relationships that by their very nature cannot be avoided because they are rooted in the very context of the professional service being provided and therefore have a high potential for conflicts of interest. Examples of this situation include reporting requirements for court-appointed therapists and military officers reporting requirements to command, both of which could impact the safety and effectiveness of the treatment setting. It is our contention that, while these potentially conflicting relationships cannot always be avoided, they must be managed in a fashion that is consistent with our ethical standards, good clinical care, and sound risk management.

To understand the problems associated with multiple relationships, one must look beyond the plethora of warnings about them and examine the ethical standards themselves. For example, Principle 3.05(a) of the APA *Code of Ethics* states that:

> Psychologists refrain from taking on a professional role when personal, scientific, professional, legal, financial, or other interests or relationships could reasonably be expected to (1) impair their objectivity, competence, or effectiveness in performing their functions as psychologists or (2) expose the person or organization with whom the professional relationship exists to harm or exploitation.
>
> (APA, 2010)

Furthermore, Standard 3.05(a) states in part that, "Multiple relationships that would not reasonably be expected to cause impairment or risk exploitation or harm are not unethical" (APA, 2010).

These standards should quickly lead the reader to see that problems only arise when competing roles create some type of a conflict of interest for the psychologist (Gottlieb, 1993). Simply put, if there is no conflict of interest, then there is no ethical dilemma, since the patient's interests remain primary.

In a perfect world, there would be no ethical dilemmas. All professional psychological services would adhere to the ethical principle of beneficence with a vigilant eye on the avoidance of any risk of harm, or non-maleficence. These are held to be the two most important of the ethical principles driving ethical healthcare delivery (Beauchamp & Childress, 2009) and form the foundation of Principle A of the *Ethical Principles of Psychologists and Code of Conduct* (APA, 2010). The next principle in an ethically perfect world would be justice. That is, the delivery of these professional services should be fair.

31

In healthcare ethics, this principle can be subdivided into three categories: fair distribution of scarce resources or distributive justice (Principle D), respect for people's rights (Principle E), and respect for morally acceptable laws or legal justice (Gillon, 1994). Finally, these services would also be founded on the principle of autonomy, which reflects respect for another's right to self-determine a course of action and the support of his or her independent decision making (Beauchamp & Childress, 2009). Unfortunately, we do not live in a perfect world; conflicts of interest arise and can be quite varied and highly complex. Consequently, the risks associated with a conflict of interest in one set of circumstances can change in another. For example, bartering professional services for goods at a fair market value might be an acceptable practice while bartering for services at a differing price for those services could be problematic. In addition, given the reality that a therapeutic relationship is actually a dynamic one, some small conflicts of interest that were not originally problematic can easily evolve into larger ones that are. Examples of such common and potentially dangerous conflicts of interest can arise when working within more confined religious or LGBT communities. Others can occur when issues of political persuasion or racial bias arise.

To only complicate these matters further, professional standards allow for the existence of conflicts of interest depending upon the nature of the service or circumstance. For example, rural psychologists are often given more flexibility regarding entering into dual relationships with their patients because such relationships are unavoidable in small communities. Military psychologists provide services where they have an obligation to the interests of both the patients and command. In situations such as these, there are increased risks that such relationships could create conflicts of interest, but increased risk in and of itself does not necessitate avoiding the relationship altogether. Rather, our ethical standards allow psychologists to engage in such relationships, but doing so also increases their responsibility for anticipating and managing potential conflicts of interest should they arise in order to protect the patient and the integrity of the treatment process.

Sometimes circumstances control the decision to allow for certain dual relationships. For example, a psychologist in a small and confined community with limited resources might be an elder in a church while also treating the minister's wife who serves as the church's treasurer. While such a circumstance might be questionable in an urban community where the woman could obtain services elsewhere, the realities of rural practice may make such an arrangement more acceptable. It does not, however, reduce the psychologist's obligation to do his/her best to minimize risk to the patient.

To continue, let us assume that during a treatment session the wife admits to her psychologist, and church elder, that she is purposely and secretly overpaying her husband. This disclosure now places the psychologist in a clear conflict of interest as she or he has fiduciary obligations to both the patient and the church. What is one to do in such a situation? Does the psychologist advocate for the church, consistent with the position of an elder, or advocate for the wife, who shared confidential information with her psychologist? Can the psychologist keep the roles separate, and if so, how does she or he manage this information? Can the psychologist keep the information secret and still fulfill the obligations of an elder? If so, how would this decision impact his or her ability to work with the wife? One way or another, the risk to both the psychologist and his or her patient has increased, and the psychologist must find an ethical solution to this unexpected conflict of interest. While these questions must be addressed, we contend that the solution is not to accuse the psychologist of being derelict by allowing the creation of such a dual relationship in the first place. What would have been the reason to refuse service to the wife in the first place? What conflict of interest was reasonably foreseeable in this situation?

We, like all psychotherapists, are not seers and do not live in a perfect or predictable world; instead, healthcare decisions often reflect a balancing between competing ethical principles (Ross, 1930). Healthcare providers are faced on a daily basis with choices that draw them away from the ethics of a perfect world and toward a reality filled by conflicting policies, vexing circumstances, competing expectations, limited resources, and ambiguous laws. Sometimes, they must make difficult choices about who gets care and who must do without it. Nowhere is this imperfect reality more evident than in the world of multiple relationships where psychologists often must face decisions that balance the competing values of delivering services when potentially conflicting roles are likely to arise or may be unavoidable.

In this chapter, we select examples of potentially unavoidable role conflicts and the issues that are unique to each of them. Specific discussion will be limited since other authors in this volume will discuss them in greater detail. Next, we will discuss ways to effectively manage these potentially competing roles that will assist psychologists in identifying when such conflicts may arise, selecting the various options for managing those conflicts, and arriving at the best choice given each specific circumstance. In doing so we caution the reader that there is nothing magic about what we propose here. Frequently, psychologists will be forced to make difficult choices that others may not understand and with which some may disagree. As some of our colleagues have noted, doing the right thing does not always feel good (Knapp et al., 2015).

## MANDATED DUAL RELATIONSHIPS

### Administrative Duality

Frequently psychologists find themselves confronted with administrative policies that could interfere with treatment. These types of difficulties can extend from professional obligations outlined in a state's administrative code, such as mandated reporting, problems and conflicts with contractual relationships with managed care companies, to conditions of employment such as mandates for centralized record keeping or electronic healthcare records, that challenge confidentiality requirements. These policies often outline additional requirements placed upon the psychologist, and by their existence, create a potential dual relationship such that the psychologist could have a conflict between the patient and some other entity such as the state, the insurance carrier, or an employer. Such requirements may be legal and enforceable, but they can threaten the effectiveness and safety of the treatment setting by requiring the professional to be loyal to both patient and some other external entity. What follows are some examples of administrative duality.

### The Managed Care/Carrier-Contracted Psychologist

There is little question that the changes in the insurance industry brought about by managed care have affected the professional relationship psychologists have with their patients. Emphasis on short-term therapy and carrier oversight create possible role conflicts and potentially serious limitations on how psychologists practice and treat their patients. The impact that managed care has had on service delivery is also shared by constraints that exist in the health insurance reimbursement system in general (Glabman, 2009; *60 Minutes,* 2014). Multiple carriers have been subject to numerous legal actions that demonstrated that they forced decisions to reduce expensive, though appropriate, care for their insureds because of their desire to limit cost (Lerner, 2015).

These restrictions can pose substantial risk for both the patient and the psychologist when trying to make decisions that are in the patient's best interest. Psychologists who find themselves dealing with the pressure to reduce service delivery must carefully navigate this common duality and consistently focus on the needs of patient and advocate for those needs.

## The Police Psychologist

By its very nature those who provide services to law enforcement run the risk of multiple conflicts of interest because, when a police psychologist provides services to police officers who work in their departments, they may find themselves in a circumstance where the administrative requirements of the department conflict with the ethics of psychological practice and duty to the patient. For example, police psychologists are often called upon to evaluate officers they are seeing clinically for a variety of purposes, and in such situations there exists the possibility that decisions might be made that are not necessarily in the best interests of the police officer they are seeing. Determinations about fitness for duty, ability to carry a firearm, and potential dangerousness are ever present in the background of the counseling services that these psychologists provide to the members of the department. Departmental policies frequently require that staff psychologists report to leadership any concerns they have about whether the officer is fit for duty. However, such administrative requirements may violate the pure ethical standards of confidentiality and fidelity and legal standards regarding fiduciary duty to patients. It is important to point out that a violation of the police department requirements does not constitute a violation of practice standards on the part of the psychologist. It is just a violation of the terms of employment.

## The Prison Psychologist

Psychologists who work in prisons frequently are confronted with institutional policies that create a duty or responsibility to serve both the inmate and the prison system. This is a clear and legal dual relationship created by the conditions of their employment and constraints placed upon a patient's civil rights following a criminal conviction. Pure confidentiality does not exist in this type of setting, and the results of treatment and assessment that may serve both the patient and the system could also conflict. For example, if a treating psychologist suspects that a prisoner is using drugs or supplying drugs to other prisoners, such information must be shared with the prison administration at the possible expense of the safety of the treatment alliance and punishment for the inmate. Psychologists in these setting must serve the system and the patient, and conflicts of interest can easily arise when to goals of the patient differ from the goals of the system.

## The School Counselor

School psychologists cope with dual relationships wherein they have concurrent obligations to students, their families, and their employer. They commonly function in a system composed of a myriad of regulations and constraints that can place them in the middle of competing duties. These include conflicts of interest between the student, the family, the school, and sometimes the state, the fulfillment of which can be mutually exclusive. For example, driven by financial concerns and limited resources, school districts are constantly under pressure to keep funding focused on the general academic population, sometimes at the expense of the individual student's specific needs; unfortunately, special needs entail special costs. So, as school psychologists provide their services they are at the same time being placed in a dual role where the needs of the student may conflict with the needs of the district.

## The Supervising Psychotherapist

Frequently psychotherapists find themselves in supervisory roles where they are forced to evaluate an individual who is in training, and do so in an environment filled with a variety of other social and administrative interactions with that supervisee. Training setting requirements can place these supervisors in a difficult circumstance where these secondary relationships can potentially create conflicts that make fulfillment of the responsibilities of a supervisor difficult to accomplish. Impossible to avoid, these other interactions need to be managed in a fashion that assures the fulfillment of the primary supervisory obligations, regardless of whether this makes the working environment more stressful and difficult to manage.

## The Court-Appointed Therapist

Psychologists may be court-appointed to treat patients in a number of circumstances such as seeing children whose parents are involved in custody disputes or convicted sex offenders. Others may treat teens, who are involved in the juvenile justice system. In all these cases, potential conflicts may arise between the patient, the court or probation officer, and parents in the case of minors. Consider the psychologist who has been ordered to see a juvenile offender. Teens cannot get to the psychologist's office by themselves and must rely on adults to bring them, but what if the adults are either unavailable due to work, or are unreliable? Here the psychologist must report the missed appointment to the probation officer, thereby risking the treatment process, even though it is not the teen's fault (for further reading, see Dewey & Gottlieb, 2011).

## CIVIL DUALITY

Frequently social policy legislation creates responsibilities for psychologists that potentially conflict with the treatment obligations that they have to their patients. Arguably with the best of intentions, society often enacts legal duties for mental health providers that create duties to protect the property and welfare of others. These laws are often designed to create dual relationships, and the failure to comply with them can create civil liability for the treating professional.

## Danger to Others

Since the advent of the Tarasoff ruling (*Tarasoff v. Regents of the University of California*, Cal. 1976), certain healthcare professionals have had a legal duty to protect others from dangerous patients. These requirements have been codified into the laws of most states, though they take differing form depending upon jurisdiction. In their most simple form, these laws require professionals to either protect others, by notifying them of the threat, or prevent the patient, who intends to harm them, from so doing. In states such as California, the mental health practitioner has to both protect and notify the intended victim. What is important to know at this juncture is that psychologists must be familiar with the laws of their particular jurisdiction.

Inherent in these laws is the civil duty a psychologist has to others with whom she or he has no professional relationship or fiduciary duty, yet which creates, *ipso facto*, a legal and mandated dual relationship. Failure to fulfill this legal duty can create exposure to licensing board complains and tort liability, a civil wrong committed by a professional that results in damage to another (*Black's Law Dictionary*, 2014). In other words, a psychologist can be sanctioned by a state board and be sued for financial damages for a failure to warn an identified potential victim. While the complexity of the process goes well beyond the purpose of this chapter, suffice it to say that a failure to warn other individuals at risk, and even to protect property, in some cases, could have significant financial impact upon the practicing professional even though the psychologist has no clear relationship with either.

## Danger to Self

Social policy has also affected the management of suicidal patients. Codified in both ethical standards and licensing regulations is the civil requirement that a psychologist must do what she or he can to protect patients from self-harm. While the process by which this is accomplished can be quite varied, society has created a duty for the professional to interfere with and prevent suicide, viewing such conduct as a social good. However, such laws may create a professional obligation to society that conflicts with the patient's desire, and failing to try and override that desire can lead to licensing board complaints and civil exposure. To make matters only more complex, the accurate prediction of risk places is extremely difficult due to such behaviors having very low base rates. Consequently, social policy creates very high risk for false-positive errors, which can harm patients and have a drastic impact upon a therapeutic alliance.

## Domestic Abuse Reporting

Some states have enacted statutes that require psychologists to report domestic abuse to a state agency in order to protect the alleged victim.

Such legislation creates laws that place the wishes of society, with whom the psychologist has no clear relationship, in conflict with those of the patient, who may wish that a report not be made. While one can debate the value of such policies, their existence and their related reporting requirements create an obligation for the psychologist that may force him or her to act contrary to the interests of the patient and consistent with the view of society with whom she or he has no formal relationship. Again this creates a legal dual relationship and the failure to fulfill this duty could have civil and administrative consequences.

Society has made fulfilling these obligations so important that it protects the good-faith fulfillment of these obligations from any type of retaliation on the part of the patient or the patient's legal representative. Simply put, the psychologist is immune from any type of legal action by fulfillment of these types of civil requirements.

## CRIMINAL DUALITY

Sometimes society has created social policy obligations to others, which, if not fulfilled by the psychologist, could constitute a crime. This is vastly different from the civil obligations previously discussed, where another party may have a financial claim against the person who failed to fulfill his or her duty to them. In this category, society has decided that the failure to fulfill defined responsibilities to some oversight agency, such as the government, is against the law.

### Child Abuse Reporting

Every jurisdiction in the USA requires psychologists, and other healthcare professionals, to report suspected child abuse. While what actually constitutes child abuse differs across jurisdictions, the law takes the position that a failure to fulfill the requirement to pro-tect children is a either a misdemeanor or a felony. For practicing psychologists, this means that they could be subject to criminal pros-ecution if they fail to fulfill their legally mandated and clearly defined obligation. Society has taken the position that fulfilling this mandate is so important that the psychologist is immune and cannot be the subject to any type of legal retaliation for having fulfilled it.

## The Military Psychologist

When psychologists provide services in the military, a unique set of rules and laws regulates their conduct. Unlike other mental health work settings, the mission of the military is primary and supersedes the needs of the individual because military members may give up their lives to accomplish a mission, a circumstance quite different from any other social system where life is valued in a different way. Therefore healthcare in the military is founded upon the assumption that when the needs of the individual run the risk of threatening the mission, those needs become secondary. For example, military psychologists find themselves in a regulatory system that allows access to healthcare records by those in a patient's chain of command to make sure that the individual is not going to jeopardize the military objective.

All military psychologists must be licensed to practice in at least one state, and such regulations might conflict with state licensing laws. Nevertheless, on federal property, the military regulations are in force and take precedence. So psychologists who work within this system clearly serve two masters: the military and the patient, but the military's needs are primary and legally enforceable.

## Risk Management, Informed Consent, and Mandatory Dual Relationships

This brief review of some of the unavoidable multiple relationships makes it obvious that they are neither uncommon, nor necessarily a violation of any law or standard of practice. However, this does not mean that the prudent psychologist should overlook them. The obvious question is, how does a psychologist manage a mandatory dual relationship when it occurs? The answer to this rests in a risk management strategy that has its foundation in the Ethical Principles of Psychologists (APA, 2010) and related professional guidelines.

As stated at the outset, one of the primary problems created by multiple relationships is that they can have a high potential for conflicts of interest. When they are unavoidable, the risk for a conflict of interest arises and must be formally addressed with the patient. Standard 3.06 of the Ethical Principles of Psychologist and Code of Conduct (Ethics Code) provides guidance when addressing such conflicts:

Psychologists refrain from taking on a professional role when personal, scientific, professional, legal, financial, or other interests or relationships could reasonably be expected to (1) impair their objectivity, competence, or effectiveness in performing their functions as psychologists or (2) expose the person or organization with whom the professional relationship exists to harm or exploitation.

(APA, 2010)

But what does one do when the conflict cannot be avoided, as is often the case? What if the dual relationship is mandated by law or inherent in the law, as has been repeatedly pointed out in this chapter? The solution to this problem rests in informed consent.

It is through the use of informed consent that the psychologist who is placed in a potential conflict fulfills his or her professional obligations to the patient and to the profession. When the patient understands the potential risks and benefits created by required disclosures, and agrees to those conditions, the psychologist will have fulfilled his or her obligations to the patient, the law, ethics and/or the employer. The informed-consent process should begin "as early as is feasible" (APA, 2010, 210.01) in the professional relationship and should include a detailed and written description outline of the applicable rules and the risks that may arise, and it should be signed by the patient. But we argue that one should go further.

Throughout the course of therapy, the patient must be reminded of the rules of the professional relationship, and they should be explained whenever the need arises. We contend that it should be woven into the very fabric of the treatment, so that noting potential problems whenever they arise is simply viewed as part of the informed-consent and therapeutic process. This recommendation applies even for those whose rights are limited, such as prison inmates, who retain a right to a clear understanding of the professional relationship

## CONCLUSION

In this chapter we have highlighted some of the more obvious situations where dual relationships and potential conflicts of interest may arise; we acknowledge that there are many others. One way or another, we hope to have shown that it is common for psychologists to find themselves in

41

situations of potential conflict, and as a result, be aware of them, and act affirmatively as a matter of patient welfare and good risk management.

This is not to say that the job of a psychologist or psychotherapist is an easy one. It is not. It is characterized by multiple obligations that may compete and conflict with each other. When psychologists find themselves in such situations, it is their responsibility to ensure that the patient clearly understands the potential conflicts that may arise and agrees to the process by which they will be managed. Following these procedures and making the related ethical decisions does not necessarily feel good, but failing to do so puts both the patient and the practitioner at risk. Fortunately, such failures are generally avoidable, and we hope this chapter assists practitioners in reducing them.

## REFERENCES

American Psychological Association. (2010). Ethical principles of psychologists and code of conduct. *American Psychologist*, 65(5), 493.

Beauchamp, T. L., & Childress, J. F. (2009). *Principles of Biomedical Ethics* (6th ed., pp. 38–39). New York, NY: Oxford University Press.

*Black's Law Dictionary* (2014), (10th ed.). Carol Steram, IL: Thomson West.

Dewey, L. M., & Gottlieb, M. C. (2011). Ethical guidelines for providing court-ordered outpatient therapy to juvenile offenders. *Journal of Forensic Psychology Practice*, 11, 1–20.

Gillon, R. (1994). Medical ethics: principles plus attention to scope. *BMJ*, 309(6948), 184–188.

Glabman, M. (2009). It's no longer just members who are suing health plans. *Managed Care*, February. Retrieved from http://www.managedcaremag.com/archives/2009/2/it's-no-longer-just-members-who-are-suing-health-plans (accessed July 31, 2016).

Gottlieb, M. C. (1993). Avoiding exploitive dual relationships: a decision-making model. *Psychotherapy: Theory, Research, Practice and Training*, 30, 41–48.

Gottlieb, M. C., & Younggren, J. N. (2009). Is there is a slippery slope? Considerations regarding multiple relationships and risk management. *Professional Psychology: Research and Practice*, 40, 564–571.

Knapp, S., Gottlieb, M., Berman, J., & Handelsman, M. (2007). When law and ethics collide: what should psychologists do? *Professional Psychology: Research and Practice*, 38(1), 54–59. doi: http://dx.doi.org/10.1037/0735-7028.38.1.54.

Knapp, S., Gottlieb, M. C., & Handelsman, M. M. (2015). *Ethics Dilemmas in Psychotherapy: Positive Approaches to Decision Making*. Washington, DC: American Psychological Association.

Lazarus, A. A., & Zur, O. (Eds.) (2002). *Dual Relationships and Psychotherapy*. New York: Springer.

Lerner, J. (2015). *Managed Care Company Settles Over Mental Health Claim Denials.* http://www.lohud.com/story/news/local/westchester/2015/03/05/mental-health-parity-settlement/24472441/ (accessed July 27, 2016).

Ross, W. D. (1930). *The Right and the Good*. Oxford: Clarendon.

*60 Minutes*, Denied (2014). http://www.cbsnews.com/news/mental-illness-health-care-insurance-60-minutes/ (accessed September 8, 2015).

*Tarasoff* v. *Regents of the University of California*, 17 Cal. 3d 425, 551 P.2d 334, 131 Cal. Rptr. 14 (Cal. 1976).

Younggren, J., & Gottlieb, M. C. (2004). Managing risk when contemplating multiple relationships. *Professional Psychology: Research and Practice*, 35, 255-260.

Zur, O. (2007). *Boundaries in Psychotherapy: Ethical and Clinical Explorations*. Washington, DC: American Psychological Association—APA Books.

# Part II

## Mandatory Multiple Relationships in Military, Police, and Forensic Settings

# INTRODUCTION

*Ofer Zur*

Part II (Chapters 3-6) discusses the clearest examples of mandatory multiple relationships. This includes the military, police, and forensic settings in which psychotherapists have no choice but to engage in the multiple relationships inherent in these settings.

In Chapter 3, Dr. Brad Johnson and his sister, Dr. Shannon Johnson, discuss the complex multiple relationships that are mandated in military settings where psychologists experience mixed agency, as their loyalties are first to the Department of Defense, then to the local commanding officer, and lastly to the individual service member whom they face in the consulting room. The chapter discusses the fact that, increasingly, military psychologists are embedded within a military unit, which means that they are deployed with the unit to combat theaters and are simultaneously a uniform-wearing member of the unit (like their clients) and a mental health provider. They end the chapter with a set of recommendations for military mental health providers on how to handle such complex, mandated, and unavoidable multiple relationships.

In Chapter 4, Dr. McCutchen discusses how police psychology also presents complex and often unavoidable multiple roles, multiple loyalties, and multiple relationship situations in which the psychologist may be concurrently involved in providing clinical services, as well as training, fitness-for-duty evaluations, pre-employment screenings, consultations with SWAT units, hostage negotiations, debriefings, consultations on suicide prevention, and other roles. Needless to say, these diverse responsibilities and multiple loyalties (i.e., to the department, officers, public, courts, own safety), can easily present conflicts of interests, conflicts of loyalties, and ethical and legal dilemmas. She goes on to articulate the benefits and risks of these complex multiple duties and suggests ways to negotiate them.

Chapters 5 and 6 detail the complexities of multiple relationships in forensic and correctional settings.

In Chapter 5, Dr. Alex Ward and Dr. Tony Ward consider how forensic mental health practitioners face highly complex and equally difficult and pressing ethical issues, whether they are assessments or therapeutic work with individuals facing trial, awaiting sentence, or serving sentences in prisons or jails. They detail how practitioners in forensic settings are part of two distinct state institutions, the criminal justice and mental health systems. These two institutions have distinct sets of functions, norms, rules, laws, acceptable conduct, and what constitutes ethical conduct.

In Chapter 6, Dr. Shapiro and Dr. Walker illuminate one of the biggest problems that psychotherapists face when it comes to dual roles. They explain why the forensic role of child custody evaluator and the therapeutic role are generally considered incompatible. They go further to explain that this incompatibility also applies to other forensic-evaluative roles. The psychotherapist's role, they explain, is that of a patient advocate, which often presents irreconcilable conflict with the objective-evaluative role of a forensic expert. They point out that psychotherapists are generally "biased" in favor of their clients, as they have a commitment to the patient's welfare. In contrast, they explain, forensic experts are committed to objective and unbiased reports to the court. The forensic evaluator's dual relationships, they assert, often present conflicts of interests and, as a result, are often unethical and should be avoided, when possible.

CHAPTER 3

# UNAVOIDABLE AND MANDATED MULTIPLE RELATIONSHIPS IN MILITARY SETTINGS

*W. Brad Johnson and Shannon J. Johnson*

Military clinical psychologists share a long and distinguished legacy of service in support of military personnel and the nation (Budd & Kennedy, 2006). At the present time, approximately 500 uniformed (active-duty) psychologists are employed around the globe in medical centers, outpatient clinics, forward-deployed combat stress units, ships at sea, and in areas ravaged by national disasters (Johnson, 2015). Increasingly, military psychologists are *embedded* within a military unit, which means that they are deployed with the unit to combat theaters and are simultaneously a uniform-wearing member of the unit and a mental health provider (Johnson, Ralph, & Johnson, 2005). The military psychologist's dual identities as provider and military officer as well as his or her embedded status within a war-fighting unit means that, quite often, multiple relationships are ubiquitous to the practice of clinical psychology in the military.

In contrast to their civilian counterparts in private practice, military psychologists must often engage clients in many different contexts and roles, daily increasing the probability for unavoidable multiple relationships (Hines, Ader, Chang, & Rundell, 1998; Kennedy & Johnson, 2009).

At times, these multiple relationships may create apparent conflicts of interest, and sometimes, distress for both clients and psychologist (particularly more junior psychologists who are fresh from graduate-school ethics classes and new to the unique culture of the military). Yet, multiple relationships in the military may also offer a number of benefits to clients, such as increased access to care and destigmatization of mental health services. Effective military psychologists acclimate to the culture of the military, increasing their tolerance of normative and mandated multiple relationships while simultaneously upholding the spirit of ethical principles and standards bearing on multiple relationships, and while working tirelessly to prevent multiple relationships from causing harm to their clients.

In this brief chapter, we describe the elements of mental health practice in military settings that create heightened probability of mandated and unavoidable multiple relationships with therapy clients. We highlight the primary types of unavoidable multiple relationships in the military and provide illustrative vignettes to shed light on how easily such relationships may occur and the ethical complexities they may create for providers. Finally, we offer several recommendations for managing unavoidable multiple relationships in military settings, always with the goal of minimizing harm to clients and maximizing the potential value of such multiple relationships.

## Military Settings Heighten the Frequency of Multiple Relationships

Multiple relationships occur when a mental health professional has more than one role with a client, or is likely to enter into another relationship with the client in the future (American Psychological Association (APA), 2010). Multiple relationships can become problematic when they place vulnerable clients at risk of exploitation. Ethics scholars warn that multiple relationships are more likely to cause harm when a mental health provider's personal interests conflict with his or her professional interests and when the practitioner holds significant power over the client (Kitchener, 2000).

At times, military psychologists have struggled with apparent conflicts between their mandated and commissioned roles as military officers and their identities as licensed healthcare providers. Notable tensions between the APA Code of Ethics (APA, 2010) and Department of Defense (DoD) statutes and regulations are most evident in the areas of confidentiality, informed consent, and multiple relationships (Jeffrey, Rankin, & Jeffrey, 1992; Johnson, 2008).

Research evidence suggests that, among these ethical tensions, multiple relationships are the most frequent area of ethical tension in the day-to-day experience of military psychologists (Orme & Doerman, 2001; Staal & King, 2000). Successfully managing unavoidable multiple relationships can be most challenging when psychologists experience *mixed-agency dilemmas* (Kennedy & Johnson, 2009); that is, when there are conflicts between loyalties or obligations to individual clients and the larger organization (DoD, federal government).

There are a number of specific features of the military context that contribute to both the frequency and the complexity of multiple relationships for uniformed mental health providers. Here are some of the most persistent among them:

- *Dual identities:* Because they are simultaneously mental health provider and military officer, military psychologists may feel occasional tension between their clinical training—emphasizing stringent avoidance of multiple roles with clients—and the requirements of their military roles—leading and interacting with clients frequently in small military units (Zur & Gonzalez, 2002).

- *Embedded assignments:* Military psychologists are increasingly likely to occupy solo, embedded assignments (officer billets) in which they find themselves the only mental health provider in a small, close-knit community of soldiers, sailors, airmen, or marines (Budd & Kennedy, 2006; Johnson et al., 2005). Consider the following reflection from a Navy aircraft carrier psychologist:

> One client stops to tell me how the last phone conversation with his wife went. Ten steps later, someone who is not a client stops to ask about whether his son has ADHD. Five more steps and I'm having a conversation with a person I've never met about his wife's history of depression . . . Finally, just before arriving at my destination, a sailor whom I've seen for a few appointments stops me to lament about why he can't ever seem to have intimate relationships with women who are not prostitutes.
>
> (Johnson et al., 2005, p. 74)

51

In such small units, members naturally expect to know more about the personal lives of others and multiple relationships between medical providers and combatants are both unavoidable and expected by members of the community. When embedded assignments are in isolated duty stations, psychologists will have limited options for social relationship and contacts with current clients outside the consultation office are not only probable, but constant and daily (Johnson, Bacho, Heim, and Ralph, 2006). As a commissioned officer in a strict chain of military command, military psychologists in embedded settings technically have multiple roles with every single client who is either enlisted (the majority of clients) or an officer of lower or higher rank.

- *Inability to refer:* Unlike most of their civilian counterparts, uniformed psychologists have little or no choice about entering or exiting clinical relationships (Johnson, 2008, 2015). Particularly in embedded positions, a psychologist may be required by the exigencies of the situation, and the fact that he or she is simply the only provider available, to handle every clinical case that "walks through their door." Quite often, the uniformed provider is mandated to accept any client who presents with a mental health service requirement, regardless of the presenting problem, diagnosis, or any pre-existing relationship with the provider. In contrast, civilian mental health providers, even those in rural settings, may feel more liberty to refer clients with whom they currently have—or are likely to have in the future—another kind of relationship.
- *Difficulty identifying the "client":* In a civilian setting, it may be easier to quickly determine the identity of the primary client in any new referral situation, and thus evaluate the probability of a multiple relationship. However, when a commanding officer requests an evaluation of an active-duty military member, it is not always clear whether the primary "client" is the individual service member, the commanding officer, or the DoD more broadly.

It is clear that the unique fusion of personal and professional interactions with clients that defines military service for psychologists is unavoidable and, at times, legally mandated. To function competently and effectively in the military milieu, mental health providers must increase their tolerance for and comfort with everyday boundary crossings (Gutheil & Gabbard, 1993). In our experience, multiple relationships with clients rarely cause harm, particularly when the psychologist demonstrates comfort with these interactions and remains attuned to the client's best interests. Moreover, multiple relationships in the military can actually improve morale, lower stigma about seeking professional assistance, and improve real-time access to care.

## COMMON VARIETIES OF MULTIPLE RELATIONSHIPS IN MILITARY SETTINGS

Gottlieb (1993) and others have cautioned psychologists to avoid multiple relationships with clients when there is a marked power differential between psychologist and client, when the relationship is likely to be of long duration, or when there is an absence of a clear termination point. Problematically, all three conditions are often in play in military settings. For instance, Kennedy and Johnson (2009) described situations in which military psychologists were required to perform evaluations of their commanding officer or have an invasive medical procedure performed by a current client. The three most common instances of unavoidable multiple relationships in military settings are described below, each with an illustrative vignette furnished by an active-duty military psychologist.

### Encountering Clients Outside the Office

While deployed with a Marine Logistic Group in Iraq, I was assigned to the one female tent on the compound. As I was unpacking my gear, I noticed that a Marine who I had treated for a personality disorder back in garrison was going to be occupying a cot nearby. I mentally prepared to maintain confidentiality and my professional boundaries with this Marine, despite having to share living quarters with her for the next 7 months. A few weeks later, I became aware that my Marine client was creating significant conflict and unnecessary drama with other women in the tent, and this was having a negative impact on unit cohesion and, more importantly, her unit's mission. In my high-visibility role as the only embedded mental health professional, it became clear that I would repeatedly be called on to serve as "group therapist" and intervene to de-escalate the tension. In addition to coming to terms with the loss of a space to escape from my therapeutic role,

53

I carefully considered how I was going to avoid "outing" my patient and maintain a supportive, empathic stance, while also acting in the best interest of the group and critical combat missions. To cope effectively, I sought alternative personal space for the quiet reflection I needed to maintain my clinical effectiveness for the duration of the deployment. In the end, my presence as a member of this "tent community" appeared reassuring for my client and helpful to the other women, who often counted on me to calm tensions before they became conflicts.

As members of very small and close-knit military communities, embedded psychologists are certain to routinely interact with many, if not all, of their clients outside of treatment (Johnson et al., 2005; Zur & Gonzalez, 2002). Sometimes, these extra-therapy contacts with clients are quite personal, even intimate, and not always possible to predict. For example, military psychologists have suddenly found themselves receiving a haircut from a client, sharing an open shower bay with clients, having their teeth cleaned or a physical examination from a client, and in at least one case we know of, having to urinate in front of a client as part of a command-required urinalysis collection. To be effective in military psychology, clinicians must assume that they will encounter clients— often in entirely unexpected ways—around the small military base or ship.

## A Colleague Becomes a Patient

During the initial months of my first Western Pacific deployment as an aircraft carrier psychologist, I had developed a close working relationship with the airwing chaplain, another Lieutenant Commander with whom I had a lot in common. Not only was I grateful for the way we were able to collaborate effectively to care for the psychological and emotional needs of over 5,000 embarked Sailors, the chaplain had also become a trusted confident with whom I appreciated being able to debrief at the end of a stressful day. I was therefore not surprised when he appeared at my office door one evening and sat down in the chair where my patients typically sat. Yet, one glance at his disheveled appearance and the pained look on this face, and it was clear to me that he was not in my office for our typical decompression session. With little prompting, he disclosed that, for the last week, he had been too anxious to sleep and increasingly haunted by disturbing and intrusive memories of the gruesome violence he witnessed while serving in the Peace Corps prior to joining the Navy. He was tearful as he acknowledged that worsening posttraumatic stress symptoms had started to undermine his effectiveness.

When he buried his face in his hands and began to sob, I became aware that the situation required me to shift from a personal to a professional interaction. After assessing his risk for self-harm, I began a series of questions to help me determine what would be in the best interest of my colleague. Should I medevac him back to the States for a higher level of care? Aware of this new multiple role, I found it impossible to maintain a professional distance as I weighed the impact of such a decision on the chaplain's career, on the crew, and inevitably on myself if I were to lose this valued friendship for the remaining months of the deployment.

It is nearly impossible for embedded military psychologists to avoid providing treatment to colleagues, friends, and even direct supervisors. Military psychologists must always be prepared to transition from a purely friendly, social, collegial relationship, to a clinical role (Johnson et al., 2006; Staal & King, 2000). On the downside, these multiple relationships can pose discomfort for both parties and tension between the best interests of a "friend" and the best interests of the military unit and ultimately the combat mission. On the upside, a pre-existing friendship with a "client" can enhance trust, empathy, and genuine care in crafting a transparent treatment plan or disposition most likely to be in the best interests of the client.

## Unanticipated Shifts from Clinical to Forensic or Administrative Roles

As the embedded psychologist with a Special Forces command, I had been treating a member of the unit for several months. He had been motivated and compliant with treatment and I deemed him to be fit for his duties providing logistical support for members of the unit down range. Despite meeting with me for bi-weekly therapy sessions and what I thought was our strong therapeutic alliance, my patient had never mentioned that he was planning on putting in a package to join an elite Special Forces community that would require him to frequently deploy to remote regions to conduct dangerous missions. I only became aware of his plan after I was asked to serve on a personnel selection and suitability determination board. As a member of the board it was my responsibility to review the packages, which included a comprehensive psychological evaluation conducted by a colleague in the operational psychology community. When I began reading through one of the packages and realized it belonged to my patient, I was stunned. Upon review, I realized that critical details of his mental health history and current functioning were missing. Since my knowledge of these details came only from confidential therapy sessions, I was unsure how to communicate my concerns to the other board members who were not clinicians. I had to weigh my commitment to protecting the confidentially of my patient with my responsibility to protect the other operators who would potentially need to depend on my patient to perform flawlessly under extremely stressful and dangerous conditions.

Although the APA Ethics Code cautions psychologists to avoid shifting roles with clients without appropriate informed consent prior to the commencement of treatment, military psychologists often find themselves assuming administrative, supervisor, or forensic roles with former or current clients with little warning or capacity to anticipate this new mandated role (APA, 2010; Johnson, 2008). Particularly in isolated duty stations, embedded assignments, and operational roles with special forces or other elite units, psychologists must be a "jack of all trades," often performing fitness-for-duty or other screening assessments, whether the object of the evaluation is a client or not. Clearly, informing clients about possible role shifts when they can be anticipated early in treatment is indicated.

## RECOMMENDATIONS FOR MILITARY MENTAL HEALTH PROVIDERS

As illustrated in the foregoing vignettes, establishing competence in military clinical psychology requires ethical dexterity in accepting and managing the many variations of unavoidable multiple relationships likely to occur daily in the life of the military psychologist. Efficacy as an embedded military psychologist or a psychologist assigned to an isolated duty station will be facilitated by a less rigid and more culturally sensitive appreciation for the unavoidable and potentially beneficial nature of multiple relationships in the military. Potential benefits of interaction with clients outside of therapy include: (a) a better appreciation for the unit culture and the specific stressors experienced by service members; (b) greater credibility within the military unit, as an "insider" who can be trusted in the community; (c) an enhanced perception that you, the provider, are available and approachable by unit members who might benefit from mental health services; and (d) a decrease in the self and unit stigma associated with talking with a mental health provider; after all, positive interactions with the psychologist have already occurred socially (Barnett & Yutrzenka, 2002; Johnson et al., 2005)! Below, we offer several specific recommendations for military mental healthcare providers designed to mitigate harm and maximize benefits for clients from multiple relationships in embedded environments.

## Provide Careful Informed Consent

At the outset and throughout any clinical relationship, be as clear and transparent as possible with clients about the high probability that the two of you will come into contact with one another around base, around the ship, or during deployments. Depending on the nature of your current assignment and the client's role in the community, openly brainstorm and then discuss all the ways the two of you might encounter one another and how you might best manage these unavoidable interactions. Ask the client how he or she would like you to respond when the two of you see each other around the unit. Also, be as specific as possible about the kinds of mental health evaluations you may be required to perform at the request of an appropriate military authority (e.g., fitness for duty, security clearance, substance use).

## Assume That Every Member of the Military is a Potential Client

It is often helpful for military mental health professionals to frame everyone they encounter socially or at work as a potential client. Adopting such a perspective may help psychologists make good decisions about levels of self-disclosure, romantic partners, and degree of social and political engagement (versus neutrality) within the work environment.

Clearly, the provider—like every other military member—will have needs for friends, emotional support, and recreation. But the degree to which one becomes engaged personally must always be tempered by the reality that any personal/social relationship may shift to a clinical role with little warning or ability to anticipate the shift.

## Maintain a Strong External Support Network, Including Professional Consultants

Particularly in isolated or embedded military assignments, providers will benefit from getting some personal and professional needs met by distal friends and colleagues not assigned to the unit. With such networks and support taking place through email, video conferencing, phone calls, and visits during leave periods, psychologists may feel less need to get all of their personal needs met within the military community. This, of course, will allow the psychologist to enjoy multiple relationships and unavoidable social interactions with clients without increasing the risk of exploitation or harm to clients.

## Engage in Self-Care and Increase Tolerance for Boundary Crossings

If military psychologists are too anxious about behaving unethically or harming clients due to extra-therapy contact, they may become isolated and perpetually upset about multiple roles and relationships about which they can do nothing (Johnson et al., 2005). To be effective, military psychologists must increase their tolerance—even their enjoyment—of routine boundary crossings and contacts with clients external to the consulting room. If psychologists can model calm acceptance of these multiple roles, while demonstrating the utmost regard for the client's confidentiality and best interests, clients too will become calmer and less anxious about these encounters. Recognize the power of intentional role modeling and allow members of the military unit to observe you engaging in exercise, occasional private time, and exchanges with all members of the community characterized by unconditional acceptance and positive regard.

SUMMARY

Multiple relationships are ubiquitous in the life and practice of the military psychologist. Uniformed mental health providers frequently encounter clients outside the confines of the consultation room. At times, these interactions are quite personal, such as when the client is the only provider of a particular medical specialty available. At other times, military psychologists must provide mental health services for friends, colleagues, and direct supervisors or commanding officers. At still other times, the uniformed psychologist may have to switch roles with a current or former client from clinical to administrative or forensic, often with little warning. Effective military mental health providers would do well to keep in mind that interaction with clients outside of therapy may include some benefits while simultaneously remaining vigilant to any adverse effects of multiple roles on the client or the therapy relationship. Military psychologists will be most effective if they provide careful informed consent regarding the frequency of multiple relationships, assume that any member of a military community may become a client eventually, maintain a strong support network external to their current military unit, engage in a robust program of self-care, and increase their tolerance for routine boundary crossings and multiple roles in military settings.

REFERENCES

American Psychological Association. (2010). *Ethical Principles of Psychologists and Code of Conduct*. Retrieved from: http://www.apa.org/ethics (accessed July 27, 2016).

Barnett, J. E., & Yutrzenka, B. A. (2002). Nonsexual dual relationships in professional practice, with special applications to rural and military communities. In A. A. Lazarus & O. Zur (Eds.), *Dual Relationships and Psychotherapy* (pp. 273–286). New York: Springer.

Budd, F., & Kennedy, C. (2006). Introduction to clinical military psychology. In C. Kennedy & E. A. Zillmer (Eds.), *Military Psychology: Clinical and Operational Applications* (pp. 21–34). New York: Guilford.

Gottlieb, M. C. (1993). Avoiding exploitive dual relationships: a decision-making model. *Psychotherapy, 30,* 41–48.

Gutheil, T. G., & Gabbard, G. O. (1993). The concept of boundaries in clinical practice: theoretical and risk-management dimensions. *American Journal of Psychiatry, 150,* 188–196.

Hines, A. H., Ader, D. N., Chang, A. S., & Rundell, J. R. (1998). Dual agency, dual relationships, boundary crossings, and associated boundary violations: a survey of military and civilian psychiatrists. *Military Medicine, 163,* 826–833.

Jeffrey, T. B., Rankin, R. J., & Jeffrey, L. K. (1992). In service of two masters: the ethical-legal dilemma faced by military psychologists. *Professional Psychology: Research and Practice, 23,* 91–95.

Johnson, W. B. (2008). Top ethical challenges for military clinical psychologists. *Military Psychology, 20,* 49–62.

Johnson, W. B. (2015). Military settings. In J. Norcross, G. R. VandenBos, & D. K. Freedheim (Eds.) *APA Handbook of Clinical Psychology: Vol. 1* (pp. 495–507). Washington, DC: American Psychological Association.

Johnson, W. B., Ralph, J., & Johnson, S. J. (2005). Managing multiple roles in embedded environments: the case of aircraft carrier psychology. *Professional Psychology: Research and Practice, 36,* 73–81.

Johnson, W. B., Bacho, R., Heim, M., & Ralph, J. (2006). Multiple-role dilemmas for military mental health care providers. *Military Medicine, 171,* 311–315.

Kennedy, C. H., & Johnson, W. B. (2009). Mixed agency in military psychology: applying the American Psychological Association ethics code. *Psychological Services, 6,* 22–31.

Kitchener, K. S. (2000). *Foundations of Ethical Practice, Research, and Teaching in Psychology.* Mahwah, NJ: Erlbaum.

Orme, D. R., & Doerman, A. L. (2001). Ethical dilemmas and U.S. Air Force clinical psychologists: a survey. *Professional Psychology: Research and Practice, 32,* 305–311.

Staal, M. A., & King, R. E. (2000). Managing a multiple relationship environment: the ethics of military psychology. *Professional Psychology: Research and Practice, 31,* 698–705.

Zur, O., & Gonzalez, S. (2002). Multiple relationships in military psychology. In A. A. Lazarus & O. Zur (Eds.), *Dual Relationships and Psychotherapy* (pp. 315–328). New York: Springer.

# Chapter 4

# MULTIPLE RELATIONSHIPS IN POLICE PSYCHOLOGY

## Common, Unavoidable, and Navigable Occurrences

*Jeni L. McCutcheon*

Ethical issues are plentiful in the specialty area of police psychology. Police psychologists routinely encounter multiple relationships. They occur commonly and are unavoidable, normal occurrences. This chapter examines types of multiple relationships that may occur in police psychology. Examples are offered. Relevant ethical codes are covered. Benefits and risks related to multiple relationships in police psychology are discussed and methods to negotiate the complexities of multiple relationships are presented.

### MULTIPLE RELATIONSHIPS AS COMMON ETHICAL DILEMMAS

Research about common ethical dilemmas in police psychology is scarce. Zelig (1988) surveyed police psychologists and found negotiating dual relationships to be among the top three encountered ethical dilemmas. Rounding out the top three were confidentiality and resolving conflicts between professional standards and the needs of the organization. This finding is consistent with research about common ethical dilemmas among psychologists in general. Multiple studies in the USA and internationally found that multiple relationships are routinely among the most prevalently experienced ethical dilemmas (Colnerud, 1997; Pettifor & Sawchuk, 2006; Slack & Wassenaar, 1999).

TYPES OF MULTIPLE RELATIONSHIPS IN
POLICE PSYCHOLOGY

Multiple relationships in police psychology are prevalent. They happen when a psychologist has more than one relationship with a current or past client or patient. They happen when a psychologist also has a relationship with someone the client or patient is associated with or close to. This could be with a family member, spouse, significant other, or friend. They also occur at an organizational level, where an agency is the client and a psychologist assumes multiple roles and has multiple loyalties within an agency. This may lead to situations where roles overlap or even conflict, and the psychologist is faced with figuring out how to provide services in multiple contexts.

Multiple relationships are increasingly common in police psychology. That stated, there are a couple of exceptions where they should be avoided. Examples include a sexual relationship with a client or doing an evaluation for a third party on a subject that is an existing client. The burden of showing that a relationship is appropriate, mandated, or unavoidable is on the police psychologist. Considerations include what is in the best interest of the client(s), that the psychologist is free from undue influence, and that the psychologist seeks to avoid harm or exploitation to the client(s), as well as avoid engaging in relationships where there is a loss of objectivity.

EXAMPLES OF MULTIPLE RELATIONSHIPS IN
POLICE PSYCHOLOGY

To understand multiple relationships in police psychology it is helpful to be aware of the different domains of practice. Police psychologists practice among four core domains (Aumiller et al., 2007). One domain is assessment-related activities. Functional competencies in this domain include pre-employment, post-offer of employment psychological evaluation of job candidates, and psychological fitness-for-duty evaluations of incumbents. Intervention services are another domain and include counseling to cope with unique or chronic job stressors and intervention-related education and training, such as teaching a stress management class for police officer recruits in a law enforcement training academy. A third domain is operational support. Functional competencies in this domain include psychological intelligence, as with criminal profiling, and crisis and hostage negotiation. A fourth domain is organizational/management consultation. Job tasks here may involve executive consultation regarding personnel-related issues, and mediation. Police psychologists typically practice in a couple of domains. It is rare that police psychologists practice in all four domains. With so many functional competencies (currently 50-plus total within all four domains), and psychologists practicing in one or more domains, it is not surprising that roles, responsibility, loyalties, and relationships overlap.

The scope and possibilities of multiple relationships in police psychology are endless. These multiple relationships can be concurrent, when the psychologist has two roles or functions with the same individual at the same time, or they can be sequential, when the different roles do not overlap and take place sequentially. Common examples are as follows. The police psychologist performs a pre-employment evaluation on a police officer candidate. This candidate is hired and the police psychologist teaches the person about working with individuals with serious mental illness in the law enforcement training academy. The contact may stop there. Or, because of the increased contact with the psychologist, the officer becomes comfortable with the psychologist and later seeks him or her out as a psychotherapist. This could be a voluntary therapy relationship where the officer seeks individual counseling, or, perhaps when he or she is mandated by the department to attend a meeting after an officer-involved shooting incident (akin to a privileged confidential therapy session, though typically with a psycho-educative focus). The contact may happen years later when the officer advances in rank and acts as the department's hiring authority. In this relationship the psychologist serves the agency and works with this past candidate/student/patient in a separate role as a consultant, providing risk ratings and recommendations to assist in hiring decisions.

Multiple relationships in police psychology are highly diverse. Another example includes showing up for a ride-along and being assigned to ride with a current or past therapy patient. Or, seeing pre-employment evaluation candidates as they apply, are hired, and laterally move and are evaluated again for work at another agency. Consider a patient who seeks relational therapy and then working as a homicide detective seeks consultation about a cold case, asking questions about a mental health condition, or requesting a psychological autopsy on a case that evolves from a suspected homicide to a confirmed suicide. What if the long hours, arduous and often-gory circumstances of this job assignment negatively impact the officer's relationship with his or her significant other? Consider the complexity involved in providing pre-employment evaluation and research services for years to a police or fire chief. When that individual faces life challenges such as retirement, he or she seeks out that same psychologist for executive consultation, information, and referrals, or even personal therapy services.

Police psychologists also run into the typical multiple relationship occurrences that other psychologists encounter in other settings. They have past and current clients as neighbors. They sometimes purchase professional services that turn out to be owned or run by a previous or current client. They run into situations where the psychologist's spouse works out at the local gym and befriends a workout partner who turns out to be a patient they helped cope with a multiple-fatality car accident where the patient was a first responder. They find themselves on the same parent–teacher association or religious committee as a patient. They show up to their child's basketball game and sit a few bleacher steps down from a police employee, also cheering on his or her own child, and recognize that they recently screened this person for membership in a police department's Critical Incident Stress Management (CISM) team. Add to that that the employee's motivation for joining the CISM team was a child drowning incident that s/he responded to two years prior, and the psychologist saw them for several therapy sessions to cope with this incident. They are contacted by an agency head and asked to reach out to help with a welfare check of a current employee reportedly in distress, only to realize that this employee's spouse was a member of a social group they belonged to last year.

More unusual examples include a crime taking place at a psychologist's residence and one of the responding officers is a past therapy patient. Also, providing therapy to an individual dealing with an unhappy marriage, and months later, three to four sessions in with a new patient with a different last name, the psychologist realizes s/he is well into a therapy relationship with the spouse of the original patient. In general, multiple relationships are likely to increase in frequency and intensity when they take place in rural or small communities and/or in small or physically isolated police departments.

As several chapters in this book detail, there are multiple relevant areas of the American Psychological Association (APA) *Ethical Principles of Psychologists and Code of Conduct.* Aspirational general principles apply and speak to the need for psychologists to do good, avoid doing harm, be aware of their influence, be trustworthy and mindful of responsibilities, be honest, truthful, and fair, exercise good judgment, recognize their own biases and limitations of competence, and avoid participation in activities that may harm others (APA).

Other sections of the Code of Ethics detailed in this book which are highly relevant to police psychology are avoiding harm, multiple relationships, conflict of interest, third-party requests for services, exploitative relationships, informed consent, psychological services delivered to or through organizations, and discussing the limits of confidentiality.

There are three major police psychologist organizations. These are the International Association of Chiefs of Police, Police Psychological Services Section (IACP PPSS); the Society for Police and Criminal Psychology (SPCP); and the APA, Division 18, Police & Public Safety Section. Membership in these organizations creates opportunities for consultation with other police psychologists, and the IACP PPSS specifically has an Ethics Consultation Committee, which is a helpful resource to section members.

Police psychologists have other resources to assist with ethical practice. There are guidelines developed in coordination with law enforcement personnel by psychologists of the IACP PPSS. Each guideline is typically revised every five years. The guidelines exist to assist police agencies and police psychologists by providing recommendations for best practice in police psychology service provision and in responding to certain types of occurrences and incidents within police agencies. The following guidelines exist: *Fitness for Duty Evaluation Guidelines* (IACP, 2013a); *Officer-Involved Shooting Guidelines* (IACP, 2013b); *Peer Support Guidelines* (IACP, 2011a); *Preemployment Psychological Evaluation Guidelines* (IACP, 2014); and *Guidelines for Consulting Police Psychologists* (IACP, 2011b). Because some competencies within police psychology are forensic in nature, the recently revised APA *Specialty Guidelines for Forensic Psychology* (2013) may also be a helpful resource.

## BENEFITS AND RISKS IN POLICE PSYCHOLOGY MULTIPLE RELATIONSHIPS

Psychologists should strive to do no harm, and to thoughtfully and competently manage multiple relationships. A goal is to take steps to safeguard that the party—whether a patient, an agency or a candidate, depending on the roles and tasks at hand—is neither exploited nor harmed. And the objectivity of the psychologist needs to remain intact. When this is done well, there are benefits to multiple relationships.

It can be argued that, similar to some military settings, the many contacts and contexts of psychologists working in police department, inevitably, create some familiarity. Much like in military and prison settings, such familiarity may decrease the stigma among police of interacting with and seeking help from psychologists. Likewise, this familiarity means that the psychologist is known and hopefully trusted by personnel. Personnel, seeing the psychologist entrenched and embedded in multiple roles and settings across the agency, begin to feel that the psychologist is relatable and "gets" them and police culture. This credibility, especially for an active in-house or consulting psychologist, means that personnel may be more likely to seek support, intervention, and consultation services. Over time, this may have a preventive effect on the health and well-being of individual employees. When psychologists are appropriately flexible and engage in ethical and correctly managed multiple relationships, police psychology is more likely to be recognized and seen as a helpful resource at organizational levels as well.

There are also risks with engaging in multiple relationships in police psychology. Boundary violations, inappropriate out-of-office experiences, and, in general, relationships that are clearly inappropriate, exploitative, and harmful bear with them a risk of harm. So do those where the psychologist loses objectivity. Consider, for example, the psychologist who accepts a request for a fitness-for-duty evaluation when s/he previously provided therapy services to this same person. Whether the employee is found fit for duty or not has negative repercussions for the agency, the past patient/subject of the evaluation, or both. Such a negligent action negatively portrays that particular psychologist, and may be generalized to psychology as a whole. In as much as positive multiple relationships can decrease stigma and do good, similarly, poorly thought-through, mishandled, and exploitative multiple relationships can create harm and have problematic consequences for those involved.

WAYS TO NEGOTIATE MULTIPLE RELATIONSHIPS
COMPLEXITIES

Certainly multiple relationships in police psychology are multi-faceted. They are, however, navigable, meaning that they are maneuverable and able to be managed. There are various methods to negotiate the complexities of multiple relationships. One primary method of resolving ethical dilemmas is to employ one or more ethical decision-making models. There are many models. They have in common a sequential and detailed method to consider the intricacies of ethical dilemmas. Steps often involve identifying the ethical dilemma or dilemmas, pinpointing the relevant ethical codes, laws, practical and business issues, recognizing potential choices that could be made with resultant risks and benefits, seeking out opportunities for consultation, deciding on a reasonable course of action, and wrapping up with some sort of an appraisal of the opted-for resolution. For an in-depth discussion of such models and their utilization in police psychology practice, see McCutcheon (2011).

There are additional ways to resolve ethical dilemmas in police psychology. Consultation with a competent police psychologist is one possible option, and such colleagues may be found among the list of Board Certified Specialists on the website of the American Board of Police and Public Safety Psychology (ABPPSP). The ABPPSP website maintains a list of current specialists, comprising psychologists who have achieved the highest level of competence as evaluated through a rigorous process by their peers. As referenced previously, presenting the dilemma to an Ethics Consultation Committee is an option. Another source of consultation would be an attorney who specializes in working with police agencies and police psychologists. Obtaining continuing education in areas of police psychology, ethics in general, and ethics in police psychology specifically, can increase competence to assist in sensible resolution of ethical dilemmas.

A final method to recognize, reflect, and resolve ethical dilemmas involves thoughtful consideration of the multiple roles of the psychologist and inherent complexities in multiple relationships. There is much writing about risk management in resolving ethical dilemmas, and while such contributions are worthwhile, that is not what this author is referring to. Focused thinking is needed. First, a consideration of aspirational ethics is important. A consideration that there may exist obligations and loyalties to multiple parties in any given multiple relationship is also important.

Aspirational ethics need to be encouraged in everyday police psychology practice. Whereas mandatory ethics sets the bar for the minimum behavior required in psychology practice, aspirational ethics asks the question, "What is the best action that can be achieved for the involved parties?" This may be a philosophical stance to assume as a way of thinking through situations, rather than a practical solution-focused model that easily solves ethical dilemmas. This author encourages a mindset of striving for good. This may serve as a sort of "moral compass" to assist in making sometimes daunting decisions regarding multiple relationships.

Ponder an example where a police psychologist sits down with a candidate to perform a pre-employment evaluation. As the psychologist walks the candidate back for the evaluation he notes the candidate's familiarity. A quick database check to look for conflict of interest is unrevealing. A few minutes into the scheduled interview, the psychologist remarks over the sense of familiarity and asks about previous relationships with this candidate. Turns out, the woman was seen 10 years ago by this psychologist for a pre-employment evaluation for another agency. At that time she was married and had a different last name. Once hired, she was called up as a reserve for military service, deployed and, upon returning stateside, she was also seen by the same psychologist 5 years ago for two visits. At that point she had reverted back to her maiden name, and was seen for a post-deployment supportive return-to-work adjustment/wellness meeting (akin to a therapy session and with subsequent confidentiality and an aim of assisting the patient with returning from military service, getting back to civilian life, and adjusting back to police work). She is now about to be seen for another pre-employment evaluation, this time under a third, newly married last name, for a new agency.

Clearly, a multiple relationship exists. In fact, as is the case with many situations in police psychology, there are several multiple relationships here. First, as a candidate and the subject of the evaluation, where an agency was the psychologist's client. In the second situation, the service is paid for and offered as a supportive service to the employee by the agency. The patient or client in this situation is defined as the employee returning home from military deployment. Finally, the client in the current requested pre-employment evaluation is the new agency. The subject of the current evaluation was (or, depending on the theoretical framework, is still) the psychologist's clinical patient.

The psychologist has a duty to both the new agency and the patient. The minimum ethical requirement is not to perform this evaluation. The psychologist is not objective and his loyalties are divided. In employing aspirational ethics, however, more than just declining the evaluation may be called for. Tasks may include clarifying with the candidate the sequence of the relationships, the psychologist's role in each, and explaining the inappropriateness of moving from a relationship where she is a clinical patient and the psychologist is privy to confidential details and the goal is care for her, to a new role where the psychologist sets aside care for her to focus on the needs and risk for the new agency. At hand are issues of maintaining confidentiality and neither divulging to the candidate what is known about her from the agency's sharing of background information for pre-employment purposes, nor sharing with the agency the details of the existing doctor–patient relationship and the specific reasons why the psychologist is unable to perform this evaluation. The ethical psychologist needs to state that there is indeed a conflict of interest. Action may be needed to help the agency to identify other objective police psychologists who can complete the needed evaluation.

Often there exists a duty to multiple parties. Police psychologists may have responsibilities to all involved parties. In times past, psychologists were encouraged to simply define their role, make this role apparent, and educate or inform others of this role. The thinking seemed to be that, if faced with an ethical dilemma or placed in a challenging situation, the right thing to do was simply cling to that original role. In the case of police psychology, this is neither a practical nor prudent stance, as psychologists often find themselves thrust into multiple roles.

Fisher (2009) wrote of the complexity of needing to serve and navigate dilemmas involving multiple parties. "Psychologists have ethical obligations to all parties in every case, regardless of the number or nature of the relationships" (p. 1). Examples include, as described in the above example, third-party requests and services provided through agencies and organizations. Fisher offered solutions of how to respond, namely being careful to recognize such multiple obligations, think through such situations carefully, and clarify relationships, recognizing a need to attend to multiple parties' needs.

A practical application of Fisher's stance is seen in Corey's remarks in reference to performing pre-employment evaluations of job candidates. "View the candidate's evaluation data first in the light most favorable to the agency's interests, and then in light of the candidate's. This helps to reduce 'primacy effect' bias" (D. Corey, personal communication, October 25, 2013). This speaks to the need to discern and address the varying roles in the context of objectively performing a pre-employment evaluation. The psychologist is working for the agency and the candidate is the subject of the evaluation. There is regard for the candidate's aspirations while there is concern for minimizing risk to the agency, and, it could be argued, potentially to the greater public to some extent.

## NAVIGABLE OCCURRENCES

This chapter focused on multiple relationships and related issues in police psychology. Such relationships are commonplace and routine within the work settings and tasks of police psychology practice. Importantly, they are navigable despite their sometimes mind-boggling complexity.

Psychologists need to tread carefully and proactively in approaching multiple relationships. They need to extricate themselves from exploitative, foreseeably harmful instances, and in cases where they are unable to maintain objectivity. When multiple relationships are inevitable, mandated, appropriate, and likely beneficial, psychologists should identify, define, and clarify their roles, aiming for transparency as much as confidentiality and competing demands will allow. Finally, psychologists should strive for practicing aspirational ethics, in considering what best action they may take while thoroughly weighing and carefully managing their obligations to multiple parties within the context of multiple relationships.

# REFERENCES

American Psychological Association (2010). *Ethics Principles of Psychologists and Code Conduct*. Retrieved from: http://www.apa.org/ethics (accessed July 27, 2016).

American Psychological Association. (2013). Specialty guidelines for forensic psychology. *American Psychologist, 68(1),* 7–19.

Aumiller, G. S., Corey, D., Allen, S., Brewster, J., Cutler, M., Gupton, H., & Honig, A. (2007). Defining the field of police psychology: core domains and proficiencies. *Journal of Police and Criminal Psychology, 22,* 65–76.

Colnerud, G. (1997). Ethical dilemmas of psychologists: a Swedish example in an international perspective. *European Psychologist, 2* (2), 164–170.

Fisher, M. A. (2009). Replacing "Who is the client?" with a different ethical question. *Professional Psychology: Research and Practice, 40*(1), 1–7.

International Association of Chiefs of Police. (2011a). *Peer Support Guidelines.* Arlington, VA. Retrieved from: http://www.theiacp.org/psych_services_section/ (accessed July 27, 2016).

International Association of Chiefs of Police. (2011b). *Guidelines for Consulting Police Psychologists.* Arlington, VA. Retrieved from: http://www.theiacp.org/psych_services_section/ (accessed July 27, 2016).

International Association of Chiefs of Police. (2013a). *Fitness for Duty Evaluation Guidelines.* Arlington, VA. Retrieved from: http://www.theiacp.org/psych_services_section/ (accessed July 27, 2016).

International Association of Chiefs of Police. (2013b). *Officer-Involved Shooting Guidelines.* Arlington, VA. Retrieved from: http://www.theiacp.org/psych_services_section/ (accessed July 27, 2016).

International Association of Chiefs of Police. (2014). *Preemployment Psychological Evaluation Guidelines.* Arlington, VA. Retrieved from: http://www.theiacp.org/psych_services_section/ (accessed July 27, 2016).

McCutcheon, J. L. (2011). Ethical issues in police psychology: challenges and decision-making models to resolve ethical dilemmas. In J. Kitaeff (Ed.), *Handbook of Police Psychology* (pp. 89–108). New York: Routledge.

Pettifor, J. L. & Sawchuk, T. R. (2006). Psychologists' perceptions of ethically troubling incidents across international borders. *International Journal of Psychology, 41*(3), 216–225.

Slack, C. M., & Wassenaar, D. R. (1999). Ethical dilemmas of South African clinical psychologists: international comparisons. *European Psychologist, 4*(3), 179–186.

Zelig, M. (1988). Ethical dilemmas in police psychology. *Professional Psychology: Research and Practice, 19*(3), 336–343.

Chapter 5

# THE COMPLEXITIES OF DUAL RELATIONSHIPS IN FORENSIC AND CORRECTIONAL PRACTICE

## Safety vs. Care

*Alex S. Ward and Tony Ward*

### Introduction

Forensic mental health practitioners face complex and pressing ethical issues in virtually every aspect of their assessment and therapeutic work with individuals facing trial, awaiting sentence, or serving a sentence within the criminal justice system. One of the major reasons that this type of work is especially ethically challenging is because it involves an interaction between two distinct state institutions, the criminal justice and mental health systems. Each of these institutions has its own set of functions and norms specifying what constitutes acceptable conduct for every role it recognizes and authorizes. The difficulty for forensic mental health practitioners is that they often have a foot in both camps. They are mental health professionals *and* criminal justice employees and therefore subject to (at least) two sets of norms, loyalties, rules, and laws and are guided by the associated professional ethical codes.

### The Dual Relationship Complexity

The difficulties associated with working as a mental health practitioner in criminal justice contexts has been identified by a number of professions, including forensic psychiatry (Sadoff, 2011), correctional clinical psychology (Bonner & Vandecreek, 2006; Ward, 2013), forensic social work (Butters & Vaughan-Eden, 2011), and law (Cooper, 2010). In their paper on dual relationships in psychiatry, Robertson and Walter (2008) define the dual relationship problem the following way:

> The problem of the dual role, variably termed 'dual agency', 'overlapping roles', and 'double agency', is a particular quandary in psychiatry. In this paper we refer to the 'dual role' and define it as a quandary in which a psychiatrist faces the dilemma of conflicting expectations or responsibilities, between the therapeutic relationship on the one hand and the interests of third parties on the other.
>
> (pp. 228–229)

Traditionally, in forensic and correctional domains, the dual relationship problem has been formulated in terms of an ethical conflict between two practice roles or sets of tasks, either in assessment or treatment contexts. In these types of situation, there may be a clash between the personal interests and needs of a defendant or offender and those of the community and state.

A central difficulty revolves around the practitioner's priorities and how he or she goes about balancing the needs and interests of the offender against the potential future possible harm the community may suffer; for example, basing a treatment plan on an individual's vocational priorities while also reducing his specific risk factors. The problem is a dual relationship one, as there is likely to be a conflict between a practitioner's commitment to promoting an offender's well-being and possibility of a better life versus the correctional system's concern about community protection—a worry he or she is likely to share by virtue of being subject to its policies and ethical code.

The complexities of dealing with dual relationships is one that continues to trouble practitioners as it reflects an ongoing concern that unjustified harm may be inadvertently inflicted on offenders and/or members of the public. While ethical codes and professional standards especially created for correctional forensic context *describe* or *label* the problem, arguably they do not provide clear and distinct ways of navigating past the obstacles (see Ward, 2013). Practitioners are advised to proceed with caution, to avoid dual relationships if and when possible, and if in them, employ informed consent, and seek advice and consult. What is absent in such professional codes are specific suggestions for addressing the problem from an ethical standpoint. Besides the emphasis on informed consent, unfortunately no guidance is given concerning *how* best to attend to the (inevitable) dual relationship conflicts that occur when working as a practitioner in forensic and correctional contexts.

## VALUE PLURALISM AND FORENSIC PRACTICE

The detection of an existing dual relationship or dual role issue is certainly informative and conveys important ethical information to a forensic mental health practitioner. It highlights the presence of normative conflicts that point to contradictory possible ways of proceeding, and which are hard to resolve; for example, increasing victim empathy as opposed to enhancing self-esteem. However, we think the problem is a deeper and more pervasive one than simply conflict between two aspects of a role. Drawing from Cooper (2010), we suggest that ethical conflicts experienced by forensic mental health practitioners involve at least four domains. That is, they reflect conflicts:

(a) between two or more professional guidelines, code of conducts, or ethical codes. The conflict may exist between different persons or within a single person who has commitments to more than one professional role or identity;

(b) between a professional ethical code and a broader, more abstract set of universal values such as human rights;

(c) between a practitioner's personal set of values that inform his or her good life plan and thus bestow a sense of meaning and purpose, and a professional code. This possible clash relates to the problem of *integrity*, where conflict between a professional ethical code and personal values could leave a person feeling fractured or trigger loss of meaning; and

(d) between universal human norms and personal values.

We propose that the problem of dual relationships is a manifestation of the wider underlying ethical issue of *value pluralism*. Value pluralism occurs when a number of distinct ethical codes or codes of conduct (ethical norms) exists within a society or community, none of which can be established as ethically superior by a rational, impartial observer (Engelhardt, 1986). The clash between the various ethical codes may be a *horizontal* one between codes at the same level of abstraction (e.g., a professional ethical code versus a criminal justice employee code) or *vertical*, where professional norms conflict with more abstract principles (e.g., human rights norms might clash with those regulating staff conduct at a high-security prison). Thus, what is apparent at an abstract level in multicultural, complex societies also occurs at the level of professional practice, and more specifically, potentially within a single clinician.

If we accept the view that the dual relationship problem is more usefully conceptualized as one of value pluralism, a number of significant practice implications follow. One obvious issue is that norms infuse all aspects of the criminal justice and correctional systems, from policy initiatives to the nature of punishment to the content of each offender's intervention plan. If there are different ethical codes or systems of norms available to guide offender assessment and treatment, it could be hard to agree on a subsequent course of action. One forensic or correctional practitioner might justify his or her actions by appealing to obligations to the court while another could refer to the needs of patients or offenders, and an obligation to ease suffering whenever possible, for example, in a report concentrating on reoffending risk rather than individuals' needs.

The problem of ethical *incommensurability* raises its head here; that is, a problem accepting the legitimacy of another person's reasons for acting as s/he does in the forensic or correctional sphere. Practitioners working from different normative frameworks, or lenses, simply do not accept another's viewpoint or choose to follow one over the other. There is no ethical common factor (or norm) capable of bridging the gap between their systems of values, as each has at its foundation a number of underlying principles that justify more specific actions. For example, a forensic practitioner might justify the treatment of an offender because of an expected reduction in offending rates (community protection) while another practitioner might appeal to the positive impact on the offender's quality of life (offender beneficence). A danger when there is no common ground is that individuals may dismiss other views as obviously mistaken or simply assume their own judgments are correct without bothering to look at the issue from another perspective. This can result in the adoption of dogmatic and intolerant attitudes or a kind of helplessness in the face of contrasting ethical professional commitments.

The norms governing the actions of a correctional system may conflict with those of mental health practitioners. To make matters worse, each practitioner may experience internal value conflicts because of allegiances to different roles and their associated codes of conduct. Thus, a correctional psychologist is both an employee of the criminal justice system and, therefore, subject to its code of conduct while also being obligated to meet the standards of his or her professional ethical code (e.g., IACFP, 2010). The difficulty is that these sets of norms and their associated standards of conduct could be at odds, and in fact may not be easily reconciled. As stated above, the scope of normative conflicts extends even further and potentially includes that between offenders' implicit life plans and police, prison officers, probation officers, mental health workers, and therapists' ethical codes. A patient's, offender's, or defendant's concerns are to ease his or her suffering, to establish genuine and caring relationships with other people.

The problem of incommensurability, or discordance between different sets of moral systems, goes even deeper than that between different moral judgments, and their respective actions. It is also evident at the underlying level of moral justification: individuals who possess different sets of moral norms are likely to justify their moral judgments by appealing to diverse foundational principles, within their own moral system. Thus, there is the real danger that people acting within the normative structure of distinct moral codes will talk past each other, and believe others are guilty of irrationality and moral capriciousness. This problem could even occur within a single practitioner or correctional worker who is subject to the standards of two or more codes; for example, ethical codes of a psychologist versus the rules of correctional agency s/he works for. The problem has its origins in the multiple systems of meaning, and their associated practices, that regulate the actions of criminal justice, health workers, and all members of a society.

## RESPONSES TO THE DUAL RELATIONSHIP PROBLEM

Typical responses to dual relationships or multiple loyalties have fallen into two broad categories: single-code primacy approaches and hybrid-code proposals. The former attempts to overcome the dual relationship problem by asserting that professional existing ethical codes (either for mental health professionals or criminal justice employees) for practitioners suffice to avoid the problem, while the latter approaches synthesize the demands of roles of mental health professional *and* servant of the justice system and distill a specialized hybrid ethical code (reduce suffering and enhance levels of well-being *and* include attention to dynamic risk factors). Both strategies, however, are deeply problematic—single-code responses inevitably either *ignore* the dual relationship or *redefine* the role of forensic practitioner to pre-empt the dual role issue, and neither of these options is intellectually or ethical attractive. Hybrid codes are more promising; however, existing proposals tend to lack specification of how procedurally to implement the hybrid model in practice situations. We contend that the *moral acquaintance framework* inspired by the work of Engelhardt (1986) avoids the problems that face the single- and hybrid-code approaches by successfully acknowledging the problem of value pluralism and multiple loyalties faced by forensic mental health practitioners, and being capable of supplying a robust series of procedures for concretely dealing with the dual relationship problem in practice.

## MORAL STRANGERS, MORAL FRIENDS, AND MORAL ACQUAINTANCES

As stated earlier, our view is that what underlies the dual relationship problem are fundamental value conflicts between those who place more stress on community protection or risk management concerns and those who stress a responsibility to assist defendants or offenders to create better lives for themselves alongside risk reduction. In our view, single-code primacy or hybrid codes cannot adequately meet the dual relationship problem, and most promising is a unified model that finds common ground through appeal to shared moral beliefs or norms. In this instance the moral acquaintance framework is pertinent to the dual relationship.

We contend that the only rationally acceptable form a unified model can take is a procedural one: the aim is to specify procedures that, if followed, will enable practitioners to engage each other in respectful discussion (or if the conflict is *within individuals,* help them to meaningfully work with different sets of norms, such as mental health versus criminal justice norms) openly with those holding opposing viewpoints, and thus to increase their chances at reaching an ethically justified consensus. A chief advantage of this model is its ability to deliver a concrete procedure to forensic practitioners; however, for the purpose of this work we do not outline this procedure in detail (for more detail, see Ward, 2013).

## Moral Acquaintances

Keeping these assumptions in mind, one possible way forward is to adopt a moral acquaintance procedure and the relational framework values of engagement, respect, and embodiment (Bergum & Dossetor, 2005; Hanson, 2009; Luban, 2007; Ward. 2011).

In a complex moral world, with diverse ethical codes and cultural perspectives, it is important to attend carefully to our concrete relationships with other people and to *engage* in dialogues that are open and intent on incorporating varying viewpoints. In other words, ethical focus should be on relationships as well as principles and norms such as rights and duties. Furthermore, it is important to acknowledge the *dignity* of others, and not to act in ways that are *disrespectful* and that denigrate their status as fellow human beings. Finally, the details or stories of individuals' lives ought to be the focus of moral decisions rather than simply abstract principles or norms.

The moral acquaintance framework agrees that in a pluralistic society there are a number of equally legitimate competing or alternative moral belief systems. The application of these different moral codes to concrete situations often results in varying responses to ethical problems. A moral acquaintance framework accepts that individuals with distinct moral codes may judge moral situations differently, and in turn, justify their actions by appealing to competing sets of principles and theories, for example, religious beliefs, political theories, or codes of ethics. In effect, such individuals are *moral strangers* to each other as they have little in common with respect to their core moral beliefs and their underlying principles. They frame problems differently and as a result may arrive at diverse judgments concerning the right course of action to take. *Moral friends*, however, share the same ethical codes and are able to solve problems by carefully attending to the relevant facts, identifying the basic ethical principles, taking care to draw valid conclusions, and then acting in ways that reflect these conclusions. Disagreements amongst moral friends are most likely due to careless reasoning, mistaken factual beliefs, or inattention to problem definition.

By contrast, *moral acquaintances* have some overlapping moral beliefs relating to the problem in question; they are not total strangers and can arrive at common decisions about how best to act (Hanson, 2009). These overlapping beliefs may be based on a shared understanding of human nature (e.g., needs for material goods, relatedness, autonomy, safety) and conditions or be oriented around a specific issue, for example, the need to protect the community from predation, or the rights of offenders to receive educational or vocational training. Moral acquaintances look for common, or overlapping, moral beliefs relating to a particular issue and view any actions proceeding from these common beliefs as justified if they are embedded within a coherent moral system, and if individuals with a different set of moral beliefs agree that their moral system is coherent. They may concur on what to do but have different reasons for doing so. The only requirement is that the reasons presented should be rationally derived from a coherent (i.e., non-contradictory and mutually supportive) set of moral norms. For example, one forensic practitioner might justify the implementation of treatment programs with offenders because of their beneficial effect on reoffending rates. The underlying principle appealed to concerns an obligation to protect the community from the harmful actions of offenders. However, another forensic practitioner might argue that offenders ought to receive treatment because they have pressing psychological needs. This justification could have its grounding in human rights principles rather than community protection concerns. However, despite working from distinct—and equally coherent—ethical systems, the two forensic practitioners might share a common moral belief that, if a certain course of action can reduce human suffering without resulting in unjustified pain to others, it ought to be undertaken.

In the example being discussed above, a treatment approach that sets out to assist offenders improve their quality of life by equipping them with the skills to manage their moods effectively could also reduce their risk of offending. The two forensic practitioners are moral acquaintances—rather than strangers—by virtue of the fact that they share some moral beliefs that are directly linked to the issue in question: whether or not to fund programs for offenders. They justify the decision to fund such programs by recourse to different moral principles and theories. They are acquaintances, not strangers, on this issue, but they are not moral friends either as they do not share the same set of moral beliefs concerning the role of programs in the criminal justice system, or more broadly, the status of offenders and their entitlements. They accept that each other's decision to fund programs is based on good reasons, within a coherent moral system, although they do not subscribe to each other's particular moral system.

We suggest that following six decision-making steps when experiencing dual relationship conflicts in the forensic and correctional domains may help practitioners to address the problem. Our procedural model is based on the one developed by Hanson (2009) in his book on ethical conflicts in bioethics.

1. Define the practice task clearly and identify any ethical issues or problems. Note any factual errors and correct them.
2. Identify the relevant group of individuals who should be participants in the discussion. Treat each person with respect and regard their contributions as of equal value.
3. Construct a narrative of all involved individuals' unique situations and perspectives, and contributions to the task at hand. Try to identify the ethical code or set of norms they are conceptualizing the case within.
4. Look for shared moral beliefs across the participants. If the conflict occurs within a single practitioner, look for common elements between the different sets of norms you hold.
5. Once any common norms have been detected, tailor them to the case at hand, using techniques such as specification and balancing, and arrive at an agreed plan of action. Ensure that all participants can justify the plan arrived at within their ethical code/set of norms.
6. If satisfied that the proposed plan can be justified within the different ethical codes/sets of norms, implement the plan and evaluate its subsequent effectiveness from both ethical and prudential viewpoints (i.e., benefits both the offender and the community).

## CONCLUSION

The ethical complexities, conflicts, and problems of the dual relationship emerge in most forensic practice contexts and represent a serious ethical issue. While theorists and practitioners in a variety of forensic and correctional disciplines agree it is a pressing ethical problem, there is little agreement concerning the best way to deal with it. Once a practitioner starts work as a correctional psychologist or psychiatrist (or social worker), or provides expert evidence in court, he or she is subject to a number of unique and ethically fraught problems centered on the issue of dual relationships. We have traced the source of the dual relationship problem to moral pluralism, and outlined a procedural moral acquaintance model that we think is capable of addressing the conflicts, at least in some situations. Although we do not think there is any infallible way of dealing with this ubiquitous ethical dilemma, the moral acquaintance procedure at least gives practitioners a reasonable chance of achieving ethical consensus when confronted with different normative viewpoints.

## REFERENCES

Bergum, V. & Dossetor, J. (2005). *Relational Ethics: The Full Meaning of Respect.* Maryland, USA: University Publishing Group.

Bonner, R. & Vandecreek, L. D. (2006). Ethical decision making for correction mental health providers. *Criminal Justice and Behavior, 33,* 542–564.

Butters, R. P. & Vaughan-Eden, V. (2011). The ethics of practicing forensic social work. *Journal of Forensic Social Work, 1,* 61–72.

Cooper, G. J. (2010). Integrity and zeal. In T. Dare & B. Wendel (Eds.) *Professional Ethics and Personal Integrity* (pp. 79–99). Newcastle, UK: Cambridge Scholars Publishing.

Engelhardt, H. T. (1986). *The Foundations of Bioethics.* New York, NY: Oxford University Press.

Hanson, S. S. (2009). *Moral Acquaintances and Moral Decisions: Resolving Conflicts in Medical Ethics.* New York, NY: Springer.

IACFP (2010). Standards for psychology services in jails, prisons, correctional facilities, and agencies, 3rd ed. *Criminal Justice and Behavior, 37,* 449–808.

Luban, D. (2007). *Legal Ethics and Human Dignity.* Cambridge, UK: Cambridge University Press.

Robertson, M. D. & Walter, G. (2008). Many faces of the dual-role relationship in psychiatric ethics. *Australian and New Zealand Journal of Psychiatry, 42,* 228–235.

Sadoff, R. L. (2011). *Ethical Issues in Forensic Psychiatry: Minimizing Harm.* Oxford, UK: Wiley-Blackwell.

Ward, T. (2011). Human rights and dignity in offender rehabilitation. *Journal of Forensic Psychology Practice, 11,* 103–123.

Ward, T. (2013). Addressing the dual relationship problem in forensic and correctional practice. *Aggression and Violent Behavior, 18,* 92–100.

# CHAPTER 6

# MULTIPLE RELATIONSHIPS IN FORENSIC SETTINGS

*David L. Shapiro and Lenore E.A. Walker*

Psychologists performing forensic evaluations are usually urged to avoid multiple relationships such as that of being both a therapist and a forensic evaluator, on the same case, for several reasons. First, the methodology in each kind of relationship is different. The therapist works within the framework of a treatment alliance, trying to help the patient or client to deal with various difficulties as the client sees them. As such, the therapist depends on the client as the source of information, and, in fact, contacting collateral sources or administering testing to explore level of motivation could interfere with the therapeutic relationship, especially in psychodynamic, humanistic, and other types of treatments. In contrast, a forensic evaluation should be atheoretical, objective, and neutral, and rely on the integration of multiple sources of data, which of course, therapy does not. Even if a therapist is asked by a client or patient to testify on his or her behalf in a court proceeding, in many cases, it may be wisest to avoid doing so, since questions could come up on cross-examination that could significantly interfere with the therapeutic relationship or even be harmful to the client (Eisner, 2010; Reid, 1998). For instance, a question about whether or not there was an assessment for malingering posed to a therapist who is testifying at his or her client's request would probably not have a definitive answer, since such an assessment may be inconsistent with the supportive nature of therapy. The therapist would need to answer based only on clinical data since there was no objective, scientific test administered to determine malingering. Thus, the therapist cannot really be sure about whether or not the client is exaggerating or even lying. This could wreak havoc with future therapeutic contact.

In other cases, such as those where clients are in trauma treatment to deal with domestic violence or other sexual assaults, it may even be therapeutic for the therapist to accede to the client's request to testify on her or his behalf in some cases, such as civil personal injury cases or even custody cases to determine parental fitness, not custody itself. Trauma survivors often have no understanding of neutrality; either the therapist is supportive and will be helpful or the client becomes fearful that the therapist will cause him or her further harm. It is also the case that a therapist may be invited to special events (such as a wedding or a celebration of an advance in business) by the client who is healing from abuse or other trauma. Here, it may solidify the therapeutic relationship in some cases for the therapist to agree to attend, although very clearly drawn boundaries must be negotiated first (Zur, 2007).

Therapists, then, should not automatically agree to or be prohibited from testifying; there may be many situations in which the therapist is called upon to testify, not as an "objective expert" but as a treater about the course of treatment, the diagnosis, the prognosis, and other materials that can be addressed based just on the treatment relationship itself. What is critical in the latter case is that the psychologist makes it clear to the attorney that he or she may not be able to answer psycholegal questions, but rather, only questions about the treatment itself. Attorneys, and sometimes even judges, may try to get the treating therapist to address issues such as causation of an injury, best custodial arrangement for a child, competency, or criminal responsibility for an incident. This needs to be resisted vigorously as the therapist usually does not have sufficient data, or even training or expertise, upon which to base such an opinion. Therefore, the therapist, while not a forensic expert, can be considered an expert on issues raised in the therapy itself. It is not necessary to contend, as is often the case (Shuman et al., 1998), that a therapist is only a "fact" witness, because the therapist is in fact an expert, but not a forensic expert, and must give his or her opinion which a fact witness may not be able to do. Further, it is the judge who ultimately declares whether a witness is an expert, not the psychologist.

One of the difficulties encountered by therapists when they attempt to testify in court is that they fail to make clear what the basis of their opinion is, leading some to conclude that they are in fact giving an expert opinion on the legal matter itself. For example, in a recent case, a therapist was testifying about her work with two children who had been severely traumatized by witnessing extreme domestic violence against their mother by their father. She was asked what custodial arrangement would be the best in this situation. Rather than declining to answer a question about custody and clarifying that she was only concerned about the children's fears as expressed in therapy, she stated that the father should only have contact with his children if the mother or another individual with whom the children felt safe was present. The father filed a complaint with the state licensing board that the therapist was making a conclusion about his parenting abilities without having examined him. Remarkably, the state board, not understanding these issues, opened a formal complaint, but after forensic expert testimony, the complaint was not sustained. This was a positive outcome in this case. However, some of the most common complaints to licensing boards and ethics committees these days involve therapists making custody recommendations without performing formal custody evaluations, or not having the proper training to do such evaluations. In short, therapists should not write letters addressing custody issues, nor should they answer questions posed by an attorney in court which address custody or visitation. The therapist must remain firmly within the parameters of her or his clinical data. In the above example, for example, the therapist might have said that the children continue to express fear of their father in therapy sessions, and not answer any questions related to visitation.

Another reason why the therapy and evaluator roles should not be mixed has to do with the nature of privileged communication in each relationship. Therapists are covered by what is called "psychotherapist-patient privilege," which has many exceptions, such as mandatory reporting of abuse, revealing material if the client has asserted some sort of mental health claim, danger to him- or herself or others for involuntary commitment and, in some states, the treatment notes of a victim of or witness to a crime. If a psychologist, on the other hand, is retained by an attorney, he or she is covered under the "umbrella" of attorney–client privilege, a much broader and more protective privilege than that of psychotherapist and patient; if the psychologist mixes roles, it becomes very murky under which definition of privilege the psychologist's work falls. This is, again, a reason to keep the roles separate.

There are, however, certain forensic settings in which the very nature of the setting makes the separation of treatment and forensic roles highly difficult, if not impossible. These settings may challenge traditional beliefs about the need to keep very firm distinctions between different kinds of professional relationships and between professional and non-professional roles. For instance, in any situation where there is a strict hierarchy, or inherent multiple roles and loyalties, such as a jail or a prison, multiple relationships are unavoidable or even mandated. The same problem may exist in forensic hospitals where the psychotherapists tasked with treating someone to restore him or her to competency to stand trial are then asked to provide testimony at a competency hearing, going against the traditional separation of therapist and forensic examiner.

The basic principle underlying all of this is of course the American Psychological Association (APA) Code of Ethics section dealing with multiple relationships. It is a popular misconception, shared even by many advanced professionals, that multiple relationships are, by their very nature, unethical. This is inaccurate, and in the 2002 Ethics Code, for the first time, it is stated that only multiple relationships that could reasonably lead to harm are unethical (APA, 2002). As this book has exemplified, not all multiple relations are unethical, or even avoidable (i.e., small, rural, rehab, and faith communities); some are mandatory (i.e., military, prisons) and in some cases, may actually be beneficial. People who maintain that all such relations are unethical speak of the "slippery slope," where involvement in one kind of multiple relationship that is not harmful will inevitably lead to one that is harmful. There, in fact, is no empirical evidence to support this position; it appears to be an "urban myth" propagated by people who feel that there is always a potential for harm and therefore we must avoid all multiple relationships. In fact, the APA Code (APA, 2010), like most other professional associations' codes of ethics, provides a good heuristic for making the determination of harm, and that is whether the relationship could reasonably lead to exploitation, loss of effectiveness, or loss of objectivity. It is the premise of this chapter that that same analysis should be performed in forensic settings. Another premise is that multiple relationships within prisons, jails, and forensic hospital are not only often unavoidable, but there are ways to minimize the risk of any harm occurring.

## Multiple Relationships in Prisons and Jails

A psychologist working within a correctional setting is exposed to multiple relationships on a daily basis, similar to those in military settings. For instance, when there is a mental health unit in the facility, or even psychiatric patients housed within the general population, psychologists may be called upon to do mental health rounds and speak to the inmates either in or out of their cells, depending on security issues (i.e., Haag, 2006; Ward, 2013, 2014). Their diagnostic impressions may be utilized in making various custodial recommendations, such as the need for seclusion, release from seclusion, number of hours of daily release from the cell for recreation, and whether or not the inmate may be moved to a less secure facility. Although participation in these types of decisions may be controversial, it is our opinion that those psychologists who insist that those decisions are purely administrative and should have nothing to do with the diagnostic or treatment input are being unrealistic, and in fact not recognizing that involvement in such administrative decisions is a routine part of working in any correctional facility. In the rare circumstances in which psychologists actually are seeing an inmate in psychotherapy, they will frequently be called upon in staff meetings to discuss the progress of the inmate, especially if it is a correctional mental health center. Issues of confidentiality also come to the fore: correctional officials are in the category of having a "need to know," especially about matters that may involve institutional security. For instance, if an inmate reveals to her or his therapist a plan to escape from the institution, the therapist is mandated, as an employee of that facility, to report the plan to the authorities. These multiple relationships are inevitable in correctional settings, and there needs to be a mechanism to handle the competing demands. There is in fact one such mechanism in the Code of Ethics, called "informed consent." Therapists working within a correctional setting need to inform the inmate of who they are, what their function is, what the nature of their services may be, and the limits of confidentiality in the relationship. Then, if a psychologist needs to report certain materials to the authorities in the prison, it needs to be discussed in the informed-consent protocol. In a similar manner, if the relationship is one of assessment, it needs to be made clear to the inmate, who may have access to the report and how it may be used (e.g., for parole decisions, for movement to a less secure facility). In this kind of setting, the multiple relationships are very entwined with issues of confidentiality. It should be clear that multiple relationships are part of working within a correctional setting.

Nevertheless, psychologists working in a correctional setting need to do their best to avoid multiple relationships that could lead to harm. For instance, one author (DLS), while working within a correctional mental health center, was asked to certify that someone was "competent" to be secluded. It was clear that correctional staff were making up a justification to do what they had already planned to do. This author refused to perform this task, citing the fact that "competence" was not a concept that should be properly utilized in this situation. It is inappropriate to use psychology to justify a deprivation of human rights, which was not included in most psychologists' scope of practice.

In another similar setting, an intern reported in supervision that she was uncomfortable with a multiple relationship in which she found herself. An inmate who had a history of psychosis had been placed in a seclusion room due to disruptive behavior and had been there several days. The defendant's attorney called the warden, expressing concern that the isolation could promote decompensation and regression in her client and the intern had been asked to look through the peephole in the cell and, based on that contact, certify that the isolation would not be psychologically harmful to the inmate. The intern was rightly concerned about the ethical issues involved in this request and she was told by her supervisor to avoid the task as this could reasonably result in harm to a psychotic inmate.

Several similar concerns may exist in a maximum-security forensic hospital which is involved in pretrial evaluations of competency to stand trial and criminal responsibility, as well as treatment of those deemed incompetent to stand trial or not guilty by reason of insanity. There have been individuals who rigidly proclaim that if they have done a pretrial evaluation, they cannot be involved in the treatment of that individual to restore him or her to competency to stand trial because it is an "unethical dual relationship." This does not appear to be logical, for if they have a baseline (the pretrial forensic assessment), then they are precisely the staff members who can view the differences from baseline, once the defendant is involved in a competency restoration program. While it could be conceived of as a multiple relationship, it is certainly not a harmful multiple relationship because the whole purpose of the treatment is to return the individual to a state of competency for trial. Again, those who insist on separating the roles are not seeing the differences between this and a harmful multiple relationship.

If the therapist becomes involved in the treatment of those found not guilty by reason of insanity, the issue of the multiple relationship can be even more problematic. There are those who insist on a strict "therapist–administrative split," where whatever goes on in therapy is not shared with the rest of the treatment team or with the review board that makes decisions about movement to a less secure environment, grounds privileges, conditional or unconditional release. This "split" is an extreme example of misunderstanding multiple relationships in such a setting; it is assumed that the therapy relationship is "pure" and the therapist cannot be perceived in any role except that of therapist. Within a maximum-security facility the insistence to separate therapist and administrative functions is, to say the least, unrealistic. It appears to be a rather archaic view based on psychoanalysis (which is not the treatment of choice in a prison) that nothing is to interfere with the transference reaction in psychotherapy, and that it would be harmful to the patient to act in any role except that of therapist. Those who adhere to this view refuse to attend treatment team meetings, refuse to go to meetings of the review board, and in fact will not share their notes with staff who attend either of those meetings. Once again, like the "slippery slope" argument discussed above, there is absolutely no empirical data that demonstrates that having a therapist interact with a treatment team or review board causes harm to the patient. In fact, quite the opposite could be argued: that the patient would be harmed more by this lack of input, because if the therapist has seen increased insight on the part of the patient, this would be important information for a review board or treatment team to be considering. On the other hand, if the patient has been discussing violent fantasies directed toward other staff members or patients, that information should certainly be shared, for the safety and security of the institution. Here too, an informed-consent process that includes limits of confidentiality regarding communications with other staff would cure most of the concerns expressed. In short, there is little evidence that sharing this information will automatically result in a relationship that was harmful, exploitative, or resulted in a loss of objectivity or effectiveness on the part of the therapist. Consider the following case.

The US Court of Appeals for the District of Columbia handed down their decision in *White v. U.S.*, a case involving the issue of multiple relationships (1986). Dwayne White had been a patient at the forensic programs division in St. Elizabeth's Hospital in Washington, D.C., having been found not guilty by reason of insanity in 1968 of murdering a police officer. He progressed well through the treatment program and, by 1979, was allowed to have grounds privileges. While on the grounds he met, and later married (in a ceremony performed by the hospital chaplain), a woman named Genoa, who was a patient in one of the civil divisions (non-forensic units) of the hospital. After they married, Genoa White was granted convalescent leave and obtained an apartment a short distance from the hospital. Dwayne White would visit her, technically violating the conditions of his grounds privileges, which required him to stay on the hospital grounds. Staff essentially adopted an attitude of "benign indifference," reasoning that, since in all other ways White was a model patient, they did not want to get in the way of something perceived as therapeutic.

White was in therapy at the time with a senior staff member, in whom he confided that he had violent fantasies about his wife. The therapist apparently shared this material with her supervisor, but, because of the therapist–administrative split at the hospital at that time, she did not report the fantasies to any of the administrative staff. White continued to visit his wife away from the hospital grounds and on one occasion, when she showed him a picture of herself in the company of another man, he flew into a rage, and stabbed her multiple times with a pair of scissors. Genoa White survived and then filed suit against the hospital, citing two issues of potential negligence: (1) his being allowed to violate the conditions of his own ground privileges; and (2) failing to warn her about her husband's violent fantasies towards her. It was unclear whether there was any causal connection between the failure to warn and the assault, but nevertheless, the concept of a therapist–administrative split came under very sharp scrutiny by the court.

In the end, the concept that talking to the rest of the staff about what goes on in therapy as being a prohibited multiple relationship was seen by many as having no basis in fact. One of the expert witnesses for the plaintiff contended that utilizing a therapist–administrative split in a maximum-security hospital was "ludicrous." Once again, we have a case where an untested assumption about the harmful nature of a multiple relationship could not be demonstrated, and while, as noted above, we cannot make a clear causal connection between the fantasies and White's later acting out, had the therapist shared that information with the treatment team there could have been a temporary suspension of White's ground privileges until such time as he could work through the violent fantasies.

## CONCLUSION

In sum, while there are many compelling reasons in the private sector to avoid the multiple roles of forensic examiner and therapist, in correctional settings and in forensic hospital settings these distinctions cannot be realistically maintained. In fact, within such settings, as with battered women and trauma survivors, the multiple relationship may in fact be of assistance to the inmate or patient. The assumption that the multiple relationship is inherently harmful is not borne out in such settings. With this in mind, it becomes all the more important to delineate just what is the nature of acceptable and unacceptable relationships in secure settings. Especially in light of the recent revelations about psychologists' involvement in coercive interrogations, it becomes all the more compelling to delineate these parameters before the psychologists in such settings come under the scrutiny of an ethics committee or licensing board.

## REFERENCES

American Psychological Association. (2002). *Ethical Principles of Psychologists and Code of Conduct.* Washington DC: Author.
American Psychological Association. (2010). *Ethical Principles of Psychologists and Code of Conduct.* Washington, DC: Author.
Eisner, D. A. (2010). Expert witness mental health testimony: handling deposition and trial traps. *American Journal of Forensic Psychology,* 28, 47–65.
Haag, A. M. (2006). Ethical dilemmas faced by correctional psychologists in Canada. *Criminal Justice and Behavior,* 33(1), 93–109.
Reid, W. H. (1998). Treating clinicians and expert testimony. *Journal of Practical Psychiatry and Behavioral Health,* March, 1–3.

Shuman, D. W., Greenberg, S., Heilbrun, K., & Foote, W. (1998). Special perspective: An immodest proposal: should treating mental health professionals be banned from testifying about their patients? *Behavioral Sciences and the Law,* 16(4), 509–523.

Ward, T. (2013). Addressing the dual relationship problem in forensic and correctional practice. *Aggression and Violent Behavior,* 18(1), 92–100.

Ward, T. (2014). The dual relationship problem in forensic and correctional practice: community protection or offender welfare? *Legal and Criminological Psychology,* 19(1), 35–39.

*White* v. *U.S.* 780 F.2d 97 (D.C. Cir. 1986).

Zur, O. (2007). *Boundaries in Psychotherapy: Ethical and Clinical Explorations.* Washington, DC: American Psychological Association—APA Books.

# Part III

## Unavoidable Multiple Relationships

# INTRODUCTION

*Ofer Zur*

Part III (Chapters 7–11) examines unavoidable multiple relationships in rural, sport, rehabilitation, and total institutions settings, which refers to an enclosed and isolated social system which controls most aspects of its participants' lives.

In Chapter 7, Dr. Barnett discusses the numerous unavoidable multiple relationships that take place in rural psychology. He provides statistics regarding the small number of practitioners available in rural and small communities and explains how members of rural communities are reportedly suspicious of outsiders and need to develop trust in health professionals before they feel comfortable seeking professional services from them. That often means that members of these communities are more likely to choose clinicians who reside in the community and whom they know in the community. That means that multiple relationships are often inherent and unavoidable in rural and small communities. He then goes on to explore more specifically the various types of boundaries, multiple roles, multiple relationships, and incidental contacts in rural and small communities.

In Chapter 8, Dr. Sanders discusses the rarely examined but very common occurrence of multiple relationships in faith, spiritual, and religious communities. He explains how multiple relationships are very common and at times challenging and complicated in these communities because religious congregations and communities tend to be close-knit enclaves, where people bond, share common values, and have a strong sense of affiliation, and equally strong feelings of interdependence. As a result, he states, they often choose members of their congregation for their mental health needs, whom they trust and who obviously share their spiritual beliefs.

Chapter 9 focuses on the rapidly growing field of sports psychology and the inherent multiple relationships involved in this setting. Dr. Bucky and Dr. Stolberg, both experienced sport psychologists, explain that there is a growing number of athletes at all levels, from graduate school to professional athletes, who acknowledge working with a psychologist, and an untold number who do so without sharing that information with others. They state that social dual relationships are unavoidable, widespread, and at times complex; however, they are an inherent part of the milieu, when, for example, a team psychologist travels and interacts with the team and spends long hours on buses, in airports, airplanes, dining halls, and hotels. They discuss the multi roles they simultaneously assume in relationships the individual athletes, the teams, and organizations. They also introduce and refer to codes of ethics that were developed especially for sport psychologists, as well.

Chapter 10 is on multiple relationships in rehabilitation communities, residential and non-residential 12-step and recovery programs. Dr. Silberstein and Ms. Boone explain that the main reasons for these multiple relationships are that almost all rehabilitation psychotherapists are actively in recovery for themselves. Therefore, it is not uncommon for the psychotherapists to encounter current or former clients at 12-step meetings, Rational Recovery, or other recovery gatherings. They go further to explain that, not only does this often create unavoidable dual relationships between client and therapist, but these relationships are reported to have positive effects on clients, since therapists model, encourage, and support their sobriety via 12-step programs.

Chapter 11, the last chapter in this part, by Dr. Reamer, discusses multiple relationships in total institutions, a term that was coined in the 1950s by the renowned sociologist Erving Goffman. Total institutions are defined as an enclosed and isolated social system which controls most aspects of its participants' lives. These include psychiatric hospitals, correctional facilities, group homes, residential treatment centers, wilderness therapy programs, inpatient rehabilitation programs, and military bases. The chapter discusses the mandated multiple relationships in some total institutions and the unavoidable or common multiple relationships in others. Dr. Reamer then elucidates the increased risk of unethical multiple relationships presented by intense 24/7 connections between therapists and clients in some total institutions, such as in wilderness programs.

# Chapter 7

# UNAVOIDABLE INCIDENTAL CONTACTS AND MULTIPLE RELATIONSHIPS IN RURAL PRACTICE

*Jeffrey E. Barnett*

While there may be many differences between individual rural communities, overall they can be characterized by their small size, low population density, and general geographic isolation. The US Census Bureau (2010) defines rural as all those communities and settings with a population of fewer than 2,500 residents and a population density of fewer than 1,000 people per square mile. The results of the most recent US Census (2010) found that 19.3 percent of the population was rural (59.5 million people), yet geographically over 95 percent of the USA is classified as rural (Health Resources and Services Administration, 2015). This small number of people distributed over such a large geographic area results in the general isolation and limited resources associated with many rural communities.

Rural communities frequently have very limited mental health treatment resources. As described by Hastings and Cohn (2013), in comparison with urban areas, rural communities tend to have many fewer mental health and medical providers and services available to their residents. It has been found that there is not even a single psychologist or social worker in one-half of US counties with populations between 2,500 and 20,000 (Holzer, Goldsmith, & Ciarlo, 2000). Hastings and Cohn (2013) also point out that the majority of the communities the federal government has identified as "critically in need of mental health practitioners" (mental health professional shortage areas) are located in rural areas (p. 38).

Members of rural communities in general have been reported to be suspicious of outsiders and to need to develop trust in health professionals before they feel comfortable seeking professional services from them. They additionally frequently associate mental health issues and mental health treatment with stigma, focusing on self-reliance and family support instead of seeking out professional assistance. Yet, as is widely known, many mental health issues are not amendable to avoidance, minimization, and self-care. Unfortunately, many rural residents seek out healthcare services at a significantly lower rate than their urban counterparts and, when they do, they tend to do so much later after symptoms and interference with functioning are experienced (DeLeon, Wakefield, & Hagglund, 2003).

Psychologists living and working in rural communities need to be engaged in the life of their community as citizens of the communities. Failure to participate in community activities and events will likely result in alienating the psychologist from the community and lead its members to view the psychologist with suspicion and mistrust. Consider, for example, a psychologist who never shops in local stores, never participates in community activities or events, never attends local religious services, and withholds her or his children from local schools and from socializing with local children. This psychologist is not likely to be known within the community or to be a person with whom community members will be comfortable speaking about their life challenges and difficulties.

Some may make the argument that in a small community it is important to keep one's professional and personal lives separate so as to minimize the risk of ethics violations, endeavoring to avoid all possible multiple relationships. In reality this is highly impractical. As will be seen, the goal for rural psychologists is not to avoid all multiple relationships within their community, but rather to manage these inevitable multiple relationships ethically and thoughtfully.

## ON BEING A RURAL PSYCHOLOGIST

Schank and Skovholt (2006) highlight that multiple relationships in rural communities are inevitable and not always to be avoided. In fact, due to the stigma typically associated with seeking mental health treatment services, these authors recommend active involvement in the local community to "help with becoming known and gaining trust" (p. 538). It is likely that through interactions with members of the community we are most likely to develop relationships of trust that are needed for community members to feel comfortable enough to seek out our professional services.

Many authors (e.g., Campbell & Gordon, 2003; Schank, Helbok, Haldeman, & Gallardo, 2010; Zur, 2006) have described life in the rural setting as being like living in a fishbowl. In essence, psychologists living and working in rural communities have high visibility within the community. How we interact with salespeople in local stores, how we treat our children when they are misbehaving in public, if and how we participate in community activities, how we resolve conflicts with neighbors, and even how we negotiate the price of a new car we are purchasing are all likely to be closely observed and then shared and discussed among members of the community (Helbok, 2003). Further, DeLeon (2002) advises psychologists of a moral imperative as members of one of the learned professions to become actively engaged in our community, contributing our knowledge and skills to support and enhance the local community through service and leadership activities.

Hopefully, observations of rural psychologists in these non-psychologist roles and other similar situations in the community can demonstrate to community members how caring, thoughtful, fair, honest, and reasonable we are as people. Informal interactions in the community can demonstrate the qualities that community members seek out in professionals (Osborn, 2012). Community members may also test us out by asking "hypothetical" questions about mental health issues or by asking for advice informally when interacting with us in the community. Each of these types of interactions may help integrate the rural psychologist into the community and help community members feel more comfortable seeking her or him out for professional services. At the same time, these same community roles and interactions create multiple relationship challenges for rural psychologists with current, past, and future clients.

Thus, while active engagement in one's community is strongly recommended, these actions will in effect be promoting numerous incidental contacts and multiple relationships. Rural psychologists will therefore need a firm grounding in ethical principles and standards along with flexibility and an understanding of the need to apply ethical standards in the context of rural practice.

Many psychologists are trained within an urban model of ethical practice that espouses a strict application of boundaries, avoidance of multiple relationships, and making referrals whenever multiple relationship issues or concerns arise (Helbok, Marinelli, & Walls, 2006; Murray & Keller, 1991; Zur, 2006). In urban settings it is much easier to take a strict view of boundaries and recommend that psychologists create clear lines of demarcation between their professional and personal lives. There also tend to be numerous referral options in urban settings, making the referral of clients an easy option when multiple relationship concerns are raised. Urban psychologists may have the luxury of espousing a multiple-relationship high road, not having to struggle with the ethics challenges that are everyday events in rural practice.

## BOUNDARIES, MULTIPLE ROLES, AND MULTIPLE RELATIONSHIPS

The *Ethical Principles of Psychologists and Code of Conduct* (American Psychological Association Ethics Code; American Psychological Association, 2010), like most other professions' ethics codes, makes it clear that all multiple relationships do not need to be avoided and that only those that hold a significant potential for harm to or exploitation of the client and those that create a significant potential to adversely impact the psychologist's objectivity and judgment should be avoided.

It is important to point out that, just because multiple relationships in general are seen as inevitable in the rural setting, this does not mean that all multiple relationships should be engaged in. Rural psychologists should give careful forethought to all potential multiple relationships and consider their ability to fulfill the ethics criteria described above. In doing so, it is vital that each potential multiple relationship be examined on its own merits, with attention being given to the level of intimacy and power differential in the secondary relationship, how the secondary relationship may impact the dynamics of the psychotherapy relationship, reasonably available options and alternatives for effectively meeting the client's treatment needs, such as referrals in person and via telepsychology, motivations for entering into the multiple relationship, and the presence or absence of a legitimate need to enter into the multiple relationship (Gottlieb, 1993; Younggren & Gottlieb, 2004).

As is highlighted in these factors to consider, multiple relationships are not all the same and not all of them need to be avoided. But, since rural psychologists who are appropriately active in their community will experience many unavoidable multiple relationship situations, it is helpful to consider the types of interactions psychologists are likely to experience with current, past, and potentially future clients in their community.

## MULTIPLE RELATIONSHIPS

Due to the nature of rural communities, it is very likely that rural psychologists will regularly find themselves in multiple relationships. The limited resources associated with rural communities and their isolation and lack of proximity to other communities can make multiple relationships more likely to occur than in other settings. Yet, as Helbok (2003) points out, this does not mean that rural psychologists must participate in all multiple relationships. Each relationship and situation must be considered for its unique characteristics to ensure its appropriateness. Accepting all multiple relationships as a requirement of clinical practice in rural communities would be inappropriate.

Multiple relationships include being in another relationship with a client in addition to the primary professional relationship as a psychologist with a client. The multiple relationship may be contemporary, such as simultaneously being an individual's psychotherapist and that person's close friend or business associate. Multiple relationships may also be sequential in nature, such as providing psychotherapy to an individual with whom one was previously in an intimate personal relationship or entering into a personal, business, or other relationship with a former client after treatment ends. When considering such relationships, the primary issues of unimpaired objectivity and judgment along with the obligation not to exploit or harm a client are paramount. Thus, one may see a significant difference between providing psychotherapy to the principal of your child's school and providing relationship counseling jointly to your spouse and his or her mother. In both situations the psychologist would want to have an open discussion with the client(s) as part of the informed-consent process. Policies and procedures would be discussed along with an explanation of the parameters of each relationship. Hopefully, by mutual consent the two roles would be compartmentalized. In the former situation the psychologist and client would not discuss the psychologist's child or concerns about the child's teacher during psychotherapy sessions. If such concerns exist, the psychologist would schedule an appointment to meet with the principal at the school during regular school hours. Then, during that appointment the parent and principal would only discuss matters relevant to those roles. It would be entirely inappropriate to switch from being in the parent role to the psychologist role and ask the client follow-up questions about treatment issues. Doing so would violate the parameters of the professional relationship agreed to during the informed consent process.

Even with the most comprehensive informed-consent process with open discussions and agreements, one can question if it is ever possible to provide relationship counseling to one's spouse and her or his mother. The ability to be objective and impartial in such a situation is highly doubtful. The psychologist's close personal relationships with these prospective clients and a likely conflict of interest resulting from a vested interest in possibly pleasing one of these individuals (or both!) makes providing counseling to these individuals ill advised and a referral for treatment elsewhere necessary.

## INCIDENTAL CONTACTS AND UNPLANNED MULTIPLE RELATIONSHIPS

Incidental contacts involve the wide range of situations where psychologists have passing, often unexpected, contact or brief interactions with their clients in the community. Incidental contacts are a daily fact of life for rural psychologists. This makes great sense considering the relative isolation and low population density of rural communities and the fact that residents are not likely to travel large distances to seek out mental health treatment services in other communities. Thus, running into one's psychotherapist or counselor in day-to-day activities is highly likely.

As a psychologist in a rural community you are likely to have incidental encounters, such as encountering your client in the local movie theater, farmers' market, political demonstration, or church service. If you volunteer as a chaperone on a school field trip you may unexpectedly find out that you and one of your clients have been paired together to chaperone a group of children for the afternoon. You may join a local civic organization and discover that current and former clients are also members of this organization.

These encounters of clients in the community are part of life in a rural community. Yet, how rural psychologists address them is of importance. While simply running into a client, in passing, in the community does not constitute a multiple relationship, chaperoning a field trip together, participating in a community service project together, or routinely encountering each other in religious ceremonies is likely to constitute a multiple relationship.

Such inevitable interactions in the community should be addressed through open discussion with clients at the outset of the professional relationship. But, not all community interactions can be anticipated, so that ongoing discussions should occur as circumstances arise, keeping in mind the dual obligations as an engaged member of the community and as your client's psychotherapist. When applying the relevant professional ethics code, this must be done within the context of life in the rural community, with attention given to prevailing community standards. To many rural residents, the rural psychologist is just another member of the community. Outside the treatment office s/he should interact as such.

While incidental contacts are likely to occur frequently in the rural community, this does not mean that rural psychologists have no control over them or should indiscriminately engage in all of them. At times, based on the client's treatment issues and the psychotherapy relationship, you may judge certain ongoing relationships in the community setting to be inappropriate when considering the client's best interests. Factors such as the client's difficulties with boundaries and dependence on the psychologist as well as the level of intimacy of the secondary relationship should be considered. Additionally, any power differential in the secondary relationship may be an important factor to consider. For example, serving on the same civic association committee together might be viewed differently than serving on a committee where either the psychologist or client is the leader of that committee and regularly directs the other's activities and provides the other with critical feedback or when a psychologist is contemplating buying a car from the only car dealership in town, which is owned by a current client.

In addition to considering clients' best interests, rural psychotherapists, like all psychotherapists, have the option not to do things that make them uncomfortable. While this must be balanced with the need to participate in the life of the community, the rural psychologist still has some control over the type of incidental contacts s/he is comfortable participating in. Brief incidental contacts such as passing a client on the street can usually be handled quite easily based on the initial agreement on how the client prefers the psychologist to handle such contacts. But, incidental contacts that are longer lasting and more interactive, such as chaperoning a field trip together all day, will likely be more challenging. Discussing such situations in session with clients to ensure both individuals' comfort, to reach an agreement on the parameters of the relationship, and to process any reactions to these contacts is recommended.

Barnett and Yutrzenka (1995) propose compartmentalizing roles within relationships to better manage incidental contacts. In essence, when on a field trip the psychologist and client would be in the role of two parents on a field trip and would only discuss issues relevant to that role, not slipping into the psychologist–client role. When in a treatment session they would be in their psychologist–client roles and would act accordingly, discussing issues of direct relevance to the client's treatment and not spending a significant portion of the session discussing what they thought of how the field trip was organized, how different children on the trip behaved, and the like.

Since clients will not likely know of the psychologist's desire to remain role-consistent in different settings, these issues will need to be openly discussed as part of the informed-consent process. If these issues are not explained in a caring and helpful manner, clients may feel shame about their natural inclination to "just be friendly" and feel hurt by the psychologist's apparently arbitrary limit setting. Explaining the unique nature of the psychotherapy relationship as well as the positive reasons for compartmentalizing roles within their relationship at the outset can go a long way toward ensuring successful professional and personal relationships in the rural setting.

## BARTER AND MULTIPLE RELATIONSHIPS

Barter is the practice of clients exchanging goods or services with the psychologist in exchange for psychological services. In many rural communities residents may lack health insurance and the finances needed to pay for these services. But, many members of rural communities may have goods (e.g., produce from their farm) or services (e.g., house painting, secretarial services, an auto repair business) that they can trade for psychotherapy or other psychological services. The use of barter is widely accepted in many rural communities and frequently conforms with prevailing community standards and expectations. Engaging in barter for services with a client is likely to constitute a business multiple relationship.

To engage in this important and often necessary multiple relationship ethically, it is important to ensure that barter does not take advantage of, and is not exploitative of, the client. Additionally, the informed-consent process is especially important in these situations to ensure that neither party feels taken advantage of at any time. Ongoing open discussions are essential for achieving this goal. It is also recommended that the value of the client's goods or services be agreed to up front in the informed-consent discussions along with relevant quality indicators that might impact satisfaction with the goods or services.

### RECOMMENDATIONS FOR MANAGING MULTIPLE RELATIONSHIPS IN THE RURAL SETTING

While multiple relationships are inevitable in rural communities, psychologists will need to exercise good judgment about which multiple relationships to enter into, which to avoid, and for those entered into, how to best manage them. The following recommendations are provided to assist rural psychologists to achieve an optimal balance between prevailing community standards and expectations, clients' best interests, the desire to be an active and contributing member of the community, and the realities of living and working in an isolated or remote community with limited mental health resources:

- Consider your profession's ethics code, which generally provides guidance that should be considered in the decision-making process, rather than relying on rigid proscriptions for behavior in all situations.
- When decisions about multiple relationships are unclear, utilize an ethical decision-making model and consult with knowledgeable colleagues. See Gottlieb (1993) and Younggren and Gottlieb (2004) for helpful decision-making models.

- When possible, compartmentalize roles within relationships as a means of functioning effectively both as a professional and as a member of the rural community.
- Consider all reasonably available options and alternatives. This includes colleagues in other related professions such as substance abuse counselors, social workers, physicians, members of the clergy, and others.
- When appropriate, make referrals to colleagues who can treat clients in your community via telepsychology. In those situations where the multiple relationship with a prospective client likely would impair your objectivity or judgment or risk exploitation of or harm to the client, the use of telepsychology may be an excellent option for assisting clients to get their treatment needs met.
- Consider trading offices with colleagues in other communities who possess the requisite competence to assist those of your clients with whom the nature of the multiple relationship makes a referral for treatment mandatory to best meet these clients' treatment needs. It is much easier for a psychologist to drive 2 hours or more for a day of clients than to expect individual clients to travel that much for a single treatment session.
- Anticipate incidental contact and multiple relationships with members of the community. Consider the appropriateness of these interactions with clients in the community, keeping in mind your need to be an engaged member of the community and your obligation not to risk exploitation of or harm to clients.
- Openly discuss the potential for incidental contacts and multiple relationships with each client as part of the informed-consent process. Continue these open discussions as new relationship issues arise during the course of treatment.

## REFERENCES

American Psychological Association. (2010). *Ethical Principles of Psychologists and Code of Conduct.* Retrieved from http://www.apa.org/ethics (accessed July 27, 2016).

Barnett, J. E., & Yutrzenka, B. A. (1995). Nonsexual dual relationships in professional practice, with special applications to rural and military communities. *Independent Practitioner, 14,* 243–248.

Campbell, C. D., & Gordon, M. C. (2003). Acknowledging the inevitable: understanding multiple relationships in rural practice. *Professional Psychology: Research and Practice, 34,* 430–434.

DeLeon, P. H. (2002). Presidential reflections. *American Psychologist, 57,* 425–430.

DeLeon, P. H., Wakefield, M., & Hagglund K. (2003). The behavioral health care needs of rural communities. In B. H. Stamm (Ed.), *Rural Behavioral Health Care: An Interdisciplinary Guide.* Washington, DC: American Psychological Association.

Gottlieb, M. C. (1993). Avoiding exploitative dual relationships: a decision-making model. *Psychotherapy: Theory, Research, Practice and Training, 30,* 41–48.

Hastings, S. L., & Cohn, T. J. (2013). Challenges and opportunities associated with rural mental health practice. *Journal of Rural Mental Health, 37,* 37–49.

Health Resources and Services Administration, U.S. Department of Health and Human Services. (2015). Defining the rural population. Retrieved from http://www.hrsa.gov/ruralhealth/policy/definition_of_rural.html (accessed July 27, 2016).

Helbok, C. M. (2003). The practice of psychology in rural communities: potential ethical dilemmas. *Ethics & Behavior, 13,* 367–384.

Helbok, C. M., Marinelli, R. P., & Walls, R. T. (2006). National survey of ethical practices across rural and urban communities. *Professional Psychology: Research and Practice, 37,* 36–44.

Holzer, C. E., III, Goldsmith, H. F., & Ciarlo, J. A. (2000). The availability of health and mental health providers by population density. *Journal of the Washington Academy of Sciences, 86,* 25–33.

Murray, J. D., & Keller, P. A. (1991). Psychology and rural America: current status and future directions. *American Psychologist, 46,* 220–231.

Osborn, L. (2012). Juggling personal life and professionalism: ethical implications for rural school psychologists. *Psychology in the Schools, 49,* 876–882.

Schank, J. A., & Skovholt, T. M. (2006). *Ethical practice in small communities: challenges and rewards for psychologists.* Washington, DC: American Psychological Association.

Schank, J. A., Helbok, C. M., Haldeman, D. C., & Gallardo, M. E. (2010). Challenges and benefits of ethical small-community practice. *Professional Psychology: Research and Practice, 41,* 502–510.

US Census Bureau. (2010). Frequently asked questions. Retrieved from https://ask.census.gov/faq.php?id=5000&faqId=5971 (accessed July 27, 2016).

Younggren, J. N., & Gottlieb, M. C. (2004). Managing risk when contemplating multiple relationships. *Professional Psychology: Research and Practice, 35,* 255–260.

Zur, O. (2006). Therapeutic boundaries and dual relationships in rural practice: ethical, clinical and standard of care considerations. *Journal of Rural Community Psychology. V. E9/1.* Retrieved from http://www.marshall.edu/jrcp/9_1_Zur.htm (accessed July 27, 2016).

CHAPTER 8

# MULTIPLE RELATIONSHIPS IN FAITH COMMUNITIES

*Randolph K. Sanders*

A clinical psychologist in solo practice is an active member of a large church.[1] He receives a call from a young woman and her parents who are also members of the church. A college student, the daughter, was diagnosed with cancer 6 months ago and had to drop out of school and come home. Over time, the daughter, who had never had any history of emotional problems, became increasingly anxious about her medical treatments, her health, and her future. The young woman asks the psychologist to see her for counseling. While they are not intimate friends, the psychologist and his wife taught the daughter's Sunday School class when she was in the fifth grade, and the psychologist and the parents were participants in an adult Bible study that occurred at the church a year ago. In their call, the family mentions that they have come to respect the psychologist over the years, and the daughter says that she wants to get counseling from someone who understands her faith perspective, particularly in a matter as serious as this. The psychologist, who specializes in health psychology, listens empathically. He discusses basic issues about counseling, including a situation-specific discussion of multiple relationships. After due consideration of the risks and benefits of working with the young woman, including consultation with a colleague who studies ethical issues, he agrees to work with her. He helps her with her anxiety and counsels her through her illness. Thankfully, her cancer goes into remission, and she returns to full health and is able to go back to school. When it comes time to graduate, the young woman enthusiastically invites her psychologist to attend her graduation, which in light of everything that had occurred, was an especially momentous achievement in her life.

The preceding is an example of the kind of non-sexual multiple relationships that commonly arise in faith settings. Indeed, a survey of Christian psychotherapists found that dealing with multiple relationship issues was the most frequent ethical issue they faced (Sanders, Swenson, & Schneller, 2011). This is likely due to factors that are endemic to most faith communities, no matter the specific religion. In this chapter, I will assert that there are types of multiple relationships that should always be avoided in these settings just as they are in other settings. Consistent with the ethics codes of the American Psychological Association (APA) (2010) and the American Counseling Association (2015), however, I will not assume that multiple relationships are unethical *per se*. As the APA Code states, "multiple relationships that would not reasonably be expected to cause impairment or risk exploitation or harm are not unethical" (APA, 2010, Sect. 3.05(a)). There are several types of multiple relationships in faith settings that are not easily avoided, and where managing the multiple relationship is clearly preferential to avoiding it entirely. And, as the preceding example illustrates, there are situations in which the multiple relationship benefits the process and outcome of therapy.

## WHY DO MULTIPLE RELATIONSHIPS OCCUR SO FREQUENTLY IN FAITH COMMUNITIES?

Religious congregations and communities are close-knit enclaves. In them, people gather together for fellowship, to share common values, and "bear one another's burdens." They bond together under what some have called the "sacred canopy" (Berger, 1967). Zur (2007) notes that these communities have a "strong sense of affiliation and equally strong feelings of interdependence, mutuality and affiliative philosophy," and that "the bonds among members . . . make them highly cohesive" (p. 24).

This bonding component is arguably one of the most distinct and beneficial aspects of religious life. In a large study of people from a variety of religious persuasions, Lim and Putnam (2010) found that most of the positive effects of religious attendance were related to the *relational networks* that people built in their religious communities. Members of the group worship together, share worldviews, solidify values, and nurture their families. They form relationships in countless other ways. Members participate together in social and humanitarian activities,

109

interact in business, and often find their accountants, doctors, and attorneys through their religious community.

Is it any surprise that psychotherapists who are themselves religiously committed frequently find themselves being asked to provide services to fellow adherents? When they do so, and they are also associated personally with the client (or someone close to the client), they are involved in a multiple relationship (Sanders, 2013).

Schank and Skovholt (1997, 2006) and others (Geyer, 1994; Hill & Mamalakis, 2001; Sanders, 2013) have recognized that religiously committed therapists experience the same kind of multiple relationship issues faced by therapists in rural communities where contact with clients is often unavoidable, and where prospective clients may prefer to see a therapist they are already acquainted with. Indeed, in many rural (and religious) settings, a therapist who is not known to the community and who has not earned a respected reputation in the community is looked at with some concern, and in some cases with suspicion. The therapist who attempts to avoid all multiple relationships in these settings may inadvertently end up inhibiting people from obtaining needed mental health services.

Consider, for example, the psychologist providing services in a Muslim community. Abi-Hashem (2013, 2014) notes that, relative to the individualistic cultures so prevalent in Western societies, Muslim cultures are often much more communal in nature; they are an integral part of what he calls "warm cultures." In these communities, people expect to relate to their helping professionals outside the confines of the consultation room (Turkes-Habibovic, 2015) as long as certain rules of decorum are followed. Instead of the pejorative term, multiple relationships, Abi-Hashem (personal communication, September 22, 2015) calls these relationships "multi-faceted relationships."

Many Asian cultures see talking to a stranger about personal matters as inappropriate, even taboo (Sue & Capodilupo, 2015). Many of these people would prefer to talk to someone they "know or trust," and this "trust is usually gained from a pre-existing relationship" (Mok, 2003, p. 116).

Some would argue that, while multiple relationships in rural, religious settings are understandable, they should not occur in large urban settings where there are surely other religious therapists in the city available to see the client. While this may be true at times, it does not fully appreciate the fact that many faith communities really do represent ethnic enclaves within the larger urban culture. In such settings, previous contact with or knowledge about the psychotherapist is frequently seen as essential, particularly in a relationship as consequential as counseling.

Multiple relationships are more likely in faith communities for another reason. Recently, religious and para-religious bodies have taken a more substantive and direct role in serving the needs of people with emotional and relationship problems. In some sense, this is not really new. It has been recognized for decades that priests, ministers, rabbis, and other religious leaders are on the "front line" in providing support and pastoral care to members struggling with mental health concerns (Gurin, Verhoff, & Feld, 1960) and adherents frequently consult clergy before they will consult a mental health professional. Increasingly, however, religious and para-religious bodies are establishing their own counseling centers staffed by licensed mental health professionals. Some of these centers serve the community at large, but some work mostly with members of the sponsoring religious body. Having licensed professionals working in an agency sponsored by a religious group amplifies the probability that multiple relationships of the kind we have been describing will arise. In fact, our research indicated that Christian therapists who work in church-related agencies are more likely to confront multiple relationship dilemmas than are Christian therapists who work in other settings (Sanders, Swenson, & Schneller, 2011). Consider the therapist who serves on the counseling staff of a church. Such a therapist, especially if she is also a member of the church, is likely to have some type of multiple relationship, however slight, with almost every client she sees from the church.

## WHAT DO WE KNOW ABOUT HOW THERAPISTS RESPOND TO MULTIPLE RELATIONSHIPS IN RELIGIOUS SETTINGS?

It may be helpful to review survey research that considers the actual incidence and types of multiple relationships that take place in religious settings (McMinn & Meek, 1996; Oordt, 1990; Sanders, 2013; Sanders, Swenson, & Schneller, 2011; Schneller, Swenson, & Sanders, 2010; Swenson, Schneller, & Sanders, 2009). While the surveys were all conducted with Christian therapists, it is possible that the results generalize to other religious groups. The results confirm that, like rural settings (Helbok et al., 2006), multiple relationships occur with some frequency among Christian therapists, especially those working in church-based settings. Over 50 percent of our sample had at least sometimes or more often attended the same church as a client, and about 44 percent had at least sometimes provided therapy to a member of their church with whom they had limited outside contact. Some 34 percent of our sample had at least sometimes belonged to the same community organization as a former client and about 44 percent believed that it was appropriate to do so (Sanders, Swenson, & Schneller, 2011).

Having said this, the sample seemed sensitive to the dangers involved with some multiple relationships. For example, survey participants overwhelmingly avoided multiple relationships that involved the mixing of finances or business, or of doing therapy with employees. They were cautious about providing therapy to someone in their church that they knew well. They appeared to recognize that not all multiple relationships are created equal, that some carry more real or potential danger than others, and therefore need to be avoided.

## MULTIPLE RELATIONSHIPS IN RELIGIOUS SETTINGS

The actual types of multiple relationships faced by therapists in religious settings take a variety of forms. Several examples serve to illustrate that some situations should be avoided and others managed.

Consider the therapist asked to see someone that she participates in a religious study group with. While the presenting problem is depression, the individual is also suffering from borderline personality disorder, and is locked in conflict with her family, several of whom the therapist knows from participating in activities within the religious body.

The therapist in this case would likely need to assist the client in seeking an alternative referral, assuming that one is available. The nature of the client's personality issues raises questions about the client's ability to maintain appropriate boundaries, and there is also an array of problems that could arise because of the therapist's prior interaction with the client and her family.

In contrast to the previous case, consider the psychologist who is a member of a small church in a university town. Another member is an assistant campus minister at the university, and the two know each other fairly well. They participate in a weekly Sunday School class, and serve on several church committees together. The minister asks the psychologist to see her for counseling concerning a conflict she is having with her superior in the campus ministry office at the university. She cites the fact that the psychologist has some seminary training and understands "denominational politics." Furthermore, the assistant campus minister believes the psychologist knows her well enough to assess her weaknesses and strengths in dealing with the situation at her office, and will be able to give her feedback in a timely way. The psychologist, after deliberation and a discussion of the multiple relationship issue with the minister, provided brief, focused counseling on the minister's problem at work.

Suppose the counselor works in a church counseling center where the church administration expects the counselor to see all parishioners referred without exception. In this case (and in any case where the expectations of the organization conflict with ethical practice), the counselor, before taking employment with the church, would do well to explain the issue of multiple relationships to church leaders and obtain an agreement allowing her to use her own clinical judgment regarding multiple relationships.

Sometimes a multiple relationship emerges after therapy begins, or one that was benign at the outset of therapy intensifies during the course of therapy. Suppose a therapist sees a client that he has occasional contact with at his synagogue. The client is seen for depression, and over the course of 17 sessions begins to show good progress in resolving her depression. At the next session, the client, who has been looking for a job, announces that a clerical position has just arisen at the synagogue, and she has applied for it. Now suppose that the therapist is a member of the synagogue's personnel committee and realizes that he will likely be part of a committee considering this woman's job application.

In this case, the complication was unforeseen and emerged after therapy was well under way and good progress was being made. First and foremost, the therapist must insure that the client continues to make progress and successfully resolves her depression. Under these conditions the therapist must consider whether it would be better to manage the multiple relationship rather than avoid it, and proceed to the conclusion of treatment. While it is ultimately the therapist's responsibility to determine a way of recusing himself from the personnel committee without betraying the client's confidentiality, it might also be appropriate for the therapist to discuss the multiple relationship with the client and obtain her input and informed consent as well. Done in a sensitive way,

113

such a discussion might not only assist the therapist in resolving the issue, but might also enhance the therapeutic relationship.

Relative to the typical mental health professional in a private practice in a big city, clergy are consistently in multiple roles and multiple relationships with their parishioners. They are seen in a number of different roles by their parishioners: friend, authority figure, shepherd, teacher and preacher, co-laborer, confidant(e), to name a few (Parent, 2005). They have to adapt to different levels of social expectation and intimacy, while not violating boundaries (Justice & Garland, 2010). This is a difficult task for even the most prudent and socially skilled clergy. Clergy who also provide counseling are vulnerable to having their motives misconstrued even when acting unintentionally. For example, parishioners can mistakenly believe that a story they hear from the pulpit is something they revealed to the minister in confidence. Combine this with the fact that many parish ministers have had little or no training in counseling, much less an understanding of multiple relationship, and it is easy to see why some faith experts suggest that the traditional minister do limited (Blackburn, 2013) or crisis counseling only (Justice & Garland, 2010). Blackburn (2013) recommends that the minister limit by-appointment, pastoral counseling to three sessions, and refer responsibly and caringly to licensed mental health professionals when a parishioner's needs exceed brief counsel.

### ISSUES TO PONDER WHEN CONTEMPLATING WHETHER TO ENGAGE IN MULTIPLE RELATIONSHIPS IN A FAITH SETTING

Before deciding whether to engage in a multiple relationship, therapists should be familiar with the ethics codes of their respective professional bodies. These provide the basic template for how one's profession expects the therapist to handle multiple relationship issues. Therapists should also be familiar with state laws and rules governing practice. In some states, regulations concerning multiple relationships are more rigid and inflexible than professional ethics codes, or at least may be interpreted that way. Moreover, therapists must realize that multiple relationships that generate a board complaint are sometimes adjudicated with hindsight bias (i.e., the board, knowing that a problem ensued, judge too quickly that the counselor should have known better) or by board members who hold a stricter personal prohibition against multiple relationships than the major ethics codes allow (Williams & Younggren, 2010).

Beyond that, the responsible therapist in a faith setting should ponder a number of issues when contemplating whether to engage in a multiple relationship. Most are similar to the concerns faced in any multiple relationships, whatever the setting. The therapist should always avoid multiple relationships where there is a real concern about exploitation or harm. Therapists must always consider the severity of the prospective client's problems, including the presence of personality disorders, and the ability of a particular client to maintain boundaries. The complexity of the treatment needed should also be considered. A comprehensive list of questions for therapists to consider is found elsewhere (Sanders, 2013). What follows are some issues most pertinent to therapists working in faith-based settings.

One of the most important is an appreciation for the client and the faith culture from which he/she comes. In these cultures, people often expect to know their professionals in a wider context (albeit with discretion). As Zur (2007) points out, the therapist who considers only the risks of engaging in the multiple relationship and does not consider the benefits to the therapy has not done a complete evaluation of the situation. At a fundamental level, the decision to engage in a multiple relationship must always be about benefit to the client, not the therapist.

The conscientious therapist will also bring the client into the discussion of the multiple relationship wherever or as soon as possible. Prospective clients and referral sources in faith-based settings may have considered only the benefits of knowing the therapist in another context, and may not have thought about how a multiple relationship could have a negative impact. Without being unduly negative, the therapist can discuss both the pros and cons of the multiple relationship with the client, seek the client's feedback and then decide how best to proceed. It must be remembered, however, that the therapist is ultimately responsible for the decision.

If you proceed with a multiple relationship, documentation of a client-centered rationale for it is very important. It can help you organize your thinking, and can also serve as proof that you considered the issues involved (including the faith setting), explained the multiple relationship to the client, and obtained the client's informed consent. It also provides a place to record any consultation you obtained.

115

As important as anything else is the relationship you have with your client. As we have seen, the close-knit, bonded culture of faith settings requires therapists not to be too quick to avoid the multiple relationship without a considered judgment of the pros and cons. The therapist who above all embodies and communicates an overarching concern for the client's welfare, and who cultivates a therapeutic relationship of mutual trust, can usually work through multiple relationship issues successfully in faith settings. The ultimate goal is to do one's best to ensure a good outcome for the client.

## NOTE

1 Case studies in this chapter are representative of the kinds of cases faced by therapists in practice. The cases are totally fictitious, are composites of a number of cases, or have been altered to ensure anonymity and confidentiality.

## REFERENCES

Abi-Hashem, N. (2013). Self-esteem. In K. D. Keith (Ed.), *The Encyclopedia of Cross-cultural Psychology* (pp. 1146–1148). Malden, MA: Wiley.

Abi-Hashem, N. (2014 Spring/Summer). Social support: a psychological and cultural perspective. *International Psychology Bulletin (Div. 52, APA), 18*, 74–77.

American Counseling Association. (2015). *ACA Code of Ethics*. Alexandria, VA: Author.

American Psychological Association. (2010). *Ethical Principles of Psychologists and Code of Conduct*. Retrieved from http://www.apa.org/ethics/code/index.aspx (accessed July 27, 2016).

Berger, P. L. (1967). *The Sacred Canopy: Elements of a Sociological Theory of Religion*. New York: Anchor Books.

Blackburn, B. (2013). Pastors who counsel. In R. K. Sanders (Ed.), *Christian Counseling Ethics: A Handbook for Psychologists, Therapists and Pastors* (2nd ed.) (pp. 368–381). Downers Grove, IL: InterVarsity Press.

Geyer, M. C. (1994). Dual role relationships and Christian counseling. *Journal of Psychology and Theology, 22*, 187–195.

Gurin, G., Veroff, J., & Feld, S. (1960). *Americans View Their Mental Health: A Nation-wide Interview Study*. New York: Basic Books.

Helbok, C. M., Marinelli, R. P., & Walls, R. T. (2006). National survey of ethical practices across rural and urban communities. *Professional Psychology: Research and Practice, 37*, 36–44.

Hill, M. R., & Mamalakis, P. M. (2001). Family therapists and religious communities: negotiating dual relationships. *Family Relations, 50*, 199–208.

Justice, J. A., & Garland, D. R. (2010). Dual relationships in congregational practice: ethical guidelines for congregational social workers and pastors. *Social Work and Christianity, 37,* 437–445.

Lim, C. & Putnam, R. (2010). Religion, social networks, and life satisfaction. *American Sociological Review. 75,* 914–933. doi: 10.1177/0003122410386686.

McMinn, M. R., & Meek, K. R. (1996). Ethics among Christian counselors: a survey of beliefs and behaviors. *Journal of Psychology and Theology, 24,* 26–37.

Mok, D. S. (2003). Multiple/dual relationships in counseling: implications for the Asian context. *Asian Journal of Counselling, 10,* 95–125.

Oordt, M. S. (1990). Ethics of practice among Christian psychologists: a pilot study. *Journal of Psychology and Theology, 18,* 255–260.

Parent, M. S. (2005). Boundaries and roles in ministry counseling. *American Journal of Pastoral Counseling, 8,* 1–25.

Sanders, R. K. (2013). Nonsexual multiple relationships. In R. K. Sanders (Ed.), *Christian Counseling Ethics: A Handbook for Psychologists, Therapists and Pastors* (2nd ed.) (pp. 139–157). Downers Grove, IL: InterVarsity Press.

Sanders, R. K., Swenson, J. E., & Schneller, G. R. (2011). Beliefs and practices of Christian psychotherapists regarding non-sexual multiple relationships, *Journal of Psychology and Theology, 39,* 330–344.

Schank, J. A., & Skovholt, T. M. (1997). Dual-relationship dilemmas of rural and small-community psychologists. *Professional Psychology: Research and Practice, 28,* 44–49.

Schank, J. A., & Skovholt, T. M. (2006). *Ethical Practice in Small Communities.* Washington, DC: APA.

Schneller, G. R., Swenson, J. E., & Sanders, R. K. (2010). Training for ethical dilemmas arising in Christian counseling: a survey of clinicians. *Journal of Psychology and Christianity, 29,* 343–353.

Sue, D. W., & Capodilupo, C. (2015). Multicultural and community perspectives on multiple relationships. In B. Herlihy & G. Corey (Eds.), *Boundaries in Counseling: Multiple Roles and Responsibilities* (3rd ed.) (pp. 92–95). Alexandria, VA: ACA.

Swenson, J. E., Schneller, G. R., & Sanders, R. K. (2009). Ethical issues in integrating Christian faith and psychotherapy: beliefs and behaviors among CAPS members. *Journal of Psychology and Christianity, 28,* 302–314.

Turkes-Habibovic, M. (2015). Boundary considerations in counseling Muslim clients. In B. Herlihy & G. Corey (Eds.), *Boundaries in Counseling: Multiple Roles and Responsibilities* (3rd ed.) (pp. 104–108). Alexandria, VA: ACA.

Williams, M. H., & Younggren, J. N. (March/April, 2010). Being right and still losing. *The National Psychologist,* 7–8.

Zur, O. (2007). *Boundaries in Psychotherapy: Ethical and Clinical Explorations.* Washington, DC: APA.

# Chapter 9

# MULTIPLE RELATIONSHIPS IN SPORT PSYCHOLOGY

*Steven F. Bucky and Ronald A. Stolberg*

## Introduction

As discussed in depth throughout this book, the American Psychological Association (APA) and other bodies governing the practice of psychotherapy have longstanding ethics codes (i.e., American Psychological Association, 1992, 2002, 2010) or guidelines, which include language regarding dual relationships. There is also substantial literature that addresses multiple/dual relationships for mental health professionals expressing a concern about the potential unethical consequences of having a multiple relationship for the patient/client. Similarly, all major professional organizations clearly acknowledge that not all multiple relationships are unethical or avoidable. This paper focuses on unavoidable, common, and even required multiple/dual relationships in working with athletes and teams.

Usual and common ethical practices of clinicians are guided by a variety of standards, yet vary greatly based on the population and setting. Clinicians working with athletes and teams often face an entirely new set of circumstances and dilemmas based on the uniqueness of working with this specific group (Gardner & Moore, 2006).

The APA *Ethical Principles and Code of Conduct* (2010) is well established and meets the needs of clients/patients in most common professional settings, which do not typically include sport psychology (Gardner & Moore, 2006), rural settings (Catalano, 1997), military settings (Johnson, 1995), and other non-traditional settings (Gardner & Moore, 2006).

The APA, in its latest code of ethics (2010), essentially talks about multiple relationships when a psychologist is in a professional role and, at the same time: (1) is in another role; or (2) is in a relationship with a person closely associated with whom the psychologist has a professional relationship; or (3) promises to enter into another role in the future with the person in the professional relationship.

It is clear that such relationships are frequently unavoidable and in some cases ethical and, in some cases, unethical. According to the APA (2010), it is only unethical when the multiple/dual relationship negatively affects the objectivity or performance of the psychologist or is exploitative.

The authors of this chapter are well versed in this important clinical issue through years of work in the field of sport psychology and their relationships with the National Football League (NFL), the San Diego Chargers, Major League Baseball (MLB), the San Diego Padres, and other lower-tier sports leagues and associations such as the World Surf League.

As it pertains to the field of sport psychology, sometimes referred to as the field of sport and exercise psychology, there are guidelines in addition to those of the APA available for clinicians working with athletes and teams. The Association for Applied Sport Psychology (AASP) is the largest sport and exercise psychology professional association in North America which offers certification to its members working in this field. Another North American group is the Canadian Society for Psychomotor Learning and Sport. Both of these associations, and several others worldwide, have developed their own set of guidelines and standards for clinicians to follow and base their actions on.

## THE FIELD OF SPORT AND EXERCISE PSYCHOLOGY

There are a growing number of athletes at all levels who acknowledge working with a psychologist and an untold number who do so without sharing that information with others. The field is growing at a record pace. Parents utilize psychologists to improve their children's chances of gaining entrance, or a scholarship, to their desired colleges and to examine their children's athletic potential for a shot at Olympic or professional status. Colleges are using sport psychology to improve the skills and win–loss record of their sports teams, and it goes without saying what impact on a career participation at the highest level means to individual athletes. These athletes are looking for any advantage in the ultra-competitive world of high-stakes athletics.

The field of sport and exercise psychology actually dates back to the late 1890s, when the first North American research studies were conducted and published (Weinberg & Gould, 2011). One of the first well-known studies was conducted by Norman Triplett (1898), who studied why cyclists sometimes rode faster when they were in a group than when they trained alone. The modern field of exercise and sport psychology became solidly established as a separate and distinct discipline in about 1980. It was in the 1980s that many of the sport psychology journals were established and that APA division 47 (Sport Psychology) and AASP were established (Weinberg & Gould, 2011).

## CODES AND GUIDELINES

More recently, groups like AASP, interested in preserving strong ethical guidelines for psychologists working with athletes, have generated their own set of standards. These guidelines are generally based on the 2002 APA ethical standards and adapted to work with athletes and teams. The overreaching principle is that those practicing sport psychology should respect the dignity of those they work with and that each individual's welfare must be foremost in one's mind (Weinberg & Gould, 2011).

The *AASP Ethical Principles and Standards, the Ethics Code* (1996), consists of an introduction, a preamble, six general principles and 25 standards (www.appliedsportpsych.org). The general principles guide an overall approach to working with teams and individuals from a position of competence, integrity, responsibility, and respect, and a general concern about the welfare of others.

The following comes directly from Section 9 of the AASP Ethics Code (www.appliedsportpsych.org/about/ethics/):

(a) AASP members must always be sensitive to the potential harmful if unintended effects of social or other nonprofessional contacts on their work and on those persons with whom they deal. Such multiple relationships might impair the AASP member's objectivity or might harm or exploit the other party.

(b) An AASP member refrains from taking on professional or scientific obligations when preexisting relationships would create a risk of such harm.

(c) AASP members do not engage in sexual relationships with students, supervisees, and clients over whom the AASP member has evaluative, direct, or indirect authority, because such relationships are so likely to impair judgment or be exploitative.

(d) AASP members avoid personal, scientific, professional, financial, or other relationships with family members of minor clients because such relationships are likely to impair judgment or be exploitative.

(e) If an AASP member finds that, due to unforeseen factors, a potentially harmful multiple relationship has arisen, the AASP member attempts to resolve it with due regard for the best interests of the affected person and maximal compliance with the Ethics Code.

(AASP, 1996)

It is easy to see a clear overlap in content and guidance between the APA (2002, 2010) Ethics Code Section 3.05 and it is well known that the AASP Ethics Code was derived in large part from the APA *Ethical Principles of Psychologists and Code of Conduct* (1992). With that said, the AASP Standard provides little additional support to those working with athletes.

The European Sport Psychology Federation (FEPSAC) is the largest association of individuals working with athletes in the world. They have their own published ethical principles (FEPSAC, 2011). Principle E: Integrity in part speaks to this issue:

> European researchers and practitioners should clearly define to all parties the roles they are performing and the obligations they adopt. European researchers and practitioners should avoid improper and potentially harmful dual (or multiple) relationship and conflicts of their personal and professional interests.

(FEPSAC, 2011)

## BALANCING MULTIPLE RELATIONSHIPS

It should be foremost in the mental health professional's thoughts that the field of sport psychology is inherently infused with opportunities for multiple relationships. While there are numerous roles and systems that we can find ourselves working in, a common scenario involves maintaining a professional relationship with individual athletes, teams, and organizations all at once. Not all of this work is this complicated, but starting from the framework of being able to anticipate potential multiple relationships affords one the opportunity to plan for them or avoid them altogether.

Sonne (1999) uses the following well-accepted definition of multiple relationships as:

> Those situations in which the psychologist functions in more than one professional relationship, as well as those in which the psychologist functions in a professional role and another definitive and intended role.
>
> (p. 227)

The APA Ethics Code does *not* explicitly prohibit these kinds of multiple relationships with clients/patients. Ethical Standard 3.05a states that psychologists are encouraged to refrain "from entering into multiple relationships" with clients (APA, 2010). The practitioner must examine the potential harm of the relationships, including one's objectivity, effectiveness of service, and possible exploitation of the client (Gardner & Moore, 2006; Pope & Vasquez, 2016; Sonne, 2006).

A common situation psychologists face in their work with professional athletes and teams is the request that they attend organizational activities, practices, and the actual sporting events or contests. Teams and organizations may request that the psychologist attend these events as a means of increasing or maintaining rapport with the athletes, staff, and other team/league officials. It is often thought that if the psychologist is frequently around the athletes, they will accept the psychologist and see the mental health professional as a reliable and trusted member of the support team. The clinician must weigh the consequence of rejecting these invitations to "hang out" which may invite multiple relationships versus the opportunity to build trust and rapport with the team and the athletes (Buceta, 1993; Gardner & Moore, 2006).

For the practicing clinician working with athletes and organizations, there are the above-mentioned guidelines and ethics codes, but there is little in the way of practical guidance. Gardner and Moore (2006) actually take a strong stance on the issue of attending team events where there is no expectation of providing clinical services:

If the clinical sport psychologist consults with a team throughout the year, attends necessary practices and games, and facilitates relationship building, rejecting an invitation to a special team event in order to maintain boundaries and avoid real or perceived multiple relationships is not setting a positive or congruent example for those team members who accepted the practitioner into the organizational family and welcomed her services. It could certainly damage the therapeutic relationships already established with specific athletes, and those athletes who resisted services in the past may be less likely to ask for assistance in the future.

(p. 216)

## CASE EXAMPLES

A frequent multiple relationship scenario involves working with an athlete in one capacity and then being asked to work for the organization, team, or league in a separate role that directly conflicts with the direct relationship and role formed with the athlete.

For example, a psychologist might be asked to work with all of the rookies recently brought into the organization or team at the beginning of training camp. One of the roles, as outlined by the organization, is to provide services to the rookies to improve their preparation, reduce stress and anxiety in their lives, and increase their readiness for competing at the highest levels. The psychologist forms strong professional relationships with each of them and learns a great deal about each athlete's strengths and weaknesses. At some point as the regular season gets closer, the team psychologist might be asked to act in another role, in this case as a consultant to the team's general manager and his staff. The team may want an evaluation of each rookie athlete, which includes those same strengths and weaknesses, as they pertain to their likelihood of actually making the team. These two roles can seem at odds with each other, as most clinicians do not actively participate in discussions which result in an individual with whom you have a strong relationship losing his job partly based on your feedback to the organization.

To some athletes, it may seem like a betrayal of the trust established in their work with the clinician. However, if the multiple roles are discussed ahead of time via the process of informed consent and the athlete understands the clinician's status with the organization, there will be less confusion about who the "client" is and what the purpose of the time spent together working on performance enhancement was about. In other words, the importance of the process of informed consent is paramount in sport psychology.

### Professional Football

The following are examples of multiple relationships with professional football players that were viewed as unavoidable and ethical.

#### Shower

In the early 1990s, a team psychologist for an NFL team was asked by the Head Coach to increase his visibility at the training facility. One day, while walking through the facility, the psychologist was passing the shower area when he heard a voice yell out his name. A player, who happened to be the psychologist's patient, walked out of the shower (with a very soapy body) and started talking about a conflict he had with his girlfriend that occurred the previous evening. The psychologist ended that interaction as quickly as was possible, recommending that they talk further once the player-patient was finished with his shower and if there was not enough time (practice was only 10 minutes later), they could continue the discussion later by phone or could schedule an extra session or could wait until the next scheduled session. Psychologists obviously do not generally talk about clinical issues or anything else with their patients while the patient is taking a shower. The authors of this chapter view the interaction as an example of an inadvertent, unavoidable, ethical, dual relationship.

#### Team Activities

Being involved in team activities (e.g., flying with the team, presence at social events, in the locker room, on the field during practice) may be inconsistent with a typical psychotherapeutic professional relationships. Such contact is frequently viewed as inconsistent and incompatible with the psychologist's role as a therapist. As a rule, psychologists in such situations inform players, as part of the informed-consent process, that during such activities, the psychologist will say "hello" as he would to any non-patient player and that such limited contact should not be interpreted as a lack of interest or friendliness, but rather as protecting the player's right to privacy. An attempt should be made that coaches, other players, and administrators cannot tell that there is a psychotherapeutic relationship with a player by virtue of visible discussion between the psychologist and the player. One solution is talking to non-patient players as often and as long as with players who are patients.

### Drunk at Party

On one occasion, a psychologist for a professional football team was invited to a fundraising activity where a number of players had been drinking. The psychologist was concerned about one of his patient's safety (the player was clearly intoxicated) because he was talking about driving home within the next few minutes. The psychologist decided to speak to the player's best friend about making sure the intoxicated player was not going to drive home. The psychologist was relieved when the player's friend pulled out the player's car keys from his pocket.

### Tickets/Autographed Footballs

The authors of this chapter have taken the position in other articles/ publications (e.g., Bucky, 2014; Bucky, Stolberg, Strack, & Landon, 2015) that it is inappropriate for psychologists to ask professional athletes for tickets for games. However, on occasion, a player, out of what might be special appreciation for what a psychologist has done, may offer his tickets or an autographed football. Such an unsolicited demonstration of appreciation is another example of an unintended ethical dual relationship.

### Involvement of Family

On occasion, psychologists are asked to help relatives of players find residential treatment for chemical dependency (as determined by the player and his family). It is the position of these authors that such requests are reasonable, though not usually part of the patient's treatment plan. Arrangements can be made for credible treatment resources and referrals in the appropriate community agencies can be found by the psychologist. While referral may be appropriate and ethical, active participation in the treatment of the professional athlete's family should be left to the appropriate mental health professionals in the relatives' community.

### Involvement with Players' Wives

In response to concern about the safety of players' wives waiting for their husbands after the game and to encourage wives' involvement in the professional lives of their husbands, psychologists have advocated for the presence of security for the wives at games and after games, and the development of women's support and psychoeducation groups with approval of the general manager, head coach, and owner. In addition to the recommended groups it was suggested that the club provide additional security in the waiting area when wives waited to meet their husbands after the game. As a result, occasionally information about player-patients may emerge from the wives. Such groups have been appreciated by the players and the wives as well as the organization.

## Professional Baseball

### Locker Room, Field, Lunch Area

At times, the psychologist's primary responsibility with professional baseball teams focuses on availability to the players in the locker room, before games, and in the dugout on the field during batting practice. As a result, the contact between the psychologist and the players can occur at any time or place (e.g., lunch room, training room, locker room, and field), and psychologists may be expected to be visible to the players and coaches on a regular basis (e.g., twice each home stand). Players who want to talk with the psychologist are usually given the opportunity to talk in a private setting (i.e., the physician's examining room); however, the players rarely take advantage of that option. The players frequently say, "This is my family," so talking in front of their teammates and coaches is acceptable. For example, on one occasion, a player approached the team's psychologist who was talking to the manager in the locker room and asked if they (the psychologist and player) could talk when the psychologist finished talking to the manager. This spoke to the issue of trust in the manager and the organization, with no observable sensitivity about his privacy.

*Medication*

MLB has strict rules about players' use of medications which have been identified as being on the MLB list of banned substances (e.g. ADHD medications). For players who are interested in obtaining MLB approval for getting such prescription medication, the psychologist's role may be: (1) to provide the initial assessment; (2) then make a referral to an MLB-approved psychiatrist; and (3) if approved by the psychiatrist and three MLB physicians, make a referral to another psychiatrist in the city in which the player lives during the season and potentially a referral to a psychiatrist in the city in which the player lives in the offseason. The initial meeting and then the referral(s) occur, at times, in addition to having a therapeutic relationship with the player (another example of what these authors view as an ethical dual relationship).

*Psychoeducation*

Another issue that presents as a common role for the psychologist working with professional athletes is providing psychoeducation to the entire team. Essentially, the psychologist is in a "teacher" role, usually in a group setting, while, at the same time, in the role of a player's therapist. These issues become difficult to separate when the topic of the training parallels issues on which the clinician is also working with a specific athlete. Common examples include trainings on relationships, anger, communication, domestic violence, and substance use/abuse.

*Stress*

A frequent role of a psychologist with a professional athlete is dealing with interpersonal stressors. At times, players seeing a psychologist may ask the psychologist to see his significant other. One option is to refer the significant other to another psychologist. However, at times, the player may have a strong preference for his significant other to see the team's psychologist. Working with significant others requires a clear discussion of the potential complications (primarily confidentiality). It should be noted that some psychologists view such therapeutic relationships, by definition, as unethical and, therefore, avoid them completely, referring the significant other to another mental health professional. However, it is important to note that the benefits may outweigh the potential complications, particularly when the athlete prefers that the significant other is seen by his psychologist.

## CONCLUSION

Professional relationships with professional athletes, teams, and organizations include frequent, inevitable, and, at times, helpful dual relationships. Psychologists need to be cautious about unintended consequences for such dual relationships which are inherently infused with opportunities for therapeutic complications. It is the position of these authors that it is possible, with the appropriate planning and caution, that such dual relationships between the athlete and psychologist may be productive as well as therapeutic. It is also the position of these authors that the informed-consent process is extremely important and, at times, an ongoing process.

## REFERENCES

American Psychological Association (1992). *Ethical Principles of Psychologists and Code of Conduct.* Retrieved from http://www.apa.org/ethics/code/code-1992.aspx (accessed July 27, 2016).

American Psychological Association (2002). Ethical principles of psychologists and code of conduct. *American Psychologist, 47*(12), 1597–1611.

American Psychological Association (2010). Ethical principles of psychologists and code of conduct. Retrieved from http://www.apa.org/ethics (accessed July 27, 2016).

Association for Applied Sport Psychology (AASP) (1996). *AASP Ethical Principles and Standards, the Ethics Code.* Retrieved from: http://www.appliedsportpsych.org/about/ethics/ (accessed on January 1, 2016).

Buceta, J. (1993). The sport psychologist/athletic coach dual role: advantages, difficulties, and ethical considerations. *Journal of Applied Sport Psychology, 5,* 64–77.

Bucky, S. F. (2014). Ethical issues in assessing/treating elite athletes. *The National Psychologist.* January Retrieved from: http://nationalpsychologist. com/2014/01/ethical-issues-in-assessing-treating-elite-athletes/102423.html (accessed July 27, 2016).

Bucky, S. F., Stolberg, R. A., Strack, B., & Landon, A. (2015). Prominent components of successful work with professional athletes. Paper presented at the meeting of San Diego Psychological Association, San Diego, CA.

Catalano, S. (1997). The challenges of clinical practice in small or rural communities: case studies in managing dual relationships in and outside of therapy. *Journal of Contemporary Psychotherapy, 27*(1), 23-35.

European Sport Psychology Federation (FEPSAC) (2011). Code of Ethics. Retrieved from http://www.fepsac.com/activities/publications/ (accessed July 27, 2016).

Gardner, F. & Moore, Z. (2006). *Clinical Sport Psychology*. Champaign, IL: Human Kinetics.

Johnson, W. (1995). Perennial ethical quandaries in military psychology: toward American Psychological Association–Department of Defense collaboration. *Professional Psychology Research and Practice, 26*(3), 281-287.

Pope, K. & Vasquez, M. J. T. (2016). *Ethics in Psychotherapy and Counseling: A Practical Guide* (5th ed.). San Francisco, CA: Jossey-Bass.

Sonne, J. (1999). Multiple relationships: does the new ethics code answer the right questions? In D. N. Bersoff (Ed.), *Ethical Conflicts in Psychology* (2nd ed., pp. 227-230). Washington, DC: American Psychological Association.

Sonne, J. L. (2006). nonsexual multiple relationships: a practical decision-making model for clinicians. *The Independent Practitioner,* Fall, 187-192.

Triplett, N. (1898). The dynamogenic factors in pacemaking and competition. *American Journal of Psychology, 9,* 507-553.

Weinberg, R. & Gould, D. (2011). *Foundations of Sport and Exercise Psychology* (5th ed.). Champaign, IL: Human Kinetics.

CHAPTER 10

# MULTIPLE RELATIONSHIPS IN RECOVERY COMMUNITIES

*Adam Silberstein and Lindsey Boone*

Clinicians who work in the addiction and recovery field are often faced with complex challenges that are inherent and unique to this population. In a traditional urban private practice, therapists more often than not engage the client in a confined setting, whereas addiction treatment routinely involves therapeutic encounters that lend to a broader array of overlapping roles, multiple relationships, and a variety of boundary crossings. Addiction therapists, particularly those who work in treatment milieu settings, often wear a variety of hats that are essential to and an inherent part of the recovery process. The addiction therapist, for example, may be required to set limits outside of the therapy session with clients, serve in the role of group therapist, family therapist, and individual therapist for the same client, or may be involved in unconventional therapeutic community activities such as eating with clients, supervising client smoking breaks, or rapport building outside of session.

## DEFINING MULTIPLE RELATIONSHIPS

As a result of the predominant communal approach to addiction treatment, therapists may often be subject to unavoidable and common multiple relationships with their clients. Professional organizations for a variety of disciplines of mental health providers address the ethics of dual relationships (American Counseling Association, 2014; American Psychological Association (APA), 2010; California Association of

Marriage and Family Therapists, 2011; National Association of Social Workers, 2008). All of the professional organizations agree that multiple relationships in and of themselves are not unethical; rather, professional codes guide therapists in regard to how to identify multiple relationships and how to assess which relationships can impair or support treatment. Nardone (2006), among many other experts, instructs clinicians working in the recovery field on how to use the Ethics Code to identify if a multiple relationship exists and how to assess whether or not it meets the ethical guidelines and is permissible.

According to Behnke (2004), the APA Ethics Code addresses how to assess if a multiple relationship is present using three distinct categories. APA Ethics Code 3.05 states:

> (a) A multiple relationship occurs when a psychologist is in a professional role with a person and (1) at the same time is in another role with the same person, (2) at the same time is in a relationship with a person closely associated with or related to the person with whom the psychologist has the professional relationship, or (3) promises to enter into another relationship in the future with the person or a person closely associated with or related to the person.
>
> (p. 66)

## Category 1

To determine if a multiple relationship is present, the therapist working in the recovery field must first establish if she is in a professional role with a client and at the same time is another role with that same client. There are numerous examples of these forms of dual relationships in the field of addiction rehabilitation. For example, it is not uncommon for therapists to be active members of 12-step communities themselves. As such, therapists may have unavoidable encounters where they belong to the same recovery support group that a client attends. A therapist may be an active participant in a meeting where she holds service positions and socializes after the meeting with her sober peers at a local coffee shop or diner. She may discover that her active client has not only elected to attend the same meeting but has also decided to participate in "fellowship" (a term to describe the supportive socializing that occurs before or after a meeting). In another scenario, a therapist's encounter

131

may involve being the main speaker at a meeting where she tells her personal story and discovers that residents of the treatment center she is employed by are also in attendance.

Additionally, individuals in recovery for addiction often pursue professional work in the recovery field and may either belong to professional organizations or are employed at treatment facilities where their previous or current therapist has an affiliation. For example, to foster ongoing recovery treatment a client who graduated from a treatment center may, after some time, become an employee of the center where her previous or current therapist may conduct groups or be employed as a staff therapist. In the same vein, a therapist may refer an active client to a sober living she refers to regularly, and that client may eventually graduate and become employed as a front-line staff or manager. The therapist may have a routine working relationship with this sober living and can find herself in a position to coordinate care of other clients she treats with the current client who is now a staff member. Another example of a multiple relationship that can occur is when an active private practice client requests admission to the treatment center where a therapist works part-time as a direct-care clinician or as a clinical director. Also, it is not uncommon for well-established professionals in the recovery field to seek out professional help by therapists who specialize in addiction. For example, a therapist may be treating the marketing director of a well-known facility and may often find herself attending the same conferences or marketing events as her client.

## Category 2

The next category of a multiple relationship involves being in a professional role with a client while at the same time being in a relationship with a person related to or closely associated with the person the therapist has a professional role with. The culture of recovery, even in larger metropolitan areas, is often close knit. Suppose two clients are treated by the same therapist in private practice and these clients meet at an Alcoholics Anonymous (AA) meeting and eventually decide to become roommates. A therapist in private practice may have a close relationship with the owner of a treatment center who employs some of her clients. Or, consider that a therapist has a sponsee in a 12-step program. The therapist's sponsee refers someone she is working with in AA to her for therapy, aware that she is also a therapist. Another common occurrence is that a therapist may treat multiple clients in private practice who are receiving services from the same sober living or treatment center. These clients are all connected to one another in that they are a part of a sober living milieu or treatment environment and attend the same meetings, recovery-related activities, or intensive therapeutic addiction services.

## Category 3

The final dimension to assess whether a multiple relationship exists involves scenarios where promises are made to enter into another relationship in the future with a client or someone closely associated with the client. This form of dual relationship may be more likely to occur in complex business endeavors. The recovery community has numerous opportunities for professional growth. For example, a therapist may be approached by an entrepreneur to assist in creating a mental health recovery phone application and discovers that this individual is pursuing financial backing from one of the therapist's clients. Suppose that a seasoned therapist is asked to consult in a weekly supervision group at a treatment center and the owner of the treatment center is also the therapist's client. Another highly complex possibility may be an active client and his family approach you to open a treatment center.

### Assessing Multiple Relationships

### Benefits

Zur (2014) provides a strategy to examine multiple relationships and how they can potentially benefit or harm clients. He discerns that multiple relationships can be helpful, neutral, or harmful. "Helpful multiple relationships are those relationships where clients clearly benefit from them. For example, social multiple relationships in one's community can enhance trust and therapeutic alliance, which, as we know, is the best predictor of positive therapeutic outcome" (p. 21). We have identified that in the field of addiction treatment there are numerous multiple relationships that can emerge in social, professional, institutional, or even business contexts. We assert that many of the relationships discussed can in fact be helpful in the context of therapy for addiction. The treatment of addiction encourages clients to actively participate in their recovery. Therapy focuses on developing a community of support and the building of coping skills to help foster healthy reintegration into life. The treating therapist can be a helpful role model to clients. As such, it can be a service to a client's treatment to see her therapist participating in AA or in professional organizations. On a similar note, there also can be benefit for those individuals who have chosen to work in the field of recovery and may have professional or institutional affiliations with their therapist. For example, the client who belongs to a professional organization and sees her therapist at a quarterly or monthly meeting may benefit from modeling of professional commitment and attending to work responsibilities, elements that are often focused on in therapy.

## Risks

Some of the multiple relationships discussed may have more inherent risk and complexities than others. For example, when two existing clients have elected to date or room together, it can create challenges in the therapeutic relationship. There is potential for discord or tensions to develop in these relationships. One of the clients may feel that confidentiality is compromised as she is aware that the therapist is seeing her partner or roommate and the therapist, because of confidentiality, cannot discuss the matter in a direct manner (unless permission to release of information is signed). Consider the scenario of a therapist who begins to conduct groups at a treatment facility where her client is a staff therapist. The therapist begins to have conflict with management or group members and her client is exposed to this information. The therapeutic relationship may be compromised since the client is now aware of information about the therapist that makes her uncomfortable and may negatively impact the therapeutic process. Another example of the complex nature of multiple relationships is a therapist who has a peer that attends the same weekly meeting. This peer invites her to join him in a business venture. After many weeks of involvement, the therapist discovers that the primary financial backer is the father of a client. If the therapist decides to remain on the project, the client may be negatively impacted.

## MANAGING MULTIPLE RELATIONSHIPS

Behnke (2004) helps guide therapists in how to utilize the APA Ethics Code to address how to assess if a multiple relationship is permissible. The 2010 APA Ethics Code 3.05 states:

> A psychologist refrains from entering into a multiple relationship if the multiple relationship could reasonably be expected to impair the psychologist's objectivity, competence or effectiveness in performing his or her functions as a psychologist, or otherwise risks exploitation or harm to the person with whom the professional relationship exists. Multiple relationships that would not reasonably be expected to cause impairment or risk exploitation or harm are not unethical.

Behnke (2004) instructs the therapist to evaluate if the nature of the identified multiple relationship could reasonably be expected to impair objectivity or competence or if it can lend harm or exploitation to the client being served. Kaplan (2005) recommends that clinicians seek regular consultation and supervision to address issues of confidentiality and clinical practices that can impact treatment services and to implement relevant agency standards related to multiple relationships in the recovery field. To evaluate whether or not a multiple relationship can impair objectivity, competence, or harm and exploit a client, the therapist must assess what a "reasonable" psychologist would do in a similar situation. It is important to note that the idea of what a "reasonable" psychologist would do in similar situations is highly distinct in the field of recovery. As this chapter has illustrated, practitioners are often faced with highly complex and often times unpredictable clinical scenarios which lead to numerous opportunities for multiple relationships.

### Standard of Care and Consultation

The term "reasonable," as described above, represents what are considered the best practices amongst psychologists, the community standards specific to the recovery field. It is important to re-emphasize at this juncture that the addiction field represents a unique professional subset in the field of psychology. To appreciate what in fact is emblematic of this professional subset, the culture and nuance of the treatment community must be considered. As emphasized in this chapter, those working in the field of addiction have far more opportunities to encounter predictable and unpredictable multiple relationships than those working in more traditional urban private practice settings. It is quite common for the addiction therapist to work in milieu treatment settings while maintaining a private practice. Therapists in this field, particularly those who themselves are in recovery, can anticipate seeing their clients in different contexts within the recovery community. As the emphasis of treatment is communally based, it is also reasonable that a therapist may serve clientele that know one another.

The standard of care has often been generally referred to as the degree of care which a reasonably prudent practitioner should exercise in the same or similar circumstances. In other words, the standard of care, as this book has thoroughly emphasized, is context-based. This chapter has detailed the complex and unique set of "circumstances" that are prevalent in the context of the recovery community. The standard of care, especially when it comes to multiple relationships, is distinct and unique in the field of addiction. Multiple relationships are not only common, expected, and unavoidable, but often unpredictable in this arena.

In light of the distinct nature of the professional climate in addiction treatment, we maintain that to assess how a "reasonable" psychologist evaluates multiple relationships, it is often essential to consult with an expert, raise the issue in peer supervision, or seek supervision with other psychologists and professionals who work or have experience in the addiction field. The clinical focus of addiction treatment emphasizes the importance of community support and the building of needed coping skills to maintain sobriety, gain employment, manage time effectively, and improve interpersonal relationships. Professionals who do not work with this population or have specific modalities that may not focus on these interventions may approach the treatment in a different manner. For example, the psychodynamic or psychoanalytic practitioner who works in an urban private practice setting with a focus on treating anxiety disorders may not have a full appreciation of the nature of the addiction and recovery community. As such, the psychodynamic practitioner may not be able to determine or evaluate what constitutes "reasonable," "permissible," or "expected" multiple relationships in the culture of the addiction field.

Analysis

To further evaluate how to approach dual relationships in the addiction field we recommend employing an ethical analysis which helps determine whether or not the relationship is ethical or unethical. Zur (2014) provides a comprehensive guide to help clinicians approach multiple relationships. The therapist is asked to examine a broad array of variables, including the type of dual relationship, whether it is avoidable, unavoidable, or unexpected, the legal and ethical status of the relationship, whether it is concurrent or sequential, the intensity of the contact, and if the relationship is common or atypical in a given context. After addressing these dimensions, the clinician can better assess whether or not the multiple relationship is permissible and beneficial, neutral, or harmful.

It is essential to utilize informed consent as a vehicle to address the issue of multiple relationships. We recommend that the discussion of potential multiple relationships, including the risks, benefits, and how to address them if they arise, be included in the informed-consent written document and discussion at the onset of treatment and that continued dialogue occur throughout the treatment process as needed.

Scenario 1

Take, for example, a clinician who has been attending a Tuesday-night AA meeting for 5 years and the fellowship directly after. On one occasion, a client attends the same meeting and the clinician notices that the client is going to participate in fellowship afterwards. Using Zur's (2014) dimensions we can determine this is a social dual relationship, is somewhat expected, avoidable if needed, ethical, concurrent, involves a high intensity of contact, and is common within the context of recovery. At this juncture, we also recommend that the clinician evaluate some other clinical elements before moving forward in the relationship. The client may have other diagnoses or symptoms that may complicate being at a meeting with her therapist outside the office and outside the AA meeting. For example, the client, in addition to carrying a chemical dependency diagnosis, may also have characterological symptoms that can lend to conflict or confusion should that client attend the same meeting or fellowship as her therapist (Zur, 2014). In this scenario, when the therapist finds herself in an unexpected multiple relationship, we maintain that initially, the therapist can stay at the meeting but need not share elaborately or share at all. The therapist should decline to attend the fellowship with the client until a thorough assessment and consultation can be conducted with a peer or consultation group and, if appropriate, after discussion with the client.

During the consultation, the clinician will be able to examine how the social encounter impacts or may impact the client. The clinician may determine that the exchange is beneficial to the client. For example, the meeting and fellowship are quite sizeable and do not lend to more intimate exchange and the client's symptoms do not warrant concern. In this case, the analysis may view the multiple relationship as beneficial and not subject to potential harm or exploitation. On the other hand, the clinician may conclude that the meeting or fellowship is too small and intimate and participation can be disruptive to the client's treatment in light of her symptoms. Should the therapist determine that the multiple relationship is in fact permissible, we recommend the therapist discuss the issue with the client and develop parameters to help identify if issues arise and how to address them should they emerge. It is important to document all consultations, discussions with the client, and ongoing evaluation of the relationship.

## Scenario 2

To further examine the complexities of multiple relationships that exist in the addiction recovery field, let's explore a situation where a private practice therapist has been working with two separate clients for over a year. The therapist discovers that the clients have recently become friends after attending the same AA meeting. This professional dual relationship is somewhat unexpected, ethical, concurrent, low intensity, and common in this setting (Zur, 2014). In this situation the therapist would examine if the clients' diagnoses and session content are impacted by both of the clients working with the same therapist. If it is determined through consultation with an appropriate professional peer or peer group that this relationship is low risk and is not likely to lead to harm or exploitation or compromise the effectiveness of the delivery of services, then the therapist can move forward with the treatment of both clients. However, if both clients decide to become roommates or lovers, the level of intensity and potential for conflict increase. In this case, careful documentation and determination of how and whether to terminate the therapeutic relationship must be done in close consultation with peers and with thorough documentation.

## Scenario 3

Finally, consider a scenario where a seasoned private practice therapist has been working with a client in recovery for many years. She has also been working collaterally with the family of this client to support treatment, as the family dynamics have significantly contributed to this client's repeated relapses. After a period of prolonged abstinence, the father is very pleased and contacts the therapist to inform her that he is financing a new treatment center and wants her to be the clinical director. This type of business dual relationship is potentially unethical, concurrent, high intensity, and uncommon (Zur, 2014). Entering into a business relationship with a current client or her family member may be exploitative or perceived to be exploitative of the therapeutic relationship and generally ill advised. Documenting that this offer was made and declined by the therapist will be important and weighing the pros and cons of exploring this offer with the client will be best addressed through consultation.

## SUMMARY

In summary, therapists working in the addiction field have a unique opportunity to serve individuals who struggle with dependency issues in a variety of contexts. The addiction and rehabilitation communities are often close knit and intimate. Many providers themselves participate in community support groups such as AA. Furthermore, it is not uncommon for individuals undergoing recovery to pursue professional opportunities in the addiction field. As such, multiple relationships are often encountered, many of which are common and beneficial and can impact the therapeutic relationship in a meaningful and positive way. We recommend that clinicians engage their clients in conversations regarding the multiple relationships, and seek consultation with other professionals who work in the field of addiction and appreciate the nuanced complexities of this population and community. We also advise clinicians to utilize a system of analysis that can help to ensure appropriate adherence to ethical standards while serving the best interest of their clients.

# References

American Counseling Association (2014). *ACA Code of Ethics*. Alexandria, VA: Author.

American Psychological Association (APA) (2010). *Ethical Principles for Psychologists*. Washington, DC: Author.

Behnke, S. (2004). Multiple relationships and APA's new ethics code: values and applications. *Ethics Rounds, 35*(1), 66.

California Association of Marriage and Family Therapists (CAMFT) (2011) *Code of Ethics for Marriage and Family Therapists*. San Diego, CA: Author.

Kaplan, L. E. (2005). Dual relationships: the challenges for social workers in recovery. *Journal of Social Work Practice in the Addictions, 5/3*. Retrieved from http://www.researchgate.net/profile/Laura_Kaplan/publication/232242136_ Dual_Relationships_The_Challenges_for_Social_Workers_in_Recovery/ links/09e41507c270d9f148000000.pdf (accessed July 27, 2016).

Nardone, N. A. (2006). Analyzing the pros and cons of multiple relationships between chemical addiction therapists and their clients. *Journal of Addictive Disorders*. Retrieved from: http://www.breining.edu (accessed July 27, 2016).

National Association of Social Workers. (2008). *Code of Ethics of the National Association of Social Workers*. Washington, DC: Author.

Zur, O. (2014). Not all multiple relationships are created equal: mapping the maze of 26 types of multiple relationships. *The Independent Practitioner, 34*(1), 15–22.

# CHAPTER 11

# THE CHALLENGE OF MULTIPLE RELATIONSHIPS IN TOTAL INSTITUTIONS

*Frederic G. Reamer*

In the mid-1950s, renowned sociologist Erving Goffman did a year of field work at St. Elizabeth Hospital in Washington, DC, a mammoth federal psychiatric hospital. His principal goal was to explore the world of the patient and the relationship between what psychiatrists actually do in their work and what they say about what they do. Based on his extensive participant observation, Goffman (1961) coined the term "total institution" and, in his now-classic book, *Asylums*, described the characteristics of settings that control nearly every moment of residents' lives.

In today's world, mental health professionals provide services in a wide range of what Goffman dubbed total institutions. Psychologists, social workers, mental health counselors, psychiatrists, addiction specialists, and marriage and family therapists are employed in adult and juvenile correctional facilities, psychiatric hospitals, group homes, residential treatment and rehabilitation centers, wilderness therapy programs (also known as outdoor behavioral health programs), and on military bases. Many clients are sent to these settings involuntarily. For example, criminal and juvenile court judges order many defendants to correctional facilities and, as an alternative to incarceration and as a condition of probation, to residential treatment and outdoor behavioral health programs. Judges also commit some people who suffer from severe psychiatric illness to a psychiatric hospital, often without the individual's consent.

In settings that include features of total institutions, clinicians often face dual roles and unique multiple relationship challenges because of the possibility that informal interactions that do not have an explicit therapeutic purpose will occur outside of private offices, informal treatment space (as in wilderness therapy programs), and during "off" hours (Reamer, 2012). In psychiatric hospitals, group homes, and residential treatment programs, especially those that feature therapeutic milieu models, clinicians may find themselves socializing with residents informally in a way that can lead to problematic dual relationships if not managed skillfully. Casual conversations in such settings can sometimes lead to friendships, staffers' extraordinary disclosure of personal information, and, in extreme cases, sexual encounters.

Military settings pose special challenges. In addition to providing clinical services in formal mental health clinics on the base, some mental health professionals are now "embedded" with military units; when these units deploy to a war zone or other theater of operation, behavioral health professionals travel with them to enhance personnel's access to mental health services. These mental health clinicians may be required to share living quarters with clients. Clinicians may interact with clients informally outside of therapeutic sessions in a variety of ways that lead to challenging and, possibly, unethical dual relationships, for example, as a result of socializing, playing games, or attending entertainment events. The absence of a formal office setting and structure can increase the likelihood of casual and, ultimately, problematic dual relationships (Johnson, 2011).

Even when not embedded with deployed units, mental health professionals in the military often develop dual roles and multiple relationships with clients when both are stationed on bases. Their children may become playmates during their time as students enrolled in Department of Defense schools located on the base, requiring clinicians and clients to interact as parents during non-work hours. Their spouses may become friends and arrange social events that clinicians and clients may be invited to attend. Military therapists may be mandated to participate in field exercises with clients. A military clinician's client may outrank the clinician, which can lead to complex boundary challenges and dual roles outside of the therapy office. A military clinician may also be expected to combine both therapeutic and forensic roles—clearly a multiple relationship—especially when the clinician is instructed to conduct a fitness-for-duty evaluation and render an opinion about whether a pilot, sailor, marine, or soldier poses a safety threat.

Mental health professionals in adult and juvenile correctional settings provide counseling to inmates who struggle with mental health issues. Here, too, clinicians encounter multiple relationship challenges that are unlikely in the civilian world. These clinicians may have what ethicists refer to as "divided loyalties," where professionals assume multiple roles and are beholden simultaneously to clients, administrators, and the public at large, particularly when clinicians may have to relate to inmates as both therapists and social control agents who, for example, must assess inmates' ability to testify in an upcoming trial or whether clients pose a threat to staffers or other inmates. Such multiple relationships can lead to daunting conflicts of interest.

Mental health professionals who work in wilderness or outdoor behavioral health programs also face special multiple relationship challenges (Reamer & Siegel, 2008). Wilderness therapy programs use nature as a teacher, creating therapeutic opportunities as struggling teens and young adults face the wide range of unpredictable circumstances and challenges that emerge in nature. As part of the wilderness therapy model, therapists spend time with clients in very remote locations, such as deserts and forests. There are no counseling offices. Because of the geographical distance from the program's headquarters, clinicians may spend overnights with the group of field staffers and clients, which may entail sharing meals, hiking, playing games, and engaging in informal conversation that seems more friend-like than therapy. This unique mix of multiple relationships provides rich therapeutic opportunities for teens, many of whom have struggled with boundaries in many areas of their lives, but it can also lead to inappropriate dual roles and multiple relationships. Similar to challenges faced by embedded military clinicians, clinicians in wilderness therapy programs must be careful to distinguish between ethically appropriate flexible boundaries and problematic dual roles and relationships. Here too, the informality of the setting requires clinicians to be on their guard to prevent unethical multiple relationships, which could include inappropriate self-disclosure or physical contact with clients.

The unique multiple relationship challenges that arise in diverse total institution settings that feature a therapeutic component or mission manifest themselves in several distinct conceptual patterns in relation to intimacy issues, personal benefit, emotional and dependency issues, and altruistic instincts (Reamer, 2012).

## INTIMACY

Many multiple relationship issues in total institutions involve some element of intimacy. In extreme cases, intimacy issues involve some kind of sexual contact between mental health professionals and clients. But beyond these obvious and extreme boundary violations are much subtler issues involving intimacy, especially related to physical touch (Downey, 2001; Durana, 1998; Hunter & Struve, 1998; Zur, 2007). In some total institution settings that have a therapeutic purpose, there are likely to be more opportunities for physical contact between clinician and client than in other outpatient counseling settings.

Many forms of physical touch are appropriate and ethical, but some are not. For example, in a wilderness therapy program it may be considered appropriate for a distraught or deeply appreciative client to initiate a hug with the therapist. However, in a prison, hugs between staffers and inmates would be considered an egregious violation of institutional policy and protocol. The essential feature of inappropriate physical touch is that it is likely to involve an unethical dual relationship, cause the client psychological harm, or violate agency policy.

## PERSONAL BENEFIT

Some multiple relationship issues emerge because of pragmatic concerns, for example, the possibility that the practitioner's relationship with the client could produce tangible, material benefits or favors for the practitioner. These relationships can arise from relatively benign motives—for example, when a client with some specialized knowledge or expertise offers to assist a clinician with a personal need or challenge (for example, providing auto repair or plumbing advice as an act of kindness or a form of barter)—and some arise from more sinister motives, such as when a practitioner exploits a client for personal gain. In one case, a clinician on a military base provided counseling to a high-ranking officer who sought help with some challenging marital issues. The client was aware that the therapist's spouse, who was also a military officer, was being considered for a significant promotion. The therapist spent time during two counseling sessions soliciting the client's advice about how the therapist's spouse might enhance her chances for promotion. This is an example of an inappropriate dual role for personal benefit.

In a relatively small number of cases in total institution settings, clinicians might be accused of entering into inappropriate business and financial multiple relationships with clients. For example, a wealthy family might offer to make a generous donation to a residential program that treats high-risk adolescents to enable their child to jump the lengthy waiting list and gain immediate admission. This is an example of a business-based multiple relationship.

Other problematic boundary issues arise because clients offer clinicians personal gifts or favors. While many such gestures are appropriate—as a way of expressing appreciation—others are questionable, either because of their monetary value or the gift giver's ulterior and self-serving motives (Gutheil & Brodsky, 2008; Reamer, 2012).

## EMOTIONAL AND DEPENDENCY ISSUES

Multiple relationship challenges arising from a clinician's personal issues can take many forms in total institutions. Some constitute boundary violations that lead to harm or exploitation of clients and others. Other multiple relationship issues involve boundary crossings that do not rise to the level of actual violations but must be managed carefully nonetheless.

What many of these personal or social multiple relationship issues have in common is that they are rooted in the clinician's own emotional and dependency needs, such as those stemming from childhood experiences, marital and relationship issues, aging, career frustrations, or financial or legal problems. Research on impaired professionals provides ample evidence that troubled practitioners sometimes find themselves enmeshed in inappropriate multiple relationships (Celenza, 2007; Gutheil & Brodsky, 2008; Guy, Poelstra, & Stark, 1989; Kilburg, Kaslow, & VandenBos, 1988; Reamer, 2015; Syme, 2003; Thoreson, Miller, & Krauskopf, 1989; Zur, 2007). The ambiguous boundaries in some total institution settings can exacerbate this risk.

Examples of multiple relationship issues in total institution settings arising from a clinician's emotional and dependency needs include

145

forming friendships with clients outside of clinical sessions, engaging in excessive self-disclosure to clients, and communicating with clients too affectionately. Although these phenomena can occur in any treatment context, the unique features of total institutions exacerbate risks. For example, some total institution settings—such as group homes and therapeutic boarding schools—work hard to simulate some features of private homes, as much as possible. Many of these programs provide the equivalent of a living room or den, a basement with recreational equipment and games, kitchens, musical instruments, sports equipment, and dining rooms. Staffers encourage informality, within limits, to enhance residents' comfort and avoid sterile institutional environments. By design, clinicians may interact with residents informally outside of their offices. Mental health professionals may play ping-pong or music with clients, share a meal in the dining room, take a walk on a nature trail, or visit with residents in their rooms. Clinicians in these settings know quite well that these informal, relaxed encounters can enhance the quality of the therapeutic relationship. However, clinicians who are struggling with issues in their own lives, and who may feel lonely or isolated outside of work, may find that the informal boundaries in some 24/7 settings lead them to let down their guard and, for example, share too much personal information with clients, treat clients too affectionately, or complain about colleagues and administrators in ways that are generally considered an inappropriate personal or social multiple relationship. The risks may increase when clinicians live in on-campus housing or dormitories, which become their professional and personal home. The ambiguous boundary between work and play may be quite blurry and lead to complicated dual roles, for example, when a therapy client visits the clinician's apartment to chat informally.

The formal boundaries that one finds in more typical treatment settings are not possible in wilderness therapy programs, nor would they be appropriate. There are no office walls to contain therapeutic conversations; counseling sessions may occur during a late-evening rain shower when a teen is finally eager to talk about his childhood trauma while sitting under a tarp attached to a tree. The clinician may decide to spend the night in the field, relatively close to the client, because of the distance from program headquarters. Although this is widely regarded as appropriately flexible boundaries, a problematic multiple relationship can develop if, for example, the clinician discloses personal information to the client inappropriately during late-night "soul baring" that may seem more like an exchange between close friends than a clinician–client conversation.

These non-traditional approaches to clinical services require exceedingly skillful management of dual roles and multiple relationships by clinicians so that their own emotional issues do not complicate the therapeutic relationship. Even the most skilled clinicians must be constantly aware of "use of self" and countertransference issues. Clinicians who are struggling with their own issues or are impaired may find that the informal boundaries that are essential in many 24/7 treatment settings provide a slippery slope on which boundary crossings and violations can develop and slide. Some judicious self-disclosure and some modest physical touch by clinicians may be constructive and therapeutic, but if these gestures are self-serving or otherwise inappropriate, they can constitute problematic multiple relationships and harm clients significantly. Clinicians must always keep in mind the Latin adage, *Cui bono?* (For whose benefit?)

ALTRUISM

Clinicians who work in total institutions often get to know their clients exceedingly well. Unlike clinicians who may see clients sporadically for an hour every week or so and never see them in the environments in which they live, mental health professionals in settings such as group homes, residential treatment centers, juvenile correctional facilities, and military bases often see their clients in non-clinical contexts. Knowing that these clients do not have access to the comforts of home, clinicians, who often have deeply caring, altruistic instincts, may want to give clients modest gifts, offer favors, and share personal information that might be useful to clients. While some modest gifts, favors, and self-disclosure may be considered appropriate as a way to humanize the treatment setting and relationship, some gestures may unwittingly foster multiple relationships that are counterproductive and harmful.

Some clients, especially those who have struggled with boundaries throughout their lives—often as a result of trauma—may misinterpret even the most altruistic and well-meaning gift or favor. To some, gifts, favors, and altruistic self-disclosure convey a sign of friendship and can

147

lead to boundary confusion. In regimented settings such as prisons and the military, such altruistic gestures may violate strict no-fraternization rules and lead to disciplinary action.

In one case, a prison inmate serving a 6-year sentence for armed robbery decided to marry his longtime partner. The two had met in high school and lived together for years before the inmate went to prison. They had two children together. After much discussion during prison visits, the couple decided to marry.

During his prison stay the inmate sought counseling from the institution's mental health counselor. For over a year, the two developed a very healthy, constructive therapeutic alliance. During their counseling sessions the inmate worked hard to address the connection between his early-life trauma, drug addiction, and criminal conduct.

The inmate asked the counselor to attend the prison-based wedding ceremony, at which the prison chaplain would officiate, and serve as best man. Because of prison regulations, the inmate and his partner could not invite outside guests. The inmate told the counselor how much it would mean to him if the counselor were to attend the ceremony and serve as best man. If this had occurred outside of a prison, many clinicians would argue that attending a client's wedding (although not the post-ceremony party) could have rich therapeutic value (so long as client confidentiality is maintained), although serving as best man would likely cross the ethics line and constitute an inappropriate dual role and multiple relationship. As Zur (2007) states: "Celebrating and otherwise affirming clients' lives and accomplishments may be an important attestation for those clients who experience low self-esteem and have lacked external validation or the experience of celebrations throughout their lives" (p. 108). In a prison setting, however, a clinician who may wish to attend an inmate's wedding ceremony would have to deal with administrative rules that prohibit this sort of dual role and multiple relationship, and the possible perception among other inmates of favoritism on the clinician's part.

## MANAGING MULTIPLE RELATIONSHIP RISKS IN TOTAL INSTITUTIONS

Mental health professionals who work in total institutions can take a number of practical steps to protect clients and themselves in light of possible multiple relationship challenges (Corey & Herlihy, 2015; Gottlieb, 2003; Gutheil, 2005; Reamer, 2012; Schank & Skovholt, 2006; Younggren & Gottlieb, 2004; Zur, 2007):

1. In small communities, including residential programs, overlapping relationships are not a matter of "if" as much as "when." Ethical codes and standards are important to consider and should be supplemented with collegial consultation.

2. Attempt to set unambiguous boundaries at the beginning of all clinical relationships. Clear expectations and boundaries, whenever possible, strengthen the therapeutic relationship and minimize risk to clients and clinicians. This is especially important in situations where outside-of-therapy contact cannot be closely controlled.

3. Obtaining informed consent and documenting any unusual encounters and multiple relationships are essential.

4. Evaluate potential dual roles and multiple relationships by considering: (a) the amount of power the clinician holds over the client (for example, clinicians in prisons, military settings, wilderness therapy programs, and residential treatment centers may hold considerable power); (b) the duration and intensity of the relationship; (c) the clarity of conditions surrounding planned or actual termination; (d) the client's clinical profile and boundary-related challenges; and (e) prevailing ethical standards in relevant codes of ethics and licensing laws.

5. Consider, based on these criteria, whether a dual role or multiple relationship in any form is warranted or justifiable, assuming there is a choice. Some multiple relationships or elements of a multiple relationship may be therapeutic and ethical, while others are not. Recognize that gradations exist between a full-fledged multiple relationship and no multiple relationship.

6. Pay special attention to potentially conflicting roles in the relationship.

7. Discuss the relevant issues with all parties involved, especially clients. Whenever feasible, clients should be actively and deliberately involved in these judgments, in part as a sign of respect and in part to promote informed consent. Fully inform clients of any known risks.

8. Work under supervision whenever multiple relationship issues are complex and risk is high. When possible, be sure to develop an exit strategy in the event that a dual role or multiple relationship proves to be harmful.

149

9. If necessary and feasible, refer the client to another professional in order to minimize risk and conflicts of interest, and prevent harm.
10. Provide training about dual roles and multiple relationships to staffers in total institution settings.

When Goffman embarked on his pioneering work concerning total institutions in the 1950s, he sought to examine the unique cultures and dynamics commonly found in these settings. At the time, mental health professionals' understanding of complex ethical issues was nascent at best. The concepts of boundary issues and multiple relationships did not exist as we know them today. Since then, beginning especially in the 1970s, professionals' grasp of complex boundary issues has matured significantly, including the cultivation of conceptual frameworks and ethical standards that help mental health practitioners identify multiple relationship dilemmas and manage them constructively and ethically.

Going forward, mental health professionals will need to maintain heightened sensitivity to the ever-present challenge of problematic dual roles and multiple relationships in total institutions. There is no one-size-fits-all protocol in these circumstances. Rather, mature and principled practitioners understand that management of complex multiple relationships requires diligence, careful consideration of norms that vary among different treatment settings, and nuanced responses that promote client well-being first and foremost.

## REFERENCES

Celenza, A. (2007). *Sexual Boundary Violations: Therapeutic, Supervisory, and Academic Contexts.* Lanham, MD: Aronson.
Corey, B., & Herlihy, G. (2015). *Boundary Issues in Counseling: Multiple Roles and Responsibilities* (3rd ed.). Alexandria, VA: American Counseling Association.
Downey, D. (2001). Therapeutic touch in psychotherapy. *Psychotherapy, 36*(1), 35–38.
Durana, C. (1998). The use of touch in psychotherapy: ethical and clinical guidelines. *Psychotherapy, 35,* 269–280.
Goffman, I. (1961). *Asylums: Essays on the Social Situation of Mental Patients and Other Inmates.* New York: Doubleday.
Gottlieb, M. (2003). Avoiding exploitative dual relationships: a decision-making model. *Psychotherapy, 30,* 41–48.
Gutheil, T. (2005). Boundary issues and personality disorders. *Journal of Psychiatric Practice, 11,* 88–96.

Gutheil, T., & Brodsky, A. (2008). *Preventing Boundary Violations in Clinical Practice.* New York: Guilford.

Guy, J., Poelstra, P., & Stark, M. (1989). Personal distress and therapeutic effectiveness: national survey of psychologists practicing psychotherapy. *Professional Psychology: Practice and Research, 20,* 48–50.

Hunter, M., & Struve, J. (1998). *The Ethical Use of Touch in Psychotherapy.* Thousand Oaks, CA: Sage.

Johnson, W. B. (2011). I've got this friend: multiple roles, informed consent, and friendship in the military. In W. B. Johnson & G. P. Koocher (Eds.), *Ethical Conundrums, Quandaries, and Predicaments in Mental Health Practice* (pp. 175–182). New York: Oxford University Press.

Kilburg, R., Kaslow, F., & VandenBos, G. (Eds.), (1988). *Professionals in Distress: Issues, Syndromes, and Solutions in Psychology.* Washington, DC: American Psychological Association.

Reamer, F. G. (2012). *Boundary Issues and Dual Relationships in the Human Services.* New York: Columbia University Press.

Reamer, F. G. (2015). *Risk Management in Social Work: Preventing Professional Malpractice, Liability, and Disciplinary Action.* New York: Columbia University Press.

Reamer, F. G., & Siegel, D. H. (2008). *Teens in Crisis: How the Industry Serving Struggling Teens Helps and Hurts our Kids.* New York: Columbia University Press.

Schank, A., & Skovholt, T. (2006). *Ethical Practice in Small Communities: Challenges and Rewards for Psychologists.* Washington, DC: American Psychological Association.

Syme, G. (2003). *Dual Relationships in Counseling and Psychotherapy.* London: Sage.

Thoreson, R., Miller, M., & Krauskopf, C. (1989). The distressed psychologist: prevalence and treatment considerations. *Professional Psychology: Research and Practice, 20,* 153–158.

Younggren, J., & Gottlieb, M. (2004). Managing risk when contemplating multiple relationships. *Professional Psychology: Research and Practice, 35,* 255–260.

Zur, O. (2007). *Boundary Issues in Psychotherapy: Ethical and Clinical Explorations.* Washington, DC: American Psychological Association.

# Part IV

## Common-Normal Multiple Relationships in Higher Educational Settings

# INTRODUCTION

*Ofer Zur*

Part IV (Chapters 12–14) focuses on multiple relationships that are a common occurrence in higher educational settings.

In Chapter 12, Dr. Koocher and Dr. Keith Spiegel examine the array of possibilities for multiple relationships in higher education between teachers or instructors and students. They map the possibilities from social interactions, to mentoring, co-publishing, researching, hiring students to do work at the professors' homes, blending therapeutic and academic modalities, and many more. They discuss the complexities and the ethical issues involved in such common multiple relationships.

In Chapter 13, Dr. Austin and co-authors map the considerable range of multiple roles that professors may assume. These include teacher, coach, mentor, consultant, counselor, advisor, administrator, dissertation chair, co-teacher, evaluator, recorder and documenter, empowerer, and advocate. They also explore the complexities of supervisory relationships between professors and students and the fine line between teacher and therapist.

In Chapter 14, Dr. Corey and co-authors focus on the dynamic involved in teaching group counseling with a didactic and experiential dual focus. They detail how the combination of didactic and experiential group learning requires a high level of professionalism and awareness of the complexities involved on the part of instructors. They explain how didactic and therapeutic roles often co-exist or are even unavoidable in such settings and detail ways for instructors and teaching assistants to sensitively and ethically walk this delicate 'dual tightrope' relationships.

# Chapter 12

# MULTIPLE RELATIONSHIPS IN EDUCATIONAL SETTINGS

*Gerald P. Koocher and Patricia Keith Spiegel*

## CHALLENGING ROLES

Educational settings involving psychologists have many built-in multiple role relationships. The resulting roles can enhance or compromise the quality of students' educational experience, but too often psychology faculty members may not fully grasp the significance of the ethical challenges related to multiple roles in educational settings. On the positive side, consider the professor who invites her seminar class to socialize at informal dinners in her home, the faculty member who invites students to join a research team and offers them co-authorship on resulting publications, or faculty members inclined to mentoring who assist their students in career development years after graduation. On the negative side, consider faculty members who ask students to run personal errands, who take advantage of students' contributions to research without giving due credit, or who may get into trouble based on misunderstandings of sensitive information elicited from or revealed by students. We will highlight the most common ethical pitfalls related to multiple relationships in educational settings here, but refer readers to our other more comprehensive writings on these matters (Koocher & Keith-Spiegel, 2016).

### Multiple Relationships on Campus

Appropriate boundaries between students and educators can prove more difficult to draw than those with therapy clients. The student–teacher

155

relationship does not constitute the same kind of fiduciary relationship as between therapists and clients (Knapp & VandeCreek, 2006). Whereas therapists and their clients must willfully decide to alter their professional relationship, professors and students often do not. Encouragement to attend many of the same activities (e.g., sporting events, festivals, club parties, and receptions) outside the classroom is commonplace in academia. Because professor–student relationships usually do not involve the same level of trust or possess the emotional closeness characteristic of psychotherapy relationships, mixing the contexts in which educators interact with students on a casual basis does not intrinsically cause concerns.

Professors who wish to form closer relationships with current students must consider the misunderstandings that can arise, including the meanings that other students might attach when observing a professor and only one or selected other students go off by themselves. Educators must remember that students feel sensitive about issues of equity and believe those who operate (or appear to operate) on a tilted playing field are extremely unethical (Owen & Zwahr-Castri, 2007). Students are inclined to feel more accepting if student–educator relationships are perceived as strictly professional. Professors should also remain self-aware to assure that they do come to view students as primarily fulfilling their own needs for companionship.

Graduate students-in-training are often in a position to develop multiple role relationships with other students, both peers and undergraduates. Clinical or counseling graduate students may see other students as clients in the counseling center, as classroom teachers or assistants, or in the course of conducting research. Sometimes graduate students find themselves in the awkward position of performing in a professional role while still holding student status.

## Multiple Relationships Off-Campus

Professors should carefully monitor their behavior whenever and wherever students are around, even when not on campus. Students regularly recognize their professors, and they discuss what they see among themselves. The most conservative and safest course of action is for educators to attempt to limit social multiple relationships, such as outside social contacts with individual classroom students to social multiple relationships associated with the institution (e.g., departmental social events or other functions where other instructors or multiple students participate) until after the students graduate.

Ethical issues involving multiple role relationships with student employees become mostly defused when the students do not work in the same departmental unit or are not taking courses from the faculty member in question. However, professional multiple relationships, such as the practice of hiring students one knows for part-time work, occur so often that faculty members rarely pause to consider the attendant ethical issues. What if the student hired for yard work or dog walking accidentally cuts down the wrong tree or loses the family pet? One should take precautions for the sake of students as well as one's own professional standing to diminish the possibility of untoward fallout when establishing such professional multiple relationships. First, never employ students currently enrolled in one's classes to do non-academically related work. Second, select student employees for their competence and trustworthiness and pay them a fair wage. Third, formulate all expectations and agreements in advance, including provisions for termination predicated on respect for the needs and welfare of students. Putting these understandings in written form for all concerned will reduce misunderstandings.

Ethical ramifications of multiple relationships arise in the context of whether a student who is concurrently subject to evaluation by an educator or advisor (or will be in the future) can turn down *any* request, even if pay is involved. As an example, an advisee with artistic skills is asked to create the illustrations for her advisor's PowerPoint presentation. Dare she tell him how overwhelmed she already feels with her own workload to the point of not getting enough sleep? Educators must consider the unintended pressure involved in creating such multiple relationships and attempt to ensure that any arrangement does not disadvantage the student.


## Mentoring Students

Perhaps the most complex multiple role relationships occur between student protégés and their mentors. Professors often become close with those they mentor, usually graduate students with whom they actively collaborate, in a way that feels absorbing and satisfying for both parties. Relationships occurring toward the end of the training period can last a lifetime. Mentoring, however, is a cut above the complex role of clinical supervisor/teacher and student, involving a close alliance with a "professional parent." Mentoring often bestows protégés career opportunities by making professional connections and opening doors that might otherwise be invisible or locked. Such relationships also offer personal benefits, such as emotional intimacy and a wide range of shared activities and contexts.

In this role, mentors teach the "ropes" that matter, providing tips that may never be taught in the classroom or during routine advisement sessions. When such relationships run smoothly, protégés thrive. Successful mentoring also rewards the mentors with a collaborator and feelings of pride for bringing students-in-training under their wings and helping them fly. However, these complex relationships are also vulnerable to breakdowns and dysfunction, to the detriment of protégés as well as to the mentor and the institution.

Mentors typically expect reciprocity as the relationship unfolds, but expectations from protégés can be inappropriate for a number of reasons, including immaturity, gender, and culture (Shore, Toyokawa, & Anderson, 2008). Mismatches can readily lead to unmet expectations that, in turn, cause the relationship to become dysfunctional and even abusive (Perrewe, Zellars, Rogers, Breaux, & Young, 2010). Although responsibility for negative outcomes of dysfunctional mentoring relationships or dysfunctional multiple roles often falls on the mentor as the more powerful player, protégés can actively contribute to the dysfunction. Unfortunately, protégés may feel exploited, harassed, or demeaned, and mentors may feel unappreciated, betrayed, and disappointed. Ideally, prospective mentors have already assessed the compatibility with the pool of potential protégés and have laid out procedures for openly addressing concerns emanating from either party.

## RESPECT FOR STUDENT PRIVACY

The rules and requirements regarding confidentiality in academic settings are not the same as duties owed to psychotherapy clients. This becomes a multiple role problem when students or faculty members make incorrect assumptions or become confused about privacy issues. Whereas student academic records are protected by law, what is revealed in the classroom and informally among faculty and students is not uniformly codified. Nevertheless ethical considerations apply, and imprudent disclosures that violate a reasonable expectation of privacy can cause students harm.

## The Family Educational Rights and Privacy Act

Faculty members often have multiple institutional roles related to administration, advising, evaluation, and teaching. They also have roles as faculty colleagues and supervisors of institutional personnel, including student workers. At times the multiple role relationships may lead to situations where a request or temptation to share information across roles comes up. In such circumstances, one must strike a balance that considers legal and ethical obligations.

The Family Educational Rights and Privacy Act (FERPA), a federal law (20 U.S.C. § 1232g; 34 CFR § 99) applies to all schools that receive federal funds (including student loan funds) from programs administered by US Department of Education. FERPA imposes firm limits on disclosing students' educational records. Parents have some specific rights under FERPA, but these transfer to so-called "eligible students" upon attaining age 18 or when attending a school beyond the high school level. These rights include the ability to inspect and review any of the student's education records maintained by the school. Redress procedures exist when parents or eligible students believe the records contain errors.

Generally, schools must have written permission from the parent or eligible student to release any information from a student's education record. Schools may disclose some information without consent, including: directory information such as a student's name, address, telephone number, date and place of birth, honors and awards, and dates of attendance. FERPA also allows schools to disclose records, without consent, under certain other circumstances. Examples might include releases to school officials with legitimate educational interests; to other schools when a student seeks to transfer; to accreditation agencies, auditors, or financial aid authorities; in response to a judicial order or lawful subpoena; to officials intervening in health and safety emergencies; and to state and local authorities acting under specific state laws. Casual discussion of academic performance with other faculty or students violates FERPA protections, although lack of awareness of these policies and other multiple roles or related conversations may lead to compromising a student's privacy.

### Revealing Information about Students Outside of the Classroom

Another dilemma arises when colleagues relax with each other and talk shop, mixing professional and social roles. Teachers behave just like everyone else with a job. Flushing out frustrations in the presence of sympathetic peers can release work-related stress. However, if such conversations become a contest to see who can tell the most outrageous student story, the appropriateness and constructiveness of this social tourney falls by the wayside.

Students' behavior can be amusing (even when not intended as such). Purposely disgracing students, however, is not an ethical way to release tension, and can result in actual harm that may not be evident in the lightness of the moment. Just as gossiping about clients qualifies as unethical, we believe the same standard is as important—and perhaps even more so—regarding students. Unflattering stories used as entertainment fodder that identify the students by name or other means will likely influence the way other instructors will see them. In that sense we have an obligation to separate the casual social role from our more formal professional role obligations.

### Educational Practices Triggering Personal Disclosures by Students

Some educational programs run an ethical risk by blending elements of therapeutic intervention with academic course work, creating professional multiple relationships. When complaints do arise, they typically involve intense feelings, and the inherent role conflicts (i.e., student/quasi-client and instructor/quasi-therapist) usually constitute the root of dissatisfaction.

Consider undergraduate courses on abnormal psychology or psychopathology during which students may react to discussion of the material by blurting out their own highly personal issues in class, especially when the topic seems relevant and by this, unintentionally creating multiple relationships or multiple roles for the instructor as a teacher and a psychotherapist. Similarly, a dual role is created when some students who come to trust in and respect a faculty member's expertise and sensitivity may disclose such material during an office hour. Instructors would do well to develop strategies in advance for effectively managing such disclosures and protecting the student's welfare (Branch, Hayes-Smith, & Richards, 2011).

A variation on the self-disclosure theme that place the instruction in a dual role involves written assignments, sometimes in the form of a journal, requiring students to record their personal feelings and share private recollections. This type of assignment has also come under ethical scrutiny, with claims that it often requires inappropriate self-revelation. A required assignment to reveal a childhood trauma, for example, may exacerbate feelings of powerlessness and deference to authority figures, and violates the student's privacy.

The American Psychological Association (APA) has taken a detailed stand on the issue of requiring self-disclosure by listing specific topics that psychologist-educators may *not* require students to recount (APA, 2010: Section 7.04). These include sexual and abuse history, psychological treatment, and relationships with parents, peers, spouses, or significant others. There are two exceptions. The first is clear-cut: if the admissions criteria or program at a training program require this kind of information and clearly identify such expectations in their program and application materials (e.g., a psychoanalytic training requiring a personal analysis). This follows from the expectation that the student has enrolled with a full understanding of the requirements. The second exception requires more thoughtful judgment. Requiring such personal information is *not* unethical if doing so seems necessary to evaluate and obtain assistance for those who are not competently performing their training or other professional activities due to personal problems or who may pose a risk to others. Consider a situation in which a clinical supervisor suspects a trainee may have acted out with a client or seems to have a significant mental illness. In such contexts seeking the more personal information needed to assess ethical and professional appropriateness becomes a reasonable exception.

Some programs allow (or require) students to enter individual psychotherapy for academic credit or as part of an advanced training program. We do not recommend using faculty members who regularly teach courses in the program to simultaneously provide clinical services to their students and create complex professional multiple relationships. These multiple relationships are highly complicated and often ill advised when the professor-therapist has grading power and decision power

161

whether to pass or fail the students who participate in his/her class. Such role separation helps insulate grading for academic accomplishment from a therapeutic component. One exception may be psychoanalytic training, in which faculty members may serve as both course instructors and training analysts for candidates. In this instance, the training model is usually well described by the analytic institute and well understood and accepted by the candidates prior to entering the program.

## Title IX Reporting

Title IX, also known as "Title 9" or Public Law 92-318, mandates that all employees of educational institutions that receive federal funds (including psychology faculty members) must report knowledge of sexual harassment or abuse of students, thus putting employees in a dual role. Because of federal student loan programs, virtually all universities in the USA are covered and must have a designated Title IX officer to receive and act on all such reports. A student may incorrectly believe that sharing such experiences with a thoughtful psychology professor is a private matter. If a faculty member suspects that a conversation with a student may soon result in such a disclosure, she or he should pause the conversation and warn that if the student wishes the details to remain confidential it should take place with a clinician at the student counseling center, student health center, or a pastoral counselor. Only those employees are exempt from institutional reporting under Title IX.

### SEXUAL RELATIONSHIPS WITH STUDENTS AND TRAINEES

Stories of college professors engaging in sexual liaisons with their younger female students persist as durable an academic stereotype as ivy, football, tower clocks, caps and gowns, and founder statues in the quad. Given the trappings of most educational environments, some students and some professors will confront the temptation to enter into romantic multiple relationships based on motivations running the gambit from gaining some future advantage to consummating true love. Indeed, most of us know educators who married one (or more) of their own students. However, times have changed, and institutions of higher education have taken more vigorous stands regarding concurrent sexual relationships between students and faculty to discourage educators from dating students. This stems neither from prudishness nor pressure from feminists. Rather, the increase in sexual harassment charges and reporting requirement of Title IX against professors and trainers, sometimes resulting in lawsuits (and sometimes countersuits by the accused), has created an economic motivation to deter such relationships.

The APA Code of Ethics (2010) Section 7.07, "Sexual relationships with students and supervisees" explicitly states that "Psychologists do not engage in sexual relationships with students or supervisees who are in their department, agency, or training center or over whom psychologists have or are likely to have evaluative authority" (p. 9). Codes of Ethics of other professions have similar prohibition of concurrent (not sequential) sexual multiple relationships between instructors and students.

The ethical issues regarding sex between student and educator revolve around the abuse of power and conflicts of interest more than about sex *per se*. Whereas policies across the country may fall short of an outright ban on all student–instructor dating, most campuses have rules that prohibit, restrict, or dissuade them from dating students over whom they have direct evaluative authority, such as those currently in one's class, advisees for theses or dissertations, and supervisees. Although male educators and female students remain the most prevalent pairing, as more women have entered academia as educators, as more older individuals return to the classroom as students, and as open GLBTQ student–faculty sexual multiple relationships surface, a discussion of dating students can no longer be confined solely to male academics and their 18–22-year-old female students.

## Summary

Educational settings will by their very nature create the potentiality of many types of dual relationships and therefor call for role-blending flexibility. Much of the flexing will benefit students, but faculty members hold the positions of power and must remain on guard to protect student rights and avoid the temptation of taking advantage or slippages or multiple relationships based on thoughtlessness or ignorance of regulatory standards.

## REFERENCES

American Psychological Association (2010). *Ethical Principles of Psychologists and Code of Conduct.* Downloaded from: http://www.apa.org/ethics/code/principles.pdf (accessed July 27, 2016).

Branch, K. A., Hayes-Smith, R., & Richards, T. N. (2011). Professors' experiences with student disclosures of sexual assault and intimate partner violence: how "helping" students can inform teaching practices. *Feminist Criminology, 6,* 54–75.

Knapp, S. J., & VandeCreek, L. D. (2006). Confidentiality, privileged communications, and record keeping. In S. J. Knapp & L. D. VandeCreek (Eds.), *Practical Ethics for Psychologists: A Positive Approach* (pp. 111–128). Washington, DC: American Psychological Association.

Koocher, G. P., & Keith-Spiegel, P. C. (2016). *Ethics in Psychology and the Mental Health Professions: Professional Standards and Cases* (4th ed.). New York: Oxford University Press

Owen, P. R., & Zwahr-Castri, J. (2007). Boundary issues in academia: student perceptions of faculty–student boundary crossings. *Ethics and Behavior, 17,* 117–129.

Perrewe, P. L., Zellars, K. L., Rogers, L. M., Breaux, D. M., & Young, A. M. (2010). Mentors gone wild! When mentoring relationships become dysfunctional or abusive. In C. Schriesheim & L. Neider (Eds.), *The "Dark" Side of Management* (pp. 1–25). Charlotte, NC: Information Age Publishing.

Shore, W. J., Toyokawa, T., & Anderson, D. D. (2008). Context-specific effects on reciprocity in mentoring relationships: ethical implications. *Mentoring and Tutoring: Partnership in Learning, 16,* 17–29. DOI: 10.1080/13611260701800926.

# CHAPTER 13

# MULTIPLE RELATIONSHIPS AND MULTIPLE ROLES IN HIGHER EDUCATION

## Maintaining Multiple Roles and Relationships in Counselor Education

*Jude Austin, Julius Austin, Michelle Muratori, and Gerald Corey*

Inherent in the nature of higher educational programs is the rich and complex web of relationships among faculty, administrators, students, alumni, supervisors, and many others. Training relationships in higher education are intrinsically multifaceted and by their nature consist of overlapping roles with various expectations, responsibilities, and obligations. Faculty members in graduate counselor education programs are not only in charge of imparting knowledge to and evaluating students, but typically also serve as their advisors, supervisors, and mentors. In carrying out their various roles, faculty members need to establish and maintain strong relationships with both the academic community and those outside of academia. This web of relationships is likely to include other faculty members and graduate students, alumni, prospective students, practicum and internship site coordinators and staff, clinical supervisors, mental health care providers on campus and in the community, local schools, clientele, and/or others. Due to the intensive relational and interpersonal demands involved in this work, it is important that counselor educators are aware of the potential benefits and risks inherent in multiple roles and relationships so they can conduct themselves in an ethical and effective manner. Given the power differential that exists between professors and students, advisors and advisees, doctoral candidates and master's students, research mentors and mentees, clinical supervisors and supervisees, and counselors and clients, there is much at stake if boundary issues are mishandled. This chapter explores factors that impact these important relationships. We draw from our own unique perspectives and professional experiences, as well as research, to highlight the challenges that can take place while juggling different types of multiple roles and responsibilities.

## RELATIONSHIPS BETWEEN DOCTORAL STUDENTS AND MASTER'S STUDENTS

Compounding the complexities inherent in multiple relationships is the fact that graduate students are often in the earlier stages of their professional development, where they may be less prepared to appreciate and effectively navigate multiple relationships. In many counselor education programs, doctoral students hold a position of authority over master's-level students when they function as teaching assistants, and clinical supervisors. This may be especially confusing when they assume the concurrent role of fellow students on campus. In their review of the literature on multiple relationships and boundary issues in counselor education programs, Scarborough, Bernard, and Morse (2006) offer some guidelines for doctoral students engaged in these multiple roles:

- Doctoral students should be aware of the multiple relationships that are unavoidable in their counselor education program and have a safe context in which to explore such relationships.
- Multiple relationships between doctoral and master's students should not be discouraged; rather, there needs to be open, ongoing discussions of ways to benefit from these relationships as well as ways to prevent violations.
- Doctoral students should receive instruction concerning the power they inherently have in their relationships with master's students and how this power can be used or abused.

Faculty members and doctoral students in a counselor education program may teach a class with someone who is a current or former advisee, supervisee, mentee, fellow student, or colleague. At times, doctoral or master's-level students may find themselves teaching a class attended by fellow students who were former classmates or friends. In such cases, the professorial-evaluative relationship can introduce a clear power differential that needs to be handled with care, sensitivity, and integrity.

## Supervisory Relationships

The focus of the supervisory relationship is inherently a composite of many roles, which change as the focus of supervision changes. Some of these roles include teacher, coach, mentor, consultant, counselor, adviser, administrator, dissertation chair, co-teacher, evaluator, recorder and documenter, empowerer, and advocate (Corey, Haynes, Moulton, & Muratori, 2010). As within any supervisory relationship, clinical supervisors are responsible for defining and maintaining the relationship. It is essential for supervisors to possess both the personal and professional maturity to serve as effective gatekeepers in the counseling field and to be effective role models in establishing and maintaining appropriate boundaries. The maintenance of the supervisory relationship involves educating supervisees on the supervisor's ethical, legal, and professional responsibilities as well as the supervisee's rights and responsibilities, refraining from engaging in inappropriate relationships with supervisees (e.g., sexual or romantic relationships), and abstaining from providing direct counseling services to them.

Doctoral students often face unique challenges during co-supervision of master's students. A co-author of this chapter (Jude Austin) was assigned a role of co-supervisor with a student colleague of a clinical group. Upon perceiving the other student colleague as being ineffective and possibly even impaired, Austin notified the co-supervisor and faculty about these concerns, but was subsequently given no information regarding the faculty's progress in developing a remediation plan. For the remainder of the semester the group's supervisees were unaware that the substandard performance of the co-supervisor had been reported and were hopefully being addressed, and Austin was unaware of the faculty's action plan.

Another co-author of this chapter (Michelle Muratori) has had to be mindful of boundary issues in supervising master's students in the context of a group counseling course that she taught. In one instance, a colleague who was employed at the same center took Muratori's group course, which invariably involved considerable self-disclosure. By openly discussing in advance the shift in roles and the implications of the changing relationship (from a collegial relationship to a supervisory one for a semester), both individuals were able to adapt well to the circumstances. Cognizant of the power differential inherent in the supervisory role, Muratori was careful in evaluating her work. Muratori needed to be especially vigilant about neither being too lenient nor overly stringent in the student's case because of their prior and continuing relationship as colleagues. This is not an unusual situation and the main point here is the importance of having a frank discussion about all the potential ethical issues that could be involved.

Supervisors must often deal with balancing the sometimes conflicting roles (or concurrent multiple relationships) involved in mentoring and evaluating supervisees, which includes managing a mentoring role that involves a commitment to their supervisees, along with the obligation to evaluate and screen their supervisees' capacity for competent practice (Johnson, 2007). Such roles occasionally persist for years after school. For example, former students may become professional colleagues. Such shifting relationships may require frequent re-evaluation and conversations about the new roles and shifting power differentials. This will be discussed further in this chapter.

## On Supervision and Counseling

The codes of ethics of several professional mental health organizations stress that proper focus of the supervision process should be on the supervisee's professional development rather than on personal concerns. As personal problems or limitations of supervisees become evident, supervisors are ethically obligated to encourage their supervisees to address barriers that could inhibit their potential as therapists (Herlihy & Corey, 2015). The purpose of discussing supervisees' personal dynamics is to bring to their awareness any limitations or unresolved problems that could negatively impact their working relationship with a client. With this awareness, supervisees are then in a position of seeking their own personal therapy elsewhere to work through a problem rather than using supervision as an outlet for therapy. If the trainee needs or wants personal therapy, the best course for supervisors to follow is to make a referral to another professional (Barnett & Johnson, 2015). However the line between supervision and therapy is not always clear or distinct. Effective supervision is *therapeutic* in the sense that the supervisory process involves dealing with supervisees' personal limitations, blind spots, and impairments so that clients are not harmed. Countertransference issues can work either in favor of or against the establishment of an effective client–therapist relationship, and thus, a supervisee's countertransference reactions can be appropriately explored in supervision.

In the supervisory relationship, it is expected that a supervisee's personal concerns will be dealt with appropriately, and that referrals will be made to a therapist when a supervisee experiences a personal problem that interferes with providing adequate care to the client. A supervisor has the responsibility to help trainees identify how their personal dynamics are likely to influence their work with clients, yet this must not be confused with therapy. Serving as both supervisor and therapist could constitute a conflict of interest because those roles have different goals and necessitate different methods (Corey et al., 2010).

As a part of the informed-consent process in supervision, boundaries need to be a topic of discussion, which includes clarifying at the outset and, if necessary, at other times during the supervision how personal issues will and will not be addressed in supervision. If supervisors overextend the boundaries of a supervisory relationship to include intense focus on the supervisee's own personal concerns, their effectiveness as supervisors can become impaired.

## Changing Roles and Relationships Over Time

Roles and relationships may evolve and change over time in higher education settings. One-time students may become valued colleagues and friends. A professor may one day find him- or herself on a committee to determine tenure or advancement for a former student. Open discussions about the evolution of a relationship from student to colleague and about additional evaluative roles are helpful and essential in making the transition smoother and averting misunderstandings and tension. These discussions should be held during the transitional phases, before actual issues arise.

## Evaluative Role with Fellow Faculty Colleagues

Relationships outside of the professional realm are an important aspect of managing multiple relationships within higher education. Among the many inherent multiple relationships in higher education is one in which faculty members who are colleagues also have an evaluative role with each other. A co-author (Gerald Corey), in his role of program coordinator, had an association with two full-time faculty members whom he had formerly had the responsibility of evaluating. He had written letters each semester based on their teaching performance, scholarly work, contribution to the department, and professional endeavors and eventually was required to recommend (or not recommend) tenure status and advancement in academic rank for both of them. Fortunately, these two faculty members were of the highest caliber, which meant that the positive evaluations and recommendations for tenure and promotion could be honestly rendered. However, what if their performance in the classroom had been substandard? What if they had many complaints from their students? What if they had not produced sufficient scholarly work? What if they were not contributing to the mission of the department? Certainly, it would have been difficult to be in the position of having to write negative evaluations or to recommend against them getting tenure status. To avoid such awkward and difficult situations, Corey's guiding principle was to initiate open and ongoing discussions about any problem areas or area of concern early on. Waiting until a decision had been reached to inform faculty of their deficiencies would have been unfair and ill advised.

After many years, one of these professors became the coordinator of the program, and the formal professional relationship was reversed. A few years later, she became the dean of the school and became Corey's direct administrative supervisor. She recently became the president of a neighboring state university. These examples illustrate that changing roles and relationships are a common and unavoidable reality in our professional work. What is important is that all concerned are aware of the potential shifts in roles and relationships and feel free to express their hopes, frustrations, wants, and concerns, usually in advance and anticipation of potential difficulties that might arise.

## Extracurricular and Social Relationships

As a counselor education doctoral student, another co-author of this chapter (Julius Austin) served as a graduate assistant in the Social Justice Research Center at the University of Wyoming. The position entailed taking part in multiple campus organizations that provide a social justice voice on campus and in the community and working with his supervisees in the counseling program on these projects. The benefit of this type of social relationship to the supervisees was that they could witness how their counseling identity might translate to the practicality of social justice and advocacy, an issue which is of increasing importance within counseling and other mental health professions.

But while some multiple relationships that venture outside of the immediate professional domain, such as these described above, can have a positive impact on those involved, counselor educators and others who hold positions of power must proceed with caution when participating in extracurricular and social relationships with those who hold less power. While this does not mean that faculty members and supervisors should not be friendly towards those they are teaching or supervising and should show a genuine interest in them, they need to be careful to set appropriate social boundaries. For example, students frequently send friend requests to professors for social media sites such as Facebook. In order to respond in a considerate and ethical way, such questions should be considered as, "What is appropriate self-disclosure? How might my students and supervisees perceive me if they had access to my personal life via my Facebook page?"

## Sexual Intimacies in Counselor Education Programs

Another type of relationship that warrants discussion is sexual or romantic relationships among individuals in counselor education programs. When a power differential exists between the individuals involved, such as a professor–student or supervisor–supervisee, pursuing a sexual or romantic relationship is clearly unethical and is prohibited by the various professions' code of ethics. The American Counseling Association *Code of Ethics* (2014) clearly states, "Counselor educators are prohibited from sexual or romantic interactions or relationships with students currently enrolled in a counseling or related program and over whom they have power and authority" (F.10.a). The American Psychological Association (2010) presents one of the most restrictive codes in this regard, stating clearly that: "Psychologists do not engage in sexual relationships with students or supervisees who are in their department, agency, or training center or over whom the psychologists have or are likely to have evaluative authority" (7.07).

## Research Relationships

Managing multiple roles within the realm of research from the perspective of counselor education faculty members may entail co-presenting, co-authoring, and serving as lead or co-investigator on research projects with doctoral or master's-level students. The Association for Counselor Education and Supervision (ACES) *Guidelines for Research Mentorship* (Borders et al., 2012) identified good practice for these relationships consisting of open and honest discussions about responsibilities, expectations, and limitations of individuals involved within the relationship. The ACES guidelines also place specific focus on the important areas of conflicts, cultural differences, and power dynamics within the research relationship.

## CONCLUSION

This chapter described several types of relationships in counselor education programs that must be navigated in a careful and vigilant manner. The expectation to avoid all dual or multiple relationships in counselor training is unrealistic; therefore, faculty members and others who hold positions of power in these programs must approach their relationships with students, supervisees, mentees, advisees, and others who hold less power with integrity, good interpersonal boundaries, and a strong commitment to ethics.

## References

American Counseling Association. (2014). *Code of Ethics*. Alexandria, VA: Author.

American Psychological Association. (2010). *Ethical Principles of Psychologists and Code of Conduct*. Washington, DC: Author. Retrieved from http://apa.org/ethics/code/index.aspx (accessed July 27, 2016).

Barnett, J. E., & Johnson, W. B. (2015). *Ethics Desk Reference for Counselors* (2nd ed.). Alexandria, VA: American Counseling Association.

Borders, L. D., Wester, K. L., Granello, D. H., Chang, C. Y., Hays, D. G., Pepperell, J., & Spurgeon, S. L. (2012). Association for Counselor Education and Supervision guidelines for research mentorship: development and implementation. *Counselor Education and Supervision*, 51(3), 162–175.

Corey, G., Haynes, R., Moulton, P., & Muratori, M. (2010). *Clinical Supervision in the Helping Professions*. (2nd ed.). Alexandria, VA: American Counseling Association.

Herlihy, B., & Corey, G. (2015). *Boundary Issues in Counseling: Multiple Roles and Responsibilities* (3rd ed.). Alexandria, VA: American Counseling Association.

Johnson, W. B. (2007). *On Being a Mentor: A Guide for Higher Education Faculty*. Mahwah, NJ: Erlbaum.

Scarborough, J. L., Bernard, J. M., & Morse, R. M. (2006). Boundary considerations between doctoral students and master's students. *Counseling and Values*, 51(1), 53–65.

# Chapter 14

# MULTIPLE RELATIONSHIPS AND MULTIPLE ROLES IN HIGHER EDUCATION

## Teaching Group Counseling with a Didactic and Experiential Focus

*Gerald Corey, Marianne Schneider Corey, Michelle Muratori, Jude Austin, and Julius Austin*

This chapter addresses the main challenges and complexities involved in managing multiple roles and multiple relationships when combining didactic instruction *and* leading an experiential group in a university setting. Including both didactic and experiential group learning requires a high level of professionalism and awareness of the complexities involved on the part of instructors. It is of paramount importance that group work educators are aware of the potential benefits and risks inherent in multiple roles and multiple relationships in teaching experiential group courses, primarily due to the fact that the instruction role includes students' evaluation. It is important that faculty effectively communicate and discuss these potential benefits and risks to their students, and that they acquire the necessary competence to navigate these roles and relationships in a manner that is ethical and enhances their students' personal and professional development.

## The Professional Mandate for Experiential Group Training

Learning about group counseling solely through classroom work and didactic instruction is no longer considered sufficient for training students in acquiring the skills necessary to become effective group leaders. A survey by Shumaker, Ortiz, and Brenninkmeyer (2011) found that experiential groups are currently utilized 90 percent of the time in group work courses. The core competencies delineated in the Association for Specialists in Group Work (2000) training standards, considered the benchmarks for the education and training of group counselors, is now focused on learning experiential group process. The Council for Accreditation of Counseling and Related Educational Programs (2016) has a 10-hour requirement for direct experience as a participant in a small group, which is typically met by structuring an experiential group as part of a group counseling course. Incorporating experiential elements into a group course affords students the best opportunity to gain an understanding of group stages and dynamics and techniques that allow for meaningful interactions among the members of the group (Stockton, Morran, & Chang, 2014).

Conducting experiential group training activities in conjunction with didactic instruction in group work requires fully informed consent and a high level of competence and clarity on the instructor's part about confidentiality and multiple relationships. Ieva, Ohrt, Swank, and Young (2009) found in a qualitative study of an experiential group led by doctoral students that the master's students experienced personal growth, professional growth, and a better understanding of such issues as group process, self-awareness, empathy for future clients, and an enhanced ability to give and receive feedback.

In another study, Ohrt et al. (2014) found that counselors'-in-training personal growth, understanding of group processes and dynamics, and development of leadership qualities can be enhanced through participation in an experiential group. In line with current trends and guidelines, we consider an experiential component to be essential in teaching group counseling courses (Corey, Corey, & Corey, 2014).

## ETHICAL ISSUES IN TRAINING GROUP COUNSELORS

While most experiential learning groups are instructor-led, other models include the use of doctoral student facilitators, non-faculty clinicians with group skills, and other graduate students who take turns co-leading their group with a supervisor present in the group.

As students as well as group course instructors (Jude and Julius Austin), we have noticed that students tend to have one major question before and during the group course: "Will what happens in group be held against me in this program?" This brings up issues of confidentiality and the multiple relationships and multiple roles of group leaders as evaluators *and* instructors. In order to navigate our multiple relationships and create a safe climate in our group course, we choose not to be the group facilitators when we teach the exclusively didactic group course. Instead, to ensure that our students are taking advantage of the group experience and to avoid their own dual roles as group and as didactic course participants. We routinely have our students write a one- to two-page personal reflection statement about their experience in group. The caveat to these personal reflection papers is that students must comment only on their personal experience and leave other group members' specifics out of their reflection.

Students are less confused and threatened by multiple relationships in experiential and didactic group course work when informed consent is presented well and the guidelines pertaining to confidentiality are made clear and are frequently discussed and reiterated. Codes of ethics, such as the American Psychological Association's *Ethical Principles* clearly state:

> Psychologists do not require students or supervisees to disclose personal information in course or program-related activities . . . regarding sexual history, history of abuse and neglect, psychological treatment, and relationships with parents, peers, and spouses or significant others except if (1) the program or training facility has clearly identified this requirement in its admissions and program materials.
>
> (American Psychological Association, 2010, p. 9)

Clearly, students have a right to be informed that some aspects of their program will involve their participating in personal ways. This disclosure should not be something that is limited to a few paragraphs in the student handbook but should be addressed and discussed throughout the course.

Confidentiality is also a crucial factor in promoting a sense of safety and trust among group members. It is important to explain to students throughout the course how to talk about their own work with people outside the group (e.g., family and friends) without revealing the identity or self-disclosures of other members.

Confidentiality on the instructor's part is an especially complex issue due to the multiple roles of the instructor as both leader and evaluator. It is important to explain to students that, because the group facilitator will have a consultation role with the course instructor, the facilitator is bound by the applicable ethical standards. The dual role of students as experiential group members and students also adds complexity to issues of confidentiality and should be emphasized and enforced.

### PREPARING STUDENTS FOR A GROUP COUNSELING EXPERIENCE

In my (Gerald Corey's) syllabus for advanced group counseling that is done as an intensive, I note that students will *not be graded or evaluated* on the basis of their participation in the small groups, either in the member or leader roles. Similarly, one of the strategies that I (Michelle Muratori) use in preparing students to co-lead small groups is to inform them that I do not grade students on the basis of the content or extent of their self-disclosures. Our rationale for this is to increase the likelihood that they will behave authentically in the group and not try to "perform" for their grade. It is important to provide extensive information to students so they are informed and can prepare themselves both academically and psychologically for the group experience. Realistically, it impossible to prepare students for everything they might encounter in a group; however, thorough preparation can go a long way in helping them to derive the maximum benefit from the group and to have a positive experience. (See Corey, 2015, for a detailed treatment of combining didactic and experiential approaches to teaching group counseling.)

### REDUCING THE RISKS OF MULTIPLE RELATIONSHIPS IN EXPERIENTIAL TRAINING

Those who teach group courses must guard against exploiting students by using the group as a way of meeting their own needs as these roles may raise issues of power and control, the undue use of pressure, and bias. It is essential to be aware of the potential pitfalls that grow out of the multiple relationships involved in these types of teaching and to develop strategies to reduce chances of negative effects on students.

One potential risk of experiential training is the influence instructors have on students' professional development. The multiple roles an instructor has while teaching the group course can magnify this influence. For example, a therapeutic reflection made in the group to a student due to the evaluative role of instructor or due to the fact that the student may be also an advisee or mentee may carry additional weight. It is important for course instructors, group facilitators, and faculty members to be aware of the additional power they possess in these multiple roles.

Since it is impossible to control the way instructors are perceived by students and the impact they have on them, it is imperative for them to be vigilant in monitoring their own behavior and be mindful of the power differential that exists as part of the multiple relationships they are part of. Again, we want to stress that adequate informed consent prior to admission to the program and prior to taking courses that rely on experiential approaches, as well as high-quality supervision by competent and experienced professionals, are key factors that contribute to a successful group learning experience.

## MANAGING THE DIDACTIC GROUP FACILITATOR MULTIPLE ROLES EFFECTIVELY

Teaching a group course that utilizes a combination of didactic and experiential methods naturally, as noted above, involves unavoidable multiple relationships and multiple roles. Group work educators have the traditional role of a didactic instructor and the additional role of a group process facilitator, which often involves encouraging students' personal disclosures regarding past and present experiences and reactions. According to Goodrich (2008), too much attention has been given to the potentially negative aspects of experiential training. Goodrich, like the authors of this chapter, believes that these multiple relationships are likely to be beneficial to students in their personal and professional development because they allow students to work through these ethical concerns, experience helpful multiple relationships, and learn how to manage this multiplicity in a training program. It is our position that the potential risks of experiential methods are offset by the clear benefits to participants who become personally involved in experiential group work as a supplement to didactic approaches to group courses. When counselors-in-training become counseling professionals they will, at times, be challenged to deal with multiple roles and relationships in their professional work, and they will need to do so in an effective and ethical manner.

There are several key themes that Herlihy and Corey (2015) and others address about boundary issues in counseling that are relevant to this discussion of effectively managing multiple roles and relationships:

- Most professional codes of ethics (i.e., American Counseling Association, 2014; American Psychological Association, 2010) caution *only* against forming dual relationships that have the potential to cause harm or to exploit, yet these codes also acknowledge that the complex nature of these relationships is unavoidable in certain settings.

- There are few absolute answers that can neatly resolve all multiple relationship dilemmas. (They include do not do harm and do not have sex with current students.) The challenge is to appreciate the complexity of ethical decision making and informed consent rather than seeking an inflexible rule-based approach to ethical practice.

- In certain instances, such as described in this chapter, multiple relationships can be beneficial.

- Faculty who use experiential approaches are inherently involved in balancing multiple roles, which requires them to consistently monitor boundaries and to examine their motivations for their practices.

An ethical issue I (Jude Austin) experienced while training group counselors involved maintaining multiple relationships with group members. My Doctoral Practicum course required me to be a group facilitator for master's students. During that semester I was also a co-instructor for these same students in another course and a colleague to some of these students/group members in a mental health clinic where they worked to complete their internship requirements. For this experience, I personally defined a healthy relationship as one in which my values remained consistent and these individuals felt safe to be themselves with me as we transitioned from role to role.

The responsibilities of my various roles presented some challenges as well. As a co-instructor, it was my responsibility to evaluate the students' fitness for the profession. In my role as a group facilitator I felt that it was my responsibility to create a safe space where all group members could be open and vulnerable so growth and learning could be achieved. To create an environment where students could be vulnerable in self-disclosing I initiated an open discussion in the group about the many roles we would all share over the course of the group process. This was also part of the informed-consent process. I encouraged all group members to be honest with me and with each other about any concerns they had about how the group process might be affected by these different roles. I checked in with the group regarding this issue throughout our group process.

During initial conversations and following check-ins, I (Jude) was transparent about my perception of these multiple relationships with the group. I shared with the group members that I was aware of these multiple roles and invited the group to discuss ways in which these roles could enhance their educational experience. I also took personal steps to ensure that I maintained healthy relationships with each group member in each dimension of our relationships. To do this I sought supervision and consultation with my co-instructor, clinical supervisor, and academic advisor.

## CARRYING OUT THERAPEUTIC FUNCTIONS AND ROLES IN EXPERIENTIAL TRAINING

At various times educators may teach group process concepts, lead a demonstration group in class, set up an exercise to illustrate an intervention in a group situation, conduct experiential exercises such as an inner and outer group, and evaluate students' work (Corey et al., 2014). If a didactic instructor also facilitates a process group or an interpersonal process-oriented group, he or she will at times carry out therapeutic roles and functions with the students. One area where instructors can act therapeutically is helping students deal with issues such as transference and countertransference as these reactions are manifested. As a part of discussing the rationale for experiential work, instructors can explain that learning to participate in a group as members and facilitators is a complex process and requires learning how to manage multiple roles. Although the instructor may avoid becoming a therapist for a student group, he or she might be called upon to assist participants in identifying personal problems that are likely to interfere with their ability to function effectively in group work. Blending these roles presents some potential tensions or even conflicts, and strategies must be employed to address these issues in the preparation of group counselors.

One of the benefits of requiring students to participate in an experiential group is having the opportunity to assist them in identifying personal characteristics that may enhance or inhibit their ability to function as group workers. Counselors-in-training can gain a great deal personally by identifying potential sources of countertransference. Counselor trainees may struggle with any number of issues that might get in their way professionally: Some may be immobilized by perfectionism and hold unrealistically high expectations of themselves and/or others; some may have a history of trauma and be easily triggered when listening to group members' painful stories; others may have a tendency to expect instant gratification and may feel impatient with others' slow progress in the group. If students can identify specific areas where they may need to do further exploration, they can be encouraged to continue what they are learning about themselves in their personal counseling. We tell students that there are limitations on how extensively we can address countertransference or other personal clinical issues that often surface in their group, and we discuss in the group how they can pursue in more depth in their own counseling the personal themes that they identify. We find it important to remind students when necessary that experiential learning groups are *not* therapy groups.

## Conclusion

There is no doubt that the combination of experiential and didactic group course training methods offers the most complete learning experience. The complexities and difficulties of experiential and didactic learning, especially the dual or multiple relationships and roles inherent in this work, should be embraced with transparency, courage, clear and fair guidelines, good intentions, and a strong ethical sense.

# REFERENCES

American Counseling Association. (2014). *Code of Ethics*. Alexandria, VA: Author.

American Psychological Association. (2010). *Ethical Principles of Psychologists and Code of Conduct*. Washington, DC: Author. Retrieved from http://apa.org/ethics/code/index.aspx (accessed July 27, 2016).

Association for Specialists in Group Work. (2000). Professional standards for the training of group workers. *The Group Worker, 29*(3), 1-10.

Corey, G. (2015). Combining didactic and experiential approaches to teaching a group counseling course. In B. Herlihy & G. Corey (Eds.). *Boundary Issues in Counseling: Multiple Roles and Responsibilities* (3rd ed., pp. 177-183). Alexandria, VA: American Counseling Association.

Corey, M. S., Corey, G., & Corey, C. (2014). *Groups: Process and Practice* (9th ed.). Boston, MA: Cengage Learning.

Council for Accreditation of Counseling and Related Educational Programs. (2016). *Council for Accreditation of Counseling and Related Educational Programs (CACREP) 2016 Standards*. Retrieved from http://www.cacrep.org/for-programs/2016-cacrep-standards/ (accessed July 31, 2016).

Goodrich, K. M. (2008). Dual relationships in group training. *Journal for Specialists in Group Work, 33*(3), 221-235.

Herlihy, B., & Corey, G. (2015). *Boundary Issues in Counseling: Multiple Roles and Responsibilities* (3rd ed.). Alexandria, VA: American Counseling Association.

Ieva, K. P., Ohrt, J. H., Swank, J. M., & Young, T. (2009). The impact of experiential groups on master's students counselor and personal development: a qualitative investigation. *Journal for Specialists in Group Work, 34*(4), 351-368.

Ohrt, J. H., Prochenko, Y., Stulmaker, H., Huffman, D., Fernando, D., & Swan, K. (2014). An exploration of group and member development in experiential groups. *Journal for Specialists in Group Work, 39*(3), 212-235.

Shumaker, D., Ortiz, C., & Brenninkmeyer, L. (2011). Revisiting experiential group training in counselor education: a survey of master's-level programs. *Journal for Specialists in Group Work, 36*(2), 111-128.

Stockton, R., Morran, K., & Chang, S. (2014). An overview of current research and best practices for training beginning group leaders. In J. L. DeLucia-Waack, C. R. Kalodoner, & M. T. Riva (Eds.). *Handbook of Group Counseling and Psychotherapy* (2nd ed., pp. 133-145). Thousand Oaks, CA: Sage.

# Part V

# Multiple Relationships in Cyberspace

# INTRODUCTION

*Ofer Zur*

Part V (Chapters 15 and 16) focuses on the new and intriguing phenomenon of digital multiple relationships in cyberspace.

In Chapter 15, Dr. Kolmes describes in detail the numerous potentialities for intended and unintended, planned and unplanned, and even known or unknown multiple relationships online between therapists and clients, primarily in social media. She then maps different types of multiple relationships available online. These include social, communal, professional, institutional, forensic, evaluative, business, and sexual. She suggests ways for therapists to handle online multiple relationships and emphasizes the importance of therapists having clear social networking policies.

In Chapter 16, Dr. Reamer provides an overview of boundaries in the realm of the digital world, including telemental health, and discusses the variety of ways that clients and therapists may be blending professional and personal lives and thus creating all sorts of multiple relationships. He also describes a wide variety of issues specific to digital communication, including sexting between therapists and clients, and explains how the brave new digital world often includes a detailed and potentially impactful digital trail or digital footprint of electronic communications between therapists and clients.

# Chapter 15

# DIGITAL AND SOCIAL MEDIA MULTIPLE RELATIONSHIPS ON THE INTERNET

*Keely Kolmes*

Psychotherapists and their clients are becoming ever more connected on the internet and social media. When we speak of social media, we are referring to websites, mobile technology, and applications ("apps") that allow users to create and share content and participate in social networking. We typically think of popular sites such as Facebook, LinkedIn, Twitter, Pinterest, and Instagram as major venues for social networking. However there are countless sites that are used by individuals and businesses. Some people consider exchanging email within Google or Yahoo groups or other lists maintained by their professional psychotherapy or counseling association to be a form of social media.

It is fairly impossible to have an email address—let alone have a presence on a social media site—without introducing the possibility of some potential overlap with your psychotherapy clients, especially if you use the same email address to correspond with clients or if you post it on your website. Your email address will often be the key to exposing the social multiple relationships you share with your clients on social media. Note that that these multiple relationships exist whether or not we, psychotherapists, *ever* become aware of them; but increasingly, many people are discovering them. Zur and Donner (2009) have acknowledged the accessibility of clinicians' online information and discussed the difference between intentional disclosures made in a therapy session versus unintentional disclosures that clinicians may make online. Lehavot et al. (2010) surveyed 302 graduate students and found that 27 percent sought information online about their clients. In DeLillo and Gale's (2011) research on 854 doctoral-level psychology students, 98 percent had Googled their patients despite holding the belief that this represented unacceptable behavior. This behavior seems to be clearly increasing as more and more digital natives enter mental health services. Kolmes and Taube (2013) surveyed 227 mental health professionals and found that 48 percent reported intentionally seeking client information on the internet and another 28 percent accidentally found information about their client online. Accidental discovery included events such as performing a Google search for a service and having a client show up in the search results as a provider of that service. It also included occurrences when clinicians went on to a social networking site and was offered a list of "recommended" friends or contacts that included one of their clients. Some authors have argued that searches on one's psychotherapy patients can be seen as intrusive and a violation of the client's trust unless it is done with the client's awareness and consent (Kaslow et al., 2011). Others note that this type of investigation is more common and accepted when therapists are in a forensic role with a client. It is worth considering whether a psychotherapist offering therapy is stepping into a forensic role if she regularly seeks information on clients through social media, without the client's awareness and/or consent. The American Counseling Association (ACA) *Code of Ethics*(2014), notes that, unless given consent by clients, counselors should respect clients' privacy on social media.

Kolmes and Taube (2011) also completed research seeking critical incidents of clients finding their psychotherapist's information online. In a survey of 332 clients, 78 percent reported finding personal information about their psychotherapist and 92 percent reported finding professional information on the web. Clearly, communication protocols are shifting for both clients and clinicians. As our digital culture evolves, our examination of ethics must evolve with it. We are learning that online multiple roles between clients and therapists are becoming more common. We must understand what kind of multiple relationships these are, when they may be problematic, and when they can become a part of the therapy. Some multiple relationships may be beneficial to the therapeutic relationship if they are well managed by a sensitive, thoughtful clinician. They can even offer opportunities to enhance the clinical relationship. Other multiple roles may erode the therapy relationship in a variety of ways.

This chapter explores both the avoidable and unavoidable digital multiple relationships that occur on social media and how to ethically handle them. Ethics codes and other chapters in this book acknowledge that rural areas and other small communities create a mix of professional and personal relationships that result in unavoidable multiple relationships. Some examples of this include practicing in drug and alcohol rehab communities, small military settings, and other condensed populations such as prisons, universities, and postgraduate training. But the internet presents a unique space in which the personal and professional become blurred when we use our same professional name to interact with clients, friends, and colleagues, alike. While it may mirror small communities in some ways, it is also distinctive in that it provides a cloak of invisibility that allows both clients and psychotherapists to secretly observe one another.

## TYPES OF MULTIPLE RELATIONSHIPS ON THE INTERNET

It can be challenging to identify what exactly constitutes a multiple role on the internet or whether the multiple role one encounters could have a negative, neutral, or positive effect on treatment. To explore the possibilities and meanings of our contact with clients outside of the therapy, I offer a number of examples of the different types of multiple relationships that may occur on social media:

- *Social/professional/communal*: Realizing that your client or a significant person in the client's life (sibling, parent, partner(s), friend, ex-relationship partner, etc.) is part of your social or professional network on a social sharing site. Or you may learn that one of these people is a regular reader of your postings on Twitter, Facebook, or your blog;
- *Social/communal*: Responding to an invitation to an event hosted by a friend and seeing that you and your client are both on the invite list for the same event;
- *Social/professional/institutional*: Having an online contact in your Facebook or LinkedIn network contact you for psychotherapy;

- *Social*: Having an email exchange with a client drift into sharing links to humor, stories, or videos that are no longer related to the clinical work, but which have become "social sharing";
- *Investigatory/forensic*: Engaging in internet or Google searches on clients or the people in their lives who they have told you about;
- *Evaluative*: Discovering that a client has negatively reviewed your psychotherapy practice, or another client has publicly come to your defense in such an online forum;
- *Communal*: Participating in an online dating site and viewing your client's personal ad on the site;
- *Business*: Seeing someone in your extended LinkedIn network begin seeing you for psychotherapy and then having another contact on LinkedIn request an introduction to this client so that she may apply for a job at his company;
- *Sexual*: Joining a special-interest forum for a particular sexual fetish, and exchanging erotic messages with your client who is, like you, using a pseudonym. You discover the multiple role when one of you sends a photo or you begin making arrangements to meet in person.

These examples demonstrate the range of multiple roles that can develop between psychotherapists and patients. Note that these roles range from social, sexual, professional, business, communal, institutional, and much more. Psychotherapists and clients are learning that it is incredibly common to cross paths on social networking sites if they share cultural affiliations including race, religion, ethnicity, disability, sexual orientation(s) or interests, gender non-conforming status, or when they are members of recovery or special-interest communities. Many of us who are connected to others via these affiliations may learn that we have friends who are friends with our clients. Most of these multiple relationships likely existed *before* the social networking and the internet, but now, due to the visible sharing activity of online networks, we are able to easily discover some of these connections.

As noted above, psychotherapy ethics codes do not prohibit multiple roles. Instead, our codes invite us to analyze and explore whether a multiple role might lead to the loss of our objectivity, impair our judgment, or lead to the exploitation of a client we are seeing (American Association for

Marriage and Family Therapy, 2015; American Psychological Association, 2010; National Asssociation of Social Workers, 2008). One discipline's ethics code has been updated to *specifically prohibit* connecting in any way with one's psychotherapy clients on social networking sites (ACA, 2014).

## PROBLEMATIC MULTIPLE RELATIONSHIPS

Some online multiple relationships should almost always be avoided, such as becoming an investigator by engaging in online searches on clients or others in their lives without informing them of this practice. Some clinicians never look for client information and others may do so regularly or only when a client is in crisis. Clients have a right to know what your practices and policies are regarding these searches. This behavior can place a clinician in the awkward position of having to pretend not to know details of a client's life and can erode trust and safety—the very conditions upon which a psychotherapy relationship is built. If a clinician does engage in searches in crisis or risk situations, it can enhance the trust and be an important part of informed consent to let a client know about this practice.

Aside from the clear prohibition against engaging in digital sexual multiple relationships, another item on the "never do" list is requesting online reviews or testimonials from *current* clients since this is a direct violation of nearly every ethics. The ACA ethics code also prohibits requesting reviews from *former* clients (ACA, 2014). Asking a client to help us advertise or market our business is inviting them into a business multiple role with us.

Adding clients as friends and contacts on social media sites can be complex since it suggests a social or business type of relationship, may invite either party to engage socially or read personal information in between sessions, and it also invites clients to communicate with our friends, family members, or colleagues in unexpected and unpredictable ways. Although social multiple relationships can be common and ethical in some small-community settings, inviting clients to engage in online discussions we are hosting on our Facebook profiles can potentially compromise the therapeutic relationship by inviting interactions between them and the many other people who are part of our online communities.

## THERAPEUTIC DIGITAL MULTIPLE RELATIONSHIPS

Some online multiple relationships may be explored and accepted and can offer an opportunity to expedite trust and communication in psychotherapy. For example, a psychotherapist may be treating another psychotherapist and they may both be part of the same professional online community, on a shared listserv together, creating professional multiple relationships. This shared identity and community may foster a client's feelings of being understood. It would be useful for clinicians to regularly assume that their postings about cases and clients may potentially be read by these clients, or someone who knows other clients in the practice, and this could require more professional caution and restraint in one's online postings. It is up to a clinician to decide how much information she would be comfortable with anyone else reading, including her clients and the people who know them.

Another example of a common point of multiple roles is the discovery of membership in recovery communities when a clinician is part of an online support group and learns that a client shares that group. There may be other similar multiple roles as well, such as membership in religious groups, email lists for people living with chronic illnesses or disabilities, or those who are part of the LGBTQ, polyamorous, or kink and fetish communities. These are all examples of multiple roles in which it may make sense to acknowledge the multiple relationship, explore it clinically, and find a way for both to enjoy the benefits of the support without either party having to give up much-needed and meaningful personal space. The knowledge of such a multiple role can become treatment enhancing, and be an additional way to increase trust and connection. It is also an opportunity to remind and reassure clients that their confidentiality will still be protected.

Of course, being mindful of these multiple roles may mean that a clinician is more cautious in the content she posts. But such awareness and adjustments are quite similar to how those in rural, military, rehabilitative, or higher education settings must share community space with those who are their clients or who are in relationships with their clients (Schank et al., 2010). Confidentiality must always be carefully preserved, but one cannot leave or avoid every community circle that is shared just because a client happens to be a part of it.

If a clinician chooses to have a public professional presence online, it should be assumed that a client or someone in the client's life may be "following" that account, be privy to its content, or learn about it. Again, this would not necessarily mean that the psychotherapy relationship is compromised, and it may not negatively affect or impair one's objectivity or lead to exploitation of the client. It also doesn't mean that a clinician should stop publishing or offering psychoeducation online. However, a skilled and sensitive clinician will be able to assess the situation and facilitate conversations that help a client articulate the impact that this multiple role has or may have on the therapeutic work. It is another reason that clinicians would be wise to avoid describing clinical material that could be identified by a person in the client's life or by clients themselves.

### ONLINE REVIEWS OF PSYCHOTHERAPISTS BY CLIENTS

The case of online consumer reviews brings up interesting issues in that it places our psychotherapy clients in a business and marketing relationship with us if they are championing us. Of course, if the review is negative, they will have become a critic, and that can financially and professionally hurt us. Some clients feel compelled to protect a psychotherapist they like who has received negative online reviews (Kolmes & Taube, 2011). This introduces a challenging new dilemma in which patients who do not know one another may potentially be drawn into a public argument about their perception of the quality of our services. Considering that psychotherapy patients and psychotherapists are accustomed to the work of psychotherapy staying private, this is a contemporary predicament. It can also offer a window into the transference feelings that clients have for us, opening the door for deeper exploration of the psychotherapy relationship. It may also provide information about how private or public our clients consider their own therapy.

Many psychotherapists wishing to market their practices may be encouraged by coaches, consultants, and marketers to obtain online reviews from clients and they may have to explain to these consultants that this is against our ethical principles. Many of these well-meaning consultants will not understand our ethics codes. While therapists are ethically not allowed to ask clients to post testimonials, obviously, clients are free to do so if they wish.

An added complexity of ethics and digital culture is that most ethical standards on testimonials were written prior to the publication of this book, at times when testimonials meant printed words on a paper brochure. But these days, an online review typically refers to an internationally accessible web page, permanently archived, that links to a client's name, her other reviews, and her friend network (unless she has created a separate account with a fake email address never used for anything else). The implications of asking for the gift of a "testimonial" have changed, although our ethics codes haven't. While we may be informed enough about ethics not to ask for a review from current patients, we may wish to create space to explore the clinical meaning for clients who feel moved to post reviews on our behalf as a way of expressing gratitude for our services or defending us to the public.

## STRATEGIES FOR MANAGING MULTIPLE ROLES

Interestingly, Kolmes and Taube (2011) found that 72 percent of clients who had found personal information about their psychotherapist online did *not* let their psychotherapist know that they had found this information. For some of these participants, simply seeking the psychotherapist's personal information and sitting alone with these discoveries created feelings of guilt and embarrassment.

Introducing a social media policy (Kolmes, 2010) is a good way to head off such confusion and discomfort from the start by normalizing clients' curiosity about you, explaining your approach to activities such as performing internet searches on clients, responding to "friend" or "contact" requests on social media sites, and other forms of online engagement such as messaging between sessions. Simply thinking through your policies to create such a document offers the opportunity to review your ethics code and explore your own thinking on what you want your approach to be. The beginning of treatment is also an excellent time to acknowledge to a new client that, just as you may encounter one another outside of therapy at events, you may also come to discover information about one another online. Acknowledging these potential discoveries at the start of treatment and letting clients know they are invited to discuss these issues when needed may increase the likelihood of their letting you know if they have stumbled on to a multiple relationship or sought you out. It can help reduce any feelings of awkwardness or embarrassment.

Of course, not every situation can be anticipated or is appropriate to place in a policies document. If you are having difficulty thinking through whether a multiple role impairs your primary role as a clinician or could exploit your client, it will be important to consult with an expert who is knowledgeable about the dynamics of the internet and social media. Always document the consultation you received.

Some clinicians will encounter circumstances in which someone in our extended social media network contacts us for therapy. These may be people we met a few times in person who invited us to connect online, but with whom we do not have a close social or business relationship. In these scenarios, we are given an opportunity to help clarify how working together clinically may change our roles and what potential futures exist for us. Clients can be given the choice of how to proceed (for example, if the situation demands, "If you become my patient, I will not be able to send business your way and it will preclude our having a future social relationship if you choose to receive psychotherapy from me"). We can inform them that, if they come in for therapy, we will disconnect from them on social networking sites if necessary to preserve the clinical work, protect their confidentiality, and avoid boundary blurring. We can offer them referrals to other clinicians if they would prefer to privilege the budding business or social relationship.

Lastly, if we have concerns about clients having access to more information about us than we are comfortable, we may wish to be extra-cautious about our privacy settings on social networking sites and also talk to our family members about what kinds of information or photos they share on sites. We may also want to develop new practices and habits that mean that we do not delve deeper when we believe we have stumbled across one of our client's pages on social media. This may be counter-intuitive: backing away and avoiding exposing ourselves to information this individual has not yet revealed to us instead of clicking on links and seeing more.

## SUMMARY

Clearly the explosion of social media culture is opening up new opportunities for connection for psychotherapists and their clients. We are finding wonderful new resources for communication, information sharing, and deepening relationships. At the same time, social networking has a tendency to reveal many of the previously invisible multiple relationships we have between our lives and our psychotherapy patients. These multiple relationships include social, professional, and business relationships and they can present new challenges. We have the possibility of our patients learning much more about us than we typically would reveal, if we had the choice. We also have the opportunity to learn things about our clients before they intend to share those things in psychotherapy. We have to consider how such information may impact the clinical relationship, whether it may affect our own judgment and objectivity, and whether the different types of multiple roles we discover could be exploitative of our client.

At the same time, the magnification of these threads that exist in our relationships and networks offers ripe opportunities to explore trust, boundaries, and meaning in our clinical relationships. How we develop our policies and manage these conversations with clients will have the potential to strengthen and deepen the psychotherapy work we do, and can also give us a chance to better understand the meaning clients make of their digital lives and relationships. We can also begin to learn more about the joys or the challenges our clients may experience in their online communities and exchanges.

Clinicians who are able to explore these issues with openness and curiosity may be doing a great service to their clients. They can also help clients reduce their shame about their natural curiosity in us. They may also be able to open up an important channel in the psychotherapy to allow for deeper discussions about the connections between the offline and online experience for their clients.

## REFERENCES

American Association for Marriage and Family Therapy. (2015). *AAMFT Revised Code of Ethics*. Retrieved from https://www.aamft.org/iMIS15/AAMFT/Content/legal_ethics/code_of_ethics.aspx (accessed July 27, 2016).

American Counseling Association. (2014). *ACA Code of Ethics*. Retrieved from http://www.counseling.org/resources/aca-code-of-ethics.pdf (accessed July 27, 2016).

American Psychological Association. (2010). *Ethical Principles of Psychologist and Codes of Conduct*. Retrieved from http://www.apa.org/ethics/code/ (accessed July 27, 2016).

DeLillo, D., & Gale, E. B. (2011). To Google or not to Google: graduate students' use of the internet to access personal information about clients. *Training and Education in Professional Psychology*, 5, 160–166.

Kaslow, F. W., Patterson, T., & Gottlieb, M. (2011). Ethical dilemmas in psychologists accessing internet data: is it justified? *Professional Psychology Research and Practice, 42*, 105–111.

Kolmes, K. (2010, April). *Private Practice Social Media Policy.* Retrieved from http://www.drkkolmes.com/docs/socmed.pdf (accessed July 27, 2016).

Kolmes, K., & Taube, D. O. (2011). *Summary of Client–Therapist Encounters on the Web: The Client Experience.* Retrieved from http://drkkolmes.com/research/ – client survey (accessed July 27, 2016).

Kolmes, K., & Taube, D. O. (2013). Seeking and finding our clients on the internet: boundary considerations in cyberspace. *Professional Psychology: Research and Practice.* doi: 10.1037/a0029958.

Lehavot, K., Barnett, J., & Powers, D. (2010). Psychotherapy, professional relationships, and ethical considerations in the MySpace generation. *Professional Psychology Research and Practice, 41*, 160–166.

National Association of Social Workers. (2008). *Code of Ethics.* Washington, DC: Author. Retrieved from http://www.socialworkers.org/pubs/code/default.asp (accessed July 27, 2016).

Schank, J. A., Helbok, C. M., Haldeman, D. C., & Gallardo, M. E. (2010). Challenges and benefits of ethical small-community practice. *Professional Psychology: Research and Practice, 41*(6), 502.

Zur, O., & Donner, M. B. (2009, January/February). The Google factor: therapists' transparency in the era of Google and MySpace. *The California Psychologist, 42* (1), 23–24.

# CHAPTER 16

# MULTIPLE RELATIONSHIPS IN A DIGITAL WORLD

## Unprecedented Ethical and Risk-management Challenges

*Frederic G. Reamer*

The vast majority of contemporary practitioners began their careers when it was a foregone conclusion that they would meet with clients face to face, paying close attention to clients' body language and non-verbal cues; communicate with clients outside of the office via landline telephones; record by hand their clinical notes, which would then be stored in folders and filing cabinets; and have contact with former clients only if they bumped into each other in the local community.

Fast forward. Growing numbers of today's practitioners use digital technology to provide services to clients, some of whom they never meet in person or meet only sporadically; communicate with clients using email, text messaging, social networking websites, and Twitter; hunt for information about clients online using powerful internet search engines; maintain electronic clinical records which are stored in the proverbial cloud; and receive unsolicited online requests from current and former clients to be their social networking "friends."

In recent years, mental health practitioners and scholars have discussed and debated the relative merits and drawbacks associated with clinicians' use of digital and other technology to deliver services; communicate with clients and former clients; and gather, manage, and store clinically relevant information. Suffice it to say that the topic is hot and the debate is intense. Proponents argue that digital technology has greatly expanded mental health professionals' reach and enhanced the provision of service to vulnerable people. Distance and remote counseling have enabled people who live in remote areas far from clinicians' brick-and-mortar offices, and those whose disability makes travel difficult, to obtain much-needed help. Research evidence suggests that some people prefer the enhanced privacy that accompanies distance counseling and their ability to obtain help 24/7/365 from practitioners who offer clinical services from every imaginable time zone. Research is demonstrating increasingly the effectiveness of distance counseling and telemental health with a variety of populations and conditions (Barak & Grohol, 2011; Barak, Hen, Boniel-Nissim, & Shapira, 2008).

Among the concerns raised by professionals about digital communications and services are that distance services may not be well suited for clients with very complex, protracted mental health challenges. Distance services also limit practitioners' ability to observe and interpret clients' clinically relevant body language and non-verbal cues and can make it difficult to respond effectively to clients' crises and emergencies. Also, digital communications expand the ways in which clients' privacy and confidentiality can be breached.

One compelling issue that has received much less attention is the way in which mental health practitioners' use of digital technology introduces potentially complex challenges related to therapeutic boundaries, particularly multiple relationships. Historically, practitioners' analyses of multiple relationships have focused on phenomena such as entering into personal relationships with clients and former clients, managing overlapping personal and professional relationships in small and rural communities, responding to clients' invitations to attend social events or religious ceremonies, meeting with clients outside of the office, bartering for services, and so on (Reamer, 2012a; Zur, 2007). However, with the advent of digital technology in the mental health arena, we must now think about multiple relationships in novel and unprecedented ways (Gutheil & Simon, 2005; Reamer, 2012b, 2013). This is especially important in light of evidence that younger and newer mental health professionals (so-called digital natives) are more comfortable with digital and other electronic communications, such as online social networking, than their predecessors (so-called digital immigrants) (DeGraff, 2014; Prensky, 2001).

## THE DIGITAL CONTEXT IN MENTAL HEALTH

Mental health resources and services emerged on the internet as early as 1982 in the form of online self-help support groups (Kanani and Regehr, 2003; Reamer, 2013, 2015). The first known fee-based internet mental health service was established by Sommers in 1995; by the late 1990s, groups of clinicians were forming companies and e-clinics that offered online counseling services to the public using secure websites (Skinner and Zack, 2004).

Clinicians now have a much wider range of digital and electronic options to serve and communicate with clients. Mental health practitioners are using video counseling, email chat, social networking websites, text messaging, avatar-based websites, self-guided web-based interventions, smartphone apps, and other technology to communicate with and provide clinical services to clients, some of whom they never meet in person (Chester and Glass, 2006; Clinton, Silverman, & Brendel, 2010; Kanani and Regehr, 2003; Lamendola, 2010; Menon and Miller-Cribbs, 2002; Reamer, 2012a, 2013, 2015; Zur, 2011, 2012). Clinicians' routine use of digital technology in their daily lives has created new ways to interact with clients and form multiple relationships, even when practitioners do not use digital technology—such as online therapy or video counseling—to provide clinical services *per se*.

There are several key multiple relationship patterns that are emerging in conjunction with practitioners' use of digital technology, related to: the blending of boundaries in practitioners' and clients' professional and personal lives; the changing nature of the spatial boundaries that define the practitioner–client relationship; and changes in the complex intersection between privacy and boundaries, some of which arise from incidental digital and electronic communications.

## BLENDING PROFESSIONAL AND PERSONAL LIVES

Paula Blair is a marriage and family therapist who counsels individuals and couples experiencing relationship challenges. Her client, Fran Robinson, was recently divorced after 17 years of marriage.

Fran became more and more dependent on Blair and curious about Blair's personal life. One evening, Fran conducted a Google search about Blair and discovered in the local county's online records that Blair was recently granted a divorce by the family division of the superior court. Fran, who struggles with boundary issues, was distraught upon learning this news and wanted to commiserate with Blair. Fran looked up Blair's name on Facebook and sent Blair a Facebook friend request.

Blair is a clinician who believes strongly that it is best not to have rigid boundaries in her relationship with clients. Blair believes that one way to empower clients is "to be a real person, not a remote, robotic clinician." Also, Blair was not very knowledgeable about Facebook privacy settings and did not realize that people who were not Facebook friends had access to most of Blair's personal information and photographs posted on this social networking site. Reading through Blair's Facebook site, Fran learned a great deal about Blair's social activities, organizational memberships, vacation experiences, friendships, dating adventures, and religious and political preferences.

Blair was very concerned about Fran's efforts to cope with her recent separation from her husband. As an act of kindness, Blair, who is a serious poet, sent Fran two poems she had written, using her personal email very late one evening, with the following message: "Earlier this year I wrote these poems about the challenges of intimate relationships. I thought you might find them helpful as you move through your journey." Fran responded immediately via email, and the two exchanged several follow-up online messages.

The elements of this case are not hypothetical. Some therapists and clients gradually transition into concurrent multiple relationships when they become Facebook friends and/or begin exchanging email and text messages of a personal nature. The real-life Blair discovered that over time her client, Fran, began to view their relationship as personal as well as professional, primarily due to their online connection. During several clinical sessions, Blair and Fran had to sort through issues related to Fran's longstanding struggle with boundary issues in her relationships, including Fran's relationship with Blair.

Fran told Blair that she was frustrated with Blair's inconsistent and sporadic responses to Fran's email and Facebook messages. Blair quickly realized that her online communications with Fran added to the complexity in their relationship and interfered with their clinical work.

In many ways digital technology has enhanced clinicians' ability to serve clients. Yet this technology has also introduced a wide range of complex multiple relationship issues (primarily social dual relationships) between clinicians and clients. In Paula Blair's case, the clinician meant well but made errors in judgment with regard to protecting her private information on Facebook and using her personal email address to send poetry to her client late at night.

Sadly, in other cases practitioners use digital technology in much more sinister ways. In one case, a married psychologist who was clinical director of a school for teens who struggle with behavioral health issues developed an unhealthy attachment to a 17-year-old client. The psychologist had provided one-on-one counseling to the teen for nearly 6 months. Over time the two engaged in flirtatious behavior, primarily online and via text messages. Their relationship evolved and the two began "sexting"—exchanging sexually explicit photos. At one point the teen posted a comment on Facebook about his sexting communications with his clinician. Another school staffer saw the Facebook message and reported it to the school director. This multiple relationship, facilitated by digital technology, proved to be disastrous; the clinical relationship ruptured and the psychologist lost her job and professional license.

## THE IMPLICATIONS OF THE DIGITAL TRAIL

In another tragic case involving an unethical multiple relationship facilitated by digital technology, a mental health counselor provided services to trauma victims in a clinic at a large hospital. He engaged in sexual relationships with two long-term clients and was indicted by a grand jury after one of the former clients disclosed the relationship to police. During his criminal court case, the counselor's intimate and sexually suggestive email and text messages to both women were entered into evidence in court as documentation of his unprofessional and criminal conduct. The clinician was convicted and sentenced to 5 years in prison.

Mental health professionals should be keenly aware of the potentially dire implications of the digital trail and footprint left by their electronic communications with clients regarding their professional as well as any existing or former multiple relationships. Of course, for purely ethical reasons clinicians should always avoid salacious, prurient, and otherwise unprofessional electronic communications with clients. That said, in contrast to unrecorded in-person and telephone communications between clients and clinicians, clinicians' communications with clients using technology such as email, text messaging, and online posts on social networking sites leave a digital trail that can be, and sometimes is, used as formal evidence in malpractice lawsuits, licensing board complaints, criminal court proceedings, and other administrative queries and investigations. Naïve and unsuspecting clinicians are sometimes stunned to learn that subpoenas and court orders can lead to full, painful, and humiliating disclosure of their unprofessional digital and other electronic communications with clients regarding different aspects of their professional relationships and any ethical or unethical multiple relationships.

## AMBIGUOUS SPATIAL BOUNDARIES AND MULTIPLE RELATIONSHIPS

Digital technology has fundamentally altered the way mental health professionals think about potentially problematic multiple relationships (Gutheil & Simon, 2005; Lannin & Scott, 2013). Providing clinical services in cyberspace, without the traditional spatial boundaries provided by the physical office, has changed the nature of the professional–client relationship and opened up the possibility, although not necessarily the probability, of new forms of complex multiple relationships.

Traditionally, mental health professionals have examined multiple relationships that clinicians enter into knowingly, for example, becoming involved in a business relationship with a client's family members or dating a former client. But digital technology opens up the possibility of multiple relationships that occur in the virtual world without the practitioner's knowledge or consent.

For example, in typical office-based counseling, clinicians usher a client, couple, or family into their physical office, close the door, and begin a confidential dialogue knowing exactly who is privy to the conversation. There is no reasonable possibility of a third party being present in the room secretly merely to eavesdrop. However, with the advent of remote video and telephone counseling, for example, it is possible for a client to invite a third party into the room in which the client is sitting—unbeknownst to the clinician—in order to observe or listen in on the session. The clinician is in a novel form of a multiple relationship with a third party who is closely connected to the client, although the clinician did not initiate the relationship and is completely unaware that this is occurring.

In one case this took place when a client had some concern about the clinician's unconventional therapeutic techniques and wanted a close friend to observe and witness a session. The friend sat in a location in the room in the client's home that was not captured by the client's camera. Some clinicians attempt to prevent this kind of unbidden multiple relationship – where a clinician unwittingly has indirect contact in cyberspace with a client's friend by asking clients to agree, at the beginning of their distance counseling relationship, that no third party will participate in a telemental health session without the clinician's knowledge and consent.

Such concealment and unauthorized multiple relationship can occur in reverse as well. In one notorious case a clinician's romantic partner was contemplating a career in telemental health counseling. The clinician invited her to observe a video counseling clinical session "off camera" and without the client's knowledge or consent. The same phenomenon can occur when practitioners provide distance counseling services using speaker phones, avatar software, email therapy, and text therapy. That is, in principle either the client or clinician could allow an acquaintance to observe the clinical exchange or eavesdrop, thus introducing an unauthorized and indirect multiple relationship.

## THE RELATIONSHIP BETWEEN PRIVACY AND MULTIPLE RELATIONSHIPS

Privacy is one of the hallmarks of the clinical relationship. Mental health professionals' use of digital technology introduces novel privacy challenges that may lead to complex multiple relationships. For example, some practitioners choose to search for information about clients using online search engines. They may search for information to shed light on a clinical concern (for example, searching social networking sites for information about a client's social activities and connections), because of safety concerns (for example, searching police and court records for details related to a client's arrest and conviction record), or due to mere curiosity. A therapist whose client attempted suicide by drug overdose might conduct an online search for a suicide note posted on Facebook or information about the drugs a client may have consumed.

Occasionally an unscrupulous clinician may stalk a client online or play detective in unprofessional ways. Such online searches and electronic sleuthing may enable clinicians to access information about clients' personal lives that, for some reason, they chose not to share in therapy sessions, and that lead clinicians to initiate an inappropriate multiple relationship, either in person or in the virtual world. For example, a clinician who takes a personal interest in a client may discover from an online search that the client is actively involved in a local religious group or theater company. A therapist with poor boundaries might use this information as a point of departure to engage the client in an inappropriate multiple relationship rooted in the client's social activities.

The reverse can happen as well, where a client who struggles with boundaries conducts an extensive online search hoping to find personal information about the therapist. This appears to be occurring with greater frequency as clients become increasingly comfortable with digital technology (Fels, 2015). The client might then use this information in order to connect with the clinician in these social contexts, for example, joining the therapist's place of worship, theater group, or bicycle club. Or a client who yearns to connect with a therapist socially might try to connect with the clinician on Facebook or on an online dating site using a pseudonym.

As another example involving possible privacy intrusions that can lead to unintended multiple relationships, clinicians and clients may register independently with online dating sites with no intention of encountering each other on the site. In one case, entirely by coincidence, a client responded to a clinician's online profile, which included very limited identifying information, without knowing that this was the client's clinician. After several online exchanges, the clinician realized that her correspondent was her current client. This led to a necessary, but awkward, in-person discussion during therapy sessions about the importance of boundaries in the clinical relationship. This inadvertent and unplanned multiple relationship certainly complicated the clinical relationship; the clinician felt over-exposed, like a victim of privacy invasion, and was unsure about whether it would be best to terminate the clinical relationship and refer the client to a colleague.

## Managing Ethical Risk

In recent years, groups of mental health professionals concerned about the ethical implications of digital technology have been actively involved in the development of practical and reasonable protocols to protect clients, third parties, and practitioners. These guidelines typically address risks related to privacy, confidentiality, informed consent, and boundaries.

With specific respect to the challenge of multiple relationships made possible by digital technology, practitioners can take several steps to protect clients and others and minimize risk to their own careers. For example, an international task force appointed by the Association of Social Work Boards (chaired by this author) to develop model regulatory guidelines pertaining to practitioners' use of technology recently made the following recommendations concerning maintenance of clear boundaries and ethical management of multiple relationships (Association of Social Work Boards, 2015):

- Communicate with clients using digital and other electronic technology (such as social networking sites, online chat, email, text messages, and video) only for professional or treatment-related purposes and only with client consent.
- Take reasonable steps to prevent client access to practitioners' personal social networking sites to avoid boundary confusion and inappropriate multiple relationships. Practitioners should maintain separate professional and personal social media and websites in order to establish clear boundaries and to avoid inappropriate multiple relationships.
- Avoid posting personal information on professional websites, blogs, or other forms of social media that might create boundary confusion and inappropriate multiple relationships.
- Be aware that cultural factors may influence the likelihood of discovering shared friend networks on websites, blogs, and other forms of social media. Practitioners should be aware that shared membership in cultural groups based on race, ethnicity, language, sexual orientation, gender identity or expression, disability, religion, addiction recovery, and other personal interests may create boundary confusion and inappropriate multiple relationships. Practitioners should avoid conflicts of interest and inappropriate multiple relationships based on their personal interests and online presence.
- Refrain from accepting "friend" or contact or blog response requests from clients on social networking sites. Exceptions may be made when such contact is an explicit component of a treatment or service-delivery model and meets prevailing standards regarding the use of digital technology to serve clients.

- When avoidable, refrain from providing electronic services to a person with whom a practitioner has had a personal relationship.
- Obtain client consent when using electronic search engines to gather information about the client, with the exception of emergency circumstances when such search may provide information to help protect the client or other parties who may be at risk.

Mental health counseling has matured significantly since its inauguration in the late nineteenth century. Since then, practitioners and scholars have developed a staggering array of conceptual and theoretical frameworks, schools of thought, intervention models, evidence-based guidelines, and ethical standards. Codes of ethics have evolved. They have shifted from one-page oaths to comprehensive documents that offer considerable guidance pertaining to a wide range of ethical challenges.

Digital technology is but the latest development calling for sound ethical judgment and careful risk management, especially related to novel forms of both intentional and unanticipated multiple relationships. No doubt, digital technology in mental health is here to stay. Our daunting task is to be ever mindful of the known and emerging ethical challenges related to multiple relationships and cultivate sensible guidelines that facilitate mental health professionals' responsible efforts to assist people in need.

## REFERENCES

Association of Social Work Boards (2015). *Model Regulatory Standards for Technology and Social Work Practice.* Retrieved from https://www.aswb.org/wp-content/uploads/2015/03/ASWB-Model-Regulatory-Standards-for-Technology-and-Social-Work-Practice.pdf (accessed July 27, 2016).

Barak, A., & Grohol, J. M. (2011). Current and future trends in internet-supported mental health interventions. *Journal of Technology in Human Services, 29,* 155–196.

Barak, A., Hen, L., Boniel-Nissim, M., & Shapira, N. (2008). A comprehensive review and a meta-analysis of the effectiveness of Internet-based psychotherapeutic interventions. *Journal of Technology in Human Services, 26*(2–4), 109–160.

Chester, A., & Glass, C. A. (2006). Online counseling: a descriptive analysis of therapy services on the internet. *British Journal of Guidance and Counseling, 34,* 145–160.

Clinton, B. K., Silverman, B., & Brendel, D. (2010). Patient-targeted Googling: the ethics of searching online for patient information. *Harvard Review of Psychiatry, 18,* 103–112.

DeGraff, J. (2014). Digital natives v. digital immigrants. *Psychology Today*. Retrieved from https://www.psychologytoday.com/blog/innovation-you/201406/digital-natives-v-digital-immigrants (accessed July 27, 2016).

Fels, A. (2015). Do you Google your shrink? *New York Times*. Retrieved from http://opinionator.blogs.nytimes.com/2015/04/04/do-you-google-your-shrink/ (accessed July 27, 2016).

Gutheil, T. G., & Simon, R. (2005). E-mails, extra-therapeutic contact, and early boundary problems: the internet as a "slippery slope." *Psychiatric Annals, 35*, 952–960.

Kanani, K., & Regehr, C. (2003). Clinical, ethical, and legal issues in e-therapy. *Families in Society, 84*, 155–162.

Lamendola, W. (2010). Social work and social presence in an online world. *Journal of Technology in the Human Services, 28*, 108–119.

Lannin, D. G., & Scott, N. A. (2013). Social networking ethics: developing best practices for the new small world. *Professional Psychology: Research and Practice, 44*(3), 135–141.

Menon, G. M., & Miller-Cribbs, J. (2002). Online social work practice: Issues and guidelines for the profession. *Advances in Social Work, 3*, 104–116.

Prensky, M. (2001). Digital natives, digital immigrants, Part II: Do they really think differently? Retrieved from http://www.marcprensky.com/writing/Prensky%20-%20Digital%20Natives,%20Digital%20Immigrants%20-%20Part1.pdf (accessed July 27, 2016).

Reamer, F. G. (2012a). *Boundary Issues and Dual Relationships in the Human Services*. New York: Columbia University Press.

Reamer, F. G. (2012b). The digital and electronic revolution in social work: rethinking the meaning of ethical practice. *Ethics and Social Welfare, 7*(1), 2–19.

Reamer, F. G. (2013). Social work in a digital age: ethical and risk management challenges. *Social Work, 58*(2), 163–172.

Reamer, F. G. (2015). *Risk Management in Social Work: Preventing Professional Malpractice, Liability, and Disciplinary Action*. New York: Columbia University Press.

Skinner, A., & Zack, J. S. (2004). Counseling and the internet. *American Behavioral Scientist, 48*, 434–446.

Zur, O. (2007). *Boundaries in Psychotherapy: Ethical and Clinical Explorations*. Washington, DC: American Psychological Association.

Zur, O. (2011). I love these e-mails, or do I? The use of e-mails in psychotherapy and counseling. Retrieved from http://www.zurinstitute.com/email%5Fin%5Ftherapy.html (accessed July 27, 2016).

Zur, O. (2012). TelePsychology or TeleMentalHealth in the digital age: the future is here. *California Psychologist, 45*, 13–15.

# Part VI

## Multiple Relationships and Multiple Roles in Unique Settings of Supervision

# INTRODUCTION

*Ofer Zur*

Part VI (Chapter 17) is the final section of the book and it focuses on multiple roles, multiple responsibilities, and multiple relationships in clinical supervision.

In Chapter 17, Dr. Falender maps the inherent multiple roles, loyalties, and relationships that supervisors are engaged in during the course of supervision. She elucidates the fine lines between supervision, mentoring, and therapy and between friendships and supervision. She also details how supervisors must balance the following roles/relationships: (1) protecting the public; (2) gatekeeping to ensure no unsuitable supervisees enter the profession; (3) supporting the growth of competence (knowledge, skills, and attitudes) and professionalism of the supervisee; and (4) protecting the well-being of clients who are currently being treated by the supervisees.

# Chapter 17

# MULTIPLE RELATIONSHIPS AND CLINICAL SUPERVISION

*Carol A. Falender*

Multiple relationships and multiple roles are implicit in clinical supervision. Many are normative, some less so. Supervisors must balance the following roles/relationships: (1) protecting the public; (2) gatekeeping to ensure no unsuitable supervisees enter the profession; (3) supporting the growth of competence (knowledge, skills, and attitudes) and professionalism of the supervisee; and (4) protecting the well-being of clients who are currently being treated by the supervisees. While the supervisor values and prioritizes the supervisory relationship, he/she is also evaluating and providing corrective feedback to the supervisee and is responsible for upholding ethical, legal, local, and contextual regulations, standards, and procedures. They may be within an institution in which the supervisor's primary loyalty or legal duty (e.g., military, forensics, law enforcement) may supersede the supervisee.

Multiple relationships may be intrinsic to the role of the supervisee: being a student in the supervisor's/professor's classes, research team member, teaching or research assistant, co-therapist, co-author, departmental or graduate school committee member, attending holiday parties together in an educational institution or clinic, or in any number of other professional or social roles with the supervisor.

The complexity of the relationship and multiple roles and the inherent power differential of supervision make specialized training in clinical supervision essential. Fortunately, clinical supervision, a cornerstone of clinical training and the major way the professions are transmitted to future generations, has undergone a metamorphosis in the last decade, moving from practice by osmosis, modeling, or adapting one's personal experience of supervision to a competency-based, systematic approach, informed by evidence (Falender & Shafranske, 2007). To be a clinical supervisor, and to effectively acknowledge and manage the multiple roles, requisite training and competence are required.

Generally, many multiple relationships or multiple roles in supervision are not only unavoidable, but also beneficial. What is proposed in this chapter is a problem-solving approach in which the supervisor and supervisee reflect on the various aspects and potential for benefit and harm before embarking on a multiple relationship. Please note that even multiple relationships that may have been normative or beneficial in supervision may become problematic when a supervisee is not meeting performance criteria and the relationship changes, as the supervisee becomes the recipient of corrective feedback, remediation, and a transformation of the supervisory relationship to an administrative one or even legal process occurs, often overseen by human resources or personnel departments.

## What is Clinical Supervision?

The Association of State and Provincial Psychology Boards (ASPPB, 2015) that oversees regulation of psychology in the USA, Canada, and territories, defined supervision as:

> A distinct, competency-based professional practice...a collaborative relationship between supervisor and supervisee that is facilitative, evaluative, and extends over time. It has the goal of enhancing the professional competence of the supervisee through monitoring the quality of services provided to the client for the protection of the public, and provides a gatekeeping function for independent professional practice (Bernard & Goodyear, 2014; Falender & Shafranske, 2004).
>
> (ASPPB, 2015, p. 5)

The American Psychological Association *Guidelines for Clinical Supervision in Health Service Psychology* (2014) defined competency-based supervision as

A metatheoretical approach that explicitly identifies the knowledge, skills and attitudes that comprise clinical competencies, informs learning strategies and evaluation procedures, and meets criterion-referenced competence standards consistent with evidence-based practices (regulations), and the local/cultural clinical setting (adapted from Falender & Shafranske, 2007).

(p. 5)

Each of the various disciplines, such as psychology, social work, marriage and family therapy, and counseling, has advanced guidelines and best practices or training sequences for clinical supervision. The National Association of Social Workers (NASW) *Best Practice Standards in Social Work Supervision* defined professional supervision as the

relationship between supervisor and supervisee in which the responsibility and accountability for the development of competence, demeanor, and ethical practice take place. The supervisor is responsible for providing direction to the supervisee, who applies social work theory, standardized knowledge, skills, competency, and applicable ethical content in the practice setting. The supervisor and the supervisee both share responsibility for carrying out their role in this collaborative process.

(NASW, 2013, p. 213)

The Association for Counselor Education and Supervision introduced best practices (2011) and the American Association for Marriage and Family Therapy has defined standards for approved supervision designation (2014).

Generally, there is consensus across disciplines about the common elements of clinical supervision, including the definition, and the various roles, ethical responsibility, and specific roles, including monitoring and assessing competence, collaboration, relationship, supervision contract, multicultural competence, and ethical and legal standards, including multiple relationships. Sadly, even though the practice of clinical supervision is transforming, overwhelming consensus is lacking that it is a distinct professional practice, requiring specific training (Genuchi, Rings, Germek, & Erickson Cornish, 2014). Also, although supervisor competence, an ethical standard, is assumed, increasing evidence points to practices of harmful (Ellis et al., 2014) or multiculturally incompetent

(Green & Dekkers, 2010) supervision. Often this involves inappropriate multiple relationships that lead to misunderstanding and damage to both the supervisory relationship and the client. Specific supervision training is essential for protection of both clients and supervisees as it provides for clarity and transparency in communication and relationship. The supervisor bears responsibility for ensuring that the supervisee is informed, reflective, and actively engaged in the process of determining the relative merits of engaging in a multiple relationship, and oversees the possible outcome even when the intern declines to engage in the multiple relationship.

Generally, ethical standards for supervisors and supervision are embedded in sections of the general ethics code of the professions. Common ethics components include competence, informed consent, limits of confidentiality, role clarification, scrutiny of multiple relationships, and responsibility to monitor, provide feedback, and support the professional and personal development of the supervisee while protecting the welfare of the clients. Supervisor–supervisee relationships that are explicitly ethically and legally prohibited are exploitation, sexual relationships, harassment, and conducting personal psychotherapy with a supervisee. Zur has compiled a comprehensive website of the relevant sections of these at http://www.zurinstitute.com/ethics_of_supervision.html.

In this chapter we will consider the multiple relationships between supervisor and supervisee, strategies to prevent harm, inherent strengths and potential conflicts, and navigating and negotiating these in the complexity of clinical supervision.

## STRUCTURING THE SUPERVISION

### The Supervision Contract

An essential component of clinical supervision is the supervision contract (American Psychological Association, 2015; ASPPB, 2015), a document constructed to outline the expectations for the supervisee of the setting and the supervisor, including clarity of the multiple roles of both parties, setting specific multiple roles (e.g., recovery or wraparound models in which supervisees have purposeful multiple relationships in which they may attend school functions with the client, or obtain a refrigerator for them), and how supervision is distinct from psychotherapy. The contract is an outgrowth of the supervisory relationship, in which the supervisor is respectful, collaborative, empathic, genuine, and explicit in articulating the power differential within which supervision occurs, the complexity of roles and expectations, and processes to address conflict.

## The Supervisory Relationship and Multiple Relationships

Supervisors form strong supervisory relationships with their supervisees as a standard of practice. The relationship is associated with positive outcomes (e.g., satisfaction, diversity competence, self-disclosure of countertransference or reactivity), but may also potentially lead to a role transformation in which the supervisee would rather not disappoint the supervisor and/or the supervisor finds it difficult to give the supervisee negative performance feedback or simply loses objectivity such that liking overcomes evaluation (Gonsalvez & Crowe, 2014). The transformation of the supervisory relationship can be gradual and subtle, and can be viewed as or seem more like friendship. Some confusion about "collaboration," a significant aspect of competency-based supervision, has arisen such that supervisors are unsure how to engage in collaboration within the given power differential and still be in a position to give corrective feedback, an essential competency of clinical supervision. A skilled supervisor balances the multiple roles, giving ongoing feedback, positive and corrective, while also supporting the development of the supervisee and ensuring that the power differential is clear. An important guideline for supervisors is that supervisees have a diminished power to say "no" to a supervisory request due to the inherent power differential so it is a supervisory responsibility to ensure safety and appropriate relationships. Discussion of incompatible expectations between the two is essential.

## Multicultural Diversity

Supervisee and supervisor may share multicultural identities (e.g., religion, sexual orientation, race, country of origin), and these may be referred to as cultural borderlands (Falicov, 2014). The intersecting identities may lead to a special connection and expectations that lend depth and breadth to the supervision or to some the supervisor is not able to fulfill. Discussion of worldviews and perspectives as they relate to assessment and all aspects of treatment and relationship with the client(s) is essential.

## Friendship

As the supervisory relationship is collaborative, generally, there is a positive valence. Sharing of confidences and general supportive interactions are common. As with any multiple relationship, the impact on the less powerful is the critical component. A supervisee may misunderstand, thinking that by virtue of a "special relationship" and confidences shared, the evaluative function of the supervisor is inoperative. Supervision training places high value on ongoing assessment, monitoring, feedback, and evaluation of supervisees to ensure clarity and mutual understanding regarding competence development, or lack of such. Babysitting, house sitting, or other mixes of personal and professional roles should be carefully considered in the multiple relationship decision-making model.

## Settings

Small communities with commonalities provide unique challenges regarding multiple relationships in supervision. In these, a small group of licensed professionals and supervisees provide services to individuals with whom they naturally interact. As Schank and Skovholt (2006) concluded in their work regarding small communities (e.g., rural, communities, communities of color, LGBT community, military bases, faith communities, or cultural-ethic communities), and we extrapolate to supervision, steps are essential to ensure that neither exploitation nor harm is done and that individuals make decisions based on a collaborative, and objective assessment, informed consent with transparency, considering clinical details as well as contextual and confidentiality, utilizing consultation, and reviewing as time goes on, with the caveat that it might become necessary to curtail the multiple relationship.

Supervision of substance abuse counselors is also punctuated by multiple roles. Powell (2004) described multiple hats: when any or all of the participants are in recovery—the client, the supervisee/therapist, and/or the supervisor. The multiple relationships (e.g., potential of the supervisor and supervisee attending Alcoholics Anonymous or other recovery or self-help support groups together) must be addressed.

## ETHICAL DECISION MAKING

Several multiple relationship ethical frames are useful and essential tools for supervisors and supervisees alike. Gottlieb (1993) proposed a model with dimensions of power, duration, and termination. Although designed to be applied in client-therapist relationships, it has been extrapolated to supervision (Falender & Shafranske, 2004). Power refers to the amount of power the supervisor has over the supervisee. In supervisory relationships, as noted above, the power differential is always present and is significant, as the supervisor is a gatekeeper, determines whether a supervisee is suitable to progress to the next level of training, the quality of recommendation he/she gives, and the feedback to the supervisee's training program. Second is duration, an aspect of power, based on the assumption that power increases over time, so length of time for the relationship is relevant. Third is the termination point and the likelihood the supervisor and supervisee will have further professional contact. However, the model does not address multiple variables relevant to supervision, such as the impact on other supervisees or supervisors (Burian & Slimp, 2000). Burian and Slimp's model, designed for internship multiple relationships, weighed each party's reasons and motivations to be in the relationship, the power differential between the supervisor and the supervisee, and the parameters of the social multiple relationship as well as the probable impact on other supervisees and supervisors and the supervisee's ability to leave the activity without repercussion. Additionally, the professional role with the supervisee, location of the multiple relationships, timing in the year, and frequency are considered. Generally, fulfillment of personal needs of the more powerful (supervisor) should be subordinate to the training needs of the supervisee.

Gottlieb, Robinson, and Younggren (2007) proposed an ethical problem-solving frame for multiple relationships in supervision with the following steps:

- Is entering into a relationship in addition to the supervisory one necessary or should the supervisor avoid it?
- Can the additional relationship potentially cause harm to the supervisee?
- If harm seems unlikely or avoidable, would the additional relationship prove beneficial?
- Is there a risk the additional relationship could disrupt the supervisory relationship?
- Can the supervisor evaluate the matter objectively?

(Adapted from Gottlieb et al., 2007.)

Possible additional frames to add to this ethical problem-solving framework include considering the emotional impact of the proposed relationship on the supervisor and supervisee and whether there are multicultural or contextual considerations. Also, after concluding the problem-solving framework, consider what has been learned in the process. A conversation (i.e., informed-consent process) could ensue so the supervisor respectfully poses the potential relationship, the possible benefits versus the risks, and collaboratively arrives at a decision with the supervisee.

## Assessing Potential for Harm or Exploitation

### Vignette 1

Joan had a strong supervisory relationship with Dr. Handler and looked forward to their weekly meeting. Increasingly Dr. Handler was asking Joan to bring things to supervision; at first it was resources that were peripherally related to a case, but were extremely relevant to his research project. Next, as he saw she arrived with a Starbucks cup, he asked if she would bring him a venti latte—and gave her money to pay for it the first few weeks, but as time went on, did not—or said, I'll pay for two next week. But didn't. Then Dr. Handler mentioned co-authoring a paper, an opportunity Joan was eager to pursue. Dr. Handler described his incredible time pressures, and urged Joan to do a complete literature review on the topic, and draft a rough version of the paper. Joan expressed concern that she had never written a paper for a journal, found the idea daunting but exciting, but would need guidance. Dr. Handler dismissed that and said Joan doesn't know her own strengths.

Then, Dr. Handler invited Joan to attend a play with him next week, saying that it will give them a chance to get to know each other better. It is a play about an interreligious marriage, and Dr. Handler is especially interested in Joan's reactions as he knew she was a member of one of the religious groups in question.

## Vignette 2

Carl was delighted at the informal nature of supervision, use of first names, the supervisor's inquiry into what he did last weekend, and generally, a developing relationship of caring, warmth, and concern. However, when his supervisor continued to chat every week, observing that his supervisees are his closest friends, asking Carl for advice, and disclosing personal information that made Carl feel uncomfortable, Carl became concerned about his clients and suggested a format for supervision, but his supervisor declined, stating that he liked free flow.

## Vignette 3

Hong, a graduate student, was delighted when assigned to Dr. Zhang's supervision as he felt that working with someone who shared his Chinese heritage would be an incredible strength and, through his cultural familiarity, Dr. Zhang would be his protector. Dr. Zhang did not address that statement, the multiple relationship implied, and its potential for conflict with his supervisory responsibilities. He simply thought their shared identities (male and Chinese, from the same region) would be a strength. After several weeks of supervision Dr. Zhang became increasingly concerned that Hong's competency was nowhere near what was expected for a practicum student at his level of training. He gently gave competency-based feedback weekly relating to interventions, relationships, and assessment, cautious not to overwhelm Hong. Hong constantly thanked Dr. Zhang for his support and protection. When Dr. Zhang had to institute a remediation plan, Hong was shocked and disbelieving. Dr. Zhang, deeply saddened, acknowledged that it had not occurred to him that Hong would have performance problems as he assumed he would be an excellent supervisee.

These vignettes highlight the power differential, the complexity of the supervisory relationship—a supervisee actually is less likely to say "no" to a supervisor request that initiates a multiple relationship for a number of reasons—and that assumptions and misunderstandings may ensue. First, and most obvious, the supervisee fears negative evaluation or a strain in the supervisory relationship; second, the supervisee wants to demonstrate competence and ability to succeed across varied and complex situations; third, a supervisee does not want to be labeled or considered less than eager, forthcoming, and flexible; fourth, there may be inherent benefits to the supervisee of parts of the multiple relationship. Further, the multiple relationship interferes with supervision time. A strong supervisory relationship may not facilitate the supervisee's power to say "no."

## Beneficial Structuring of Multiple Relationships

### Vignette 1

Dr. Longly was intrigued by Jackie's excellent work with adult survivors of sexual abuse and invited her to co-author a paper. Together they developed an outline, divided the sections, and within several months had a manuscript that was ready for publication, where Jackie's name appeared as first author.

### Vignette 2

Loren was a strong supervisee but seemed to be increasingly stressed, so Dr. Sylvester gently asked her if there had been a change as her behavior in supervision seemed to have changed. Loren disclosed that when they moved for the internship she had hoped her husband would get a job, but had been unable to, so had begun to clean houses and wondered if she could let her supervisors know of the new service. Dr. Sylvester was very sympathetic, and used a decision-making process to identify possible issues that might disrupt her relationship with him or with the internship in general, but assisted her (not taking supervision time) by giving her several free local newspapers and online resources to disseminate information about the cleaning service, and her husband used those successfully.

### Vignette 3

Alexander had an idea to develop an interactive website for his internship site, a community clinic, and sell it to them. His supervisor praised his competence and initiative, reviewed various decision-making frameworks with him, especially the one about the timing of the multiple relationship, and noted that the internship was ending in 2 months. After Alexander successfully completed the internship, his supervisor set up a meeting for him with the Executive Director, who was eager to hire him to develop the website.

A supervisory responsibility is to ensure that expectations for multiple relationships are clear, and to introduce ethical decision-making protocols when potential multiple relationship situations arise. This proactive, positive modeling of ethical and respectful supervisory practice provides the supervisee with multiple levels of training in approaching ethical and relationship issues that arise during training and beyond. Further, this approach supports the normative and beneficial multiple relationships that are a protective factor and strength in professional development in all fields.

## References

American Association for Marriage and Family Therapy (2014). *Approved Supervision Designation: Standards Handbook*. Retrieved from: http://dx5br1z4f6n0k. cloudfront.net/imis15/Documents/AS-Handbook.pdf (accessed July 27, 2016).

American Psychological Association (2014) *Guidelines for Clinical Supervision in Health Service Psychology*. Retrieved from: http://www.apa.org/about/policy/guidelines-supervision.pdf (accessed July 27, 2016).

American Psychological Association (2015). Guidelines for clinical supervision in health service psychology. *American Psychologist, 70*(1), 33–46. doi:10.1037/a0038112.

Association for Counselor Education and Supervision (2011). *Best Practices in Clinical Supervision*. Retrieved from: https://c.ymcdn.com/sites/www.a4pt.org/resource/resmgr/Resource_Center/ACES_Best_Practices_in_Clini.pdf (accessed July 31, 2016).Association of State and Provincial Psychology Boards. (2015). *Supervision Guidelines for Education and Training Leading to Licensure as a Health Service Psychologist*. Retrieved from: http://c.ymcdn.com/sites/www.asppb.net/resource/resmgr/Guidelines/Final_Supervision_Guidelines.pdf (accessed July 27, 2016).

Bernard, J. M., & Goodyear, R. K. (2014). *Fundamentals of Clinical Supervision* (5th ed.). Boston: Pearson.

Burian, B. K., & Slimp, A. O. (2000). Social dual-role relationships during internship: a decision-making model. *Professional Psychology: Research and Practice, 31*, 332–338. doi:10.1037/0735-7028.31.3.332

Ellis, M. V., Berger, L., Hanus, A. E., Ayala, E. E., Swords, B. A., & Siembor, M. (2014). Inadequate and harmful clinical supervision: testing a revised framework and assessing occurrence. *The Counseling Psychologist, 42*(4), 434–472.

Falender, C. A., & Shafranske, E. P. (2004). *Clinical Supervision: A Competency-based Approach*. Washington, DC: American Psychological Association.

Falender, C. A., & Shafranske, E. P. (2007). Competence in competency-based supervision practice: construct and application. *Professional Psychology: Research and Practice, 38*(3), 232–240. doi:10.1037/0735-7028.38.3.232.

Falicov, C. J. (2014). Psychotherapy and supervision as cultural encounters: the MECA framework. In C. A. Falender, E. P. Shafransky, & C. J. Falicov (Eds.), *Multiculturalism and Diversity in Clinical Supervision: A Competency-based Approach.* Washington, DC: American Psychological Association.

Genuchi, M. C., Rings, J. A., Germek, M. D., & Erickson Cornish, J. A. (2014). Clinical supervisors' perceptions of the clarity and comprehensiveness of the supervision competencies framework. *Training and Education in Professional Psychology*, doi:10.1037/tep0000064.

Gonsalvez, C. J., & Crowe, T. P. (2014). Evaluation of psychology practitioner competence in clinical supervision. *American Journal of Psychotherapy, 68*(2), 177–193.

Gottlieb, M. C. (1993). Avoiding exploitive dual relationships: a decision-making model. *Psychotherapy, 30*, 41–48.

Gottlieb, M. C., Robinson, K., & Younggren, J. N. (2007). Multiple relations in supervision: guidance for administrators, supervisors, and students. *Professional Psychology: Research and Practice, 38*, 241–247. doi:10.1037/0735-7028.38.3.241.

Green, M. S., & Dekkers, T. D. (2010). Attending to power and diversity in supervision: an exploration of supervisee learning outcomes and satisfaction with supervision. *Journal of Feminist Family Therapy, 22*, 293–31. doi:10.1080/0895 2833.2010.528703.

National Association of Social Workers (2013). *Best Practice Standards in Social Work Supervision*. Retrieved from: http://www.naswdc.org/practice/naswstandards/ supervisionstandards2013.pdf (accessed July 27, 2016).

Powell, D. J. (2004). *Clinical Supervision in Alcohol and Drug Abuse Counseling*. San Francisco: Jossey-Bass.

Schank, J. A., & Skovholt, T. (2006). *Ethical Practice in Small Communities: Challenges and Rewards for Psychologists*. Washington, DC: American Psychological Association.

# INDEX

# Taylor & Francis eBooks

## Helping you to choose the right eBooks for your Library

Add Routledge titles to your library's digital collection today. Taylor and Francis ebooks contains over 50,000 titles in the Humanities, Social Sciences, Behavioural Sciences, Built Environment and Law.

**Choose from a range of subject packages or create your own!**

**Benefits for you**

» Free MARC records
» COUNTER-compliant usage statistics
» Flexible purchase and pricing options
» All titles DRM-free.

**Benefits for your user**

» Off-site, anytime access via Athens or referring URL
» Print or copy pages or chapters
» Full content search
» Bookmark, highlight and annotate text
» Access to thousands of pages of quality research at the click of a button.

| REQUEST YOUR **FREE** INSTITUTIONAL TRIAL TODAY | **Free Trials Available**<br>We offer free trials to qualifying academic, corporate and government customers. |
| --- | --- |

## eCollections – Choose from over 30 subject eCollections, including:

| | |
| --- | --- |
| Archaeology | Language Learning |
| Architecture | Law |
| Asian Studies | Literature |
| Business & Management | Media & Communication |
| Classical Studies | Middle East Studies |
| Construction | Music |
| Creative & Media Arts | Philosophy |
| Criminology & Criminal Justice | Planning |
| Economics | Politics |
| Education | Psychology & Mental Health |
| Energy | Religion |
| Engineering | Security |
| English Language & Linguistics | Social Work |
| Environment & Sustainability | Sociology |
| Geography | Sport |
| Health Studies | Theatre & Performance |
| History | Tourism, Hospitality & Events |

For more information, pricing enquiries or to order a free trial, please contact your local sales team:
www.tandfebooks.com/page/sales

 Routledge
Taylor & Francis Group

The home of
Routledge books

**www.tandfebooks.com**

Lightning Source UK Ltd.
Milton Keynes UK
UKHW020301220219
337666UK00020B/607/P

9 781138 937772